PSL FIELD GUIDE

Railways of the

EASTERN REGION

Volume 2: Northern operating area

PSL FIELD GUIDE

Railways of the
EASTERN
REGION

Volume 2: Northern operating area

Geoffrey Body

Patrick Stephens Limited

Title page *Night time line up of HSTs.*

First published in 1989

British Library Cataloguing in Publication Data

Body, Geoffrey, *1929–*
    Railways of the Eastern Region.
    Vol.2 : Northern operating area.—(PSL field guide; v:4)
    1.Eastern England. Railway services: British Rail. Eastern Region
    I.Title
    385.'09426

    ISBN 1–85260–072–1

Patrick Stephens Limited is part of the Thorsons Publishing Group, Wellingborough, Northamptonshire NN8 2RQ, England.

Printed by Biddles Limited, Guildford, Surrey

10 9 8 7 6 5 4 3 2 1

Contents

Acknowledgements
The compilation of this book would not have been possible without the consider-
able assistance afforded by the Eastern Region of British Rail. Arrangements for
that assistance were readily and generously made by Public Affairs Manager Bert
Porter, and implemented in the most helpful way by Stuart Rankin, the Public
Relations Officer. Thanks are also due to the Director General of the Tyne &
Wear Passenger Transport Executive for the supply of information relating to the
Tyne & Wear Metro, and to the National Railway Museum and other preservation
bodies for data on their locations and activities.

Except where otherwise indicated, the illustrations have either been provided by
British Rail or are drawn from my own collection. The maps have been prepared by
I.G. Body.

Geoffrey Body MCIT

Foreword

by John Nelson
General Manager, British Rail, Eastern Region, York

This second volume of the 'PSL Field Guide' *Railways of the Eastern Region* covers a part of the country which not only saw the very beginnings of railways in Britain, but which is still in the forefront of modern developments.

The electrification of the East Coast Main Line, the many engineering and station improvements and the new trains coming into service on Provincial routes all add up to changes every bit as exciting as anything in the past. We also look forward to major developments in the movement of freight by rail, with two depots to handle traffic via the Channel Tunnel already announced, and others certain to follow. All of this is amply demonstrating that British Rail is a strong and developing industry, poised for further expansion in most areas of its activity.

Any current survey of the Eastern Region is of course a 'snapshot in time' and Geoffrey Body, himself a retired railway manager, has composed his picture well, bringing a lifetime's experience to bear in describing what is happening today and putting it in a historical context.

The BBC's *Railwatch* programmes, shown during February 1989, demonstrated that there is considerable public interest in what goes on behind the scenes of daily railway operations. This 'Field Guide' goes a long way towards answering those 'What, How, Why and When?' questions which occur not just to rail enthusiasts, but to the ordinary traveller when looking out of the carriage window.

The Eastern Region (Northern Area) field guide

Railways could reasonably claim to be among the most interesting of British industries. The train services themselves might be seen as scenic tours, admitting the traveller in comfort to all the facets of Britain's infinitely variable town and countryside landscape. They are also works of the engineer and coach-builder's art, surrounded by an infrastructure which presents a great deal of modern technical interest—tracks, points, signals, communications, and so on. Railway structures are equally varied and fascinating and span over 150 years of civil engineering and architectural practice. Add to all this the interest of the actual operation of the system, nowhere more evident than at a large passenger station, and the claim to be among the most interesting of industries seems to be fully justified.

British Rail still cherishes some early architectural jewels and the long-standing 'block' system of signalling is still practised, but the pace of change has accelerated greatly over recent years, taking advantage of new ideas and materials. Once 60 mph was a respectable speed: now it is frequently doubled; once the single needle telegraph carried most of the system's communications: now fibre optics do the job in a hundredth of the time; once a branch line had dozens of level crossings and signal boxes: now it may have automatic barrier crossings and radio signalling between control centre and locomotive cab. Even as this book is written, more dramatic change is on the way. Masts and wires are appearing along the length of the East Coast Main Line and electric traction is due to take over from the High Speed Trains which have already set their own high standards for speed and comfort.

All this change has been taking and is continuing to take place in what is already a highly interesting industry and, in the case of the territory covered by this book, in one of its most complex regions. The whole series was founded on an attempt to present the high interest of the modern railway system—what there was to see, how it had originated, what its function was—and nowhere could this task be more worthwhile or challenging than in the Eastern Region's Northern Operating Area. Here the industrial activity of the early nineteenth century had prompted a wealth of competing lines, especially in and between the great manufacturing areas of South and West Yorkshire, and around the Tyne, Wear, Tees and Humber estuaries. Substantial freight activity still exists today—including the movement of coal, which inspired so many early lines—but the passenger business now dominates and the British Rail task has been to provide fast, frequent and arractive services over InterCity routes, operate effective cross-country services within strict financial parameters and meet local and commuter needs, the latter in conjunction with the powerful local Passenger Transport Authorities.

Over the years, technical, economic and political influences have dramatically altered the railway system and activity. Sparsely-trafficked routes have gone, competing routes have been pruned and rationalized and a new pattern of services evolved to meet new demands, including those for easy interchange between transport modes. Cleared of its clutter, the system now provides the major centres of the North East and Yorkshire with high speed services to London, cross-country services link Liverpool/Manchester and North Wales with Hull and York/Scarborough and major centres have frequent local services often operated by the new Pacer or Sprinter units.

In presenting this picture of the railways of the northern area of BR's Eastern Region, the treatment used in previous volumes has been broadly maintained. It commences, immediately after this introduction, with a summary view of the evolution of the area's railway network, designed to give a broad understanding of today's system and how it came into being. Then follows a detailed gazetteer section which contains an entry for every location of significance in the area. Further sections follow covering routes, technical and traffic matters, closures and the preservation scene. A supplementary index then helps to locate information on secondary locations or those of past rather than present significance. Together the sections attempt to present all that is interesting about the railway system of the area in a sequence of introduction, evolution, principal locations, generic activities, and closure and preservation.

The gazetteer section deals with major railway centres and locations as a single, exclusive entry, but this approach is varied to a line, or line section basis where that line is so much of a single entity that its fragmentation would be confusing. Thus the Leeds to York line has its own entry because of the self-contained service it carries, but Leeds, Bramhope Tunnel, Harrogate, Starbeck and Knaresborough are all treated in more detail separately. Cross-referencing between entries and, where appropriate, between sections enables the data to be used in whatever permutation the reader may require.

Each entry in the main gazetteer section has a sub-heading which pinpoints its location in terms of the line on which it lies, and also an official distance based on

Example of the tiled system map which still survives at a number of ex-NER stations.

Publicity photograph taken in the early part of 1984 as the new Class '141s' entered service on local lines in West Yorks.

the BR Sectional Appendix to the Working Timetable. The entry itself then provides a summary of the origins, features, functions and facilities of the location. For these purposes, physical features and train services are normally referred to in the Down direction (ie, away from London or the focal point of the original railway), information on the latter being based on the Monday to Friday service at the time of writing. Distances normally refer to the central point of the location but in the case of tunnels the distance for each portal is given in the Down direction.

The main objective of the book is to present the facts and interest of each location as it exists today. The background history is obviously an important part of this, explaining how today's situation evolved and often providing a commentary on items of past interest still to be seen. For this reason, and in order to be comprehensive, the closed lines of the area are covered by the book and normally described as part of the entry for the logical, or first junction station. Thus the old Leeds Northern route north from Harrogate is described as part of the Harrogate entry.

British Rail itself welcomes an interest in its activities and will be as helpful in encouraging that interest as is consistent with its primary task of running a modern, efficient and safe railway system. Viewing, spotting and photography are generally permitted, at the discretion of the local BR management, wherever normal public access is free or generally available. BR provides a comprehensive service of train and fare information, with travel centres in most of the main towns; and there are many special fare facilities that can be put to good use in the pursuit of a railway interest.

In preparing this book every effort has been made to ensure accuracy, and account has been taken of changes known to be coming along in the interval between writing and publication. Yet the railway scene is constantly changing—new facilities being introduced, outmoded ones being abandoned, new evidence of the past emerging, new plans being made for the future—and for the benefit of future volumes the compiler would be glad to hear from readers with additional information.

The Eastern (Northern Operating Area)

The British railway system as we know it today was born in the area covered by this book, the Northern Operating Area of the Eastern Region of British Rail. The North East was the breeding ground for the primitive wagonways built to move coal to wharfs along the Tyne, Wear and Tees rivers and thus fuel the growth of the Industrial Revolution which, in turn, was to shape the nation and its society. Not that any of this happened overnight, for the earliest wagonways date back to the seventeenth century and it was to be 1825 before Britain's first major conventional railway emerged from the motley collection of home-devised lines and horse traction used to haul the output of the scattered, individualistic collieries of the seventeenth and eighteenth centuries.

Although other railways may legitimately claim some type of first place in the railway genesis—the Middleton Railway at Leeds, for example, was the first to be authorized by Act of Parliament—the Stockton & Darlington Railway project was the one that lifted rail transport from the wagonway era to that of the modern railway. Opened on 27 September 1825 and using the steam power of George Stephenson's *Locomotion No.1*, it soon added passenger trains to the early coal haulage and, by 1830, had bridged the Tees in search of better shipping facilities, originating the town of Middlesbrough in the process. The Stockton & Darlington Railway expanded its own system, supported some adjacent railways and fought others, cherished trunk route ambitions, and generally set a pattern for railway company behaviour that was to last until the 1923 grouping.

As in other railway areas, the systems of Yorkshire and the North East were initially shaped by their traffics and the individual schemes which evolved in the search of profits from their carriage. Later lines were promoted to realize trunk route ambitions, fight off a rival or to fill in gaps in a company's territorial network, but the pioneer schemes had too many obstacles to overcome to lose sight of their traffic and profit objectives. In this situation, carrying coal to the east coast ports or inland from them, moving ironstone to the coal deposits and transporting raw materials to and finished goods from the West Riding, are all apparent among the objectives of the area's earliest railway schemes.

The experience of the 1830 Liverpool & Manchester Railway soon proved that the carriage of passengers was lucrative and that trade and commerce expanded when its representatives could travel easily between major cities. This factor became reflected in subsequent railway schemes, aided by the fact that those subscribing the money for new projects were generally both men of some substance and men with a need to travel. Being human they also wanted the new transport

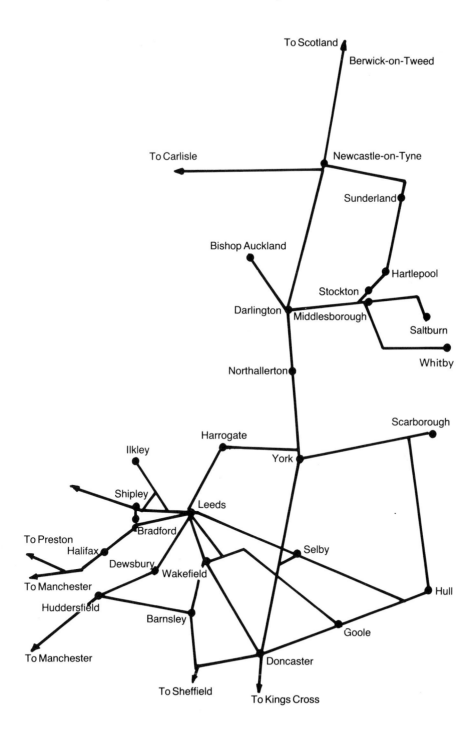

The first metal railway bridge, erected over the River Gaunless by the Stockton & Darlington Railway.

facilities for their own locality, particularly if a rival was about to acquire them!

As a whole, the area covered by this book still has most of its original trunk lines. The notable exception is that of the Leeds Northern concern, whose south-north route from the West Riding to the Tees has lost its middle section between Harrogate and Northallerton. There are some variations between the original course of the Stockton & Darlington Railway and that followed by today's Bishop Auckland-Saltburn trains, and the Manchester & Leeds Railway's 1840–41 route nearly closed when a derailed oil train blaze damaged Summit Tunnel, but otherwise the earliest of the area's railway lines are still in existence and still performing a useful function.

In looking at the development of this rail network, it is best seen as three major groupings, the lines of the West Riding and South Yorkshire, those of the North East of England, and a group made up of the East Coast Main Line and its offshoots. Each of these three groupings had some distinct characteristics. The West Riding was a sort of traffic Mecca for the pre-grouping railways which evolved from the independent pioneer lines. Six of them had a major presence there and it took a long while for competition and conflict to make concessions to common sense and co-operation. By that time, many duplications existed and these joined the branch lines as later targets for cuts and closures. The North East, with a much earlier railway tradition of independent, insular wagonways, derived the benefits of combination rather later than elsewhere. However, once the North Eastern Railway eventually emerged, it grew into a progressive and profitable concern which dominated the area from the Humber to the Tweed. In further contrast, the East Coast Main Line grew from half a dozen constituent schemes which, right from the start, showed ambitions beyond their own territory and gave the emergence of this great trunk route an air of inevitability.

Following in the wake of the Stockton & Darlington Railway came other pioneers of considerable stature, including the Leeds & Selby and the Newcastle & Carlisle schemes. The former was incorporated by an Act of 29 May 1830 and opened its 20 mile line from Marsh Lane, Leeds, to the west bank of the River Ouse at Selby on 22 September 1834. The long-debated railway had been planned to continue on to Hull, but initially passengers transferred to a steamer at Selby and completed their journey by heading down the Ouse to the Humber estuary. Fearing that the original intentions would never be realized, the citizens of Hull promoted the Hull & Selby Railway to complete the project, obtaining their Act on 21 June 1836 and opening their end of the route on 1 July 1840.

Like its contemporaries, the Newcastle & Carlisle Railway's proposals had been under discussion for many years. They obtained real substance with the Royal Assent to the company's Act on 22 May 1829, but this was a project with a difference. It proposed a major east-west trunk route, running for 60 miles across the 'neck' of Britain and involving significant physical obstacles, as well as crossing tracts of country with very sparse traffic prospects. Prompted by strategic as well as traffic motives, and using the valley of the Tyne and South Tyne rivers to good advantage, the route was brought into use progressively from 9 March 1835; but not without then having to close down again for a period as a result of an objection to its use of locomotives!

In 1836, three other railways deserving of the 'pioneer' accolade were authorized. Senior by a short head was the York & North Midland Railway which obtained its Act on 21 June of that year, and which is remembered most as the vehicle for the ambitions of George Hudson, the so-called 'Railway King'. Following, on 4 July, were the schemes of the North Midland Railway—to extend north from the Birmingham & Derby Junction to Leeds—and of the Manchester & Leeds, which had been conceived as an eastward extension of the 1830 Liverpool & Manchester Railway. With hindsight, both of these concerns can be seen to have made serious mistakes, the North Midland in allowing Stephenson's easy-gradient policy to result in bypassing Sheffield, and the Manchester & Leeds in choosing the Calder valley to cross the Pennines instead of a shorter course along the Colne. Sheffield got its direct main line later, but the Lancashire & Yorkshire Railway, as successor

An interesting example of Stockton & Darlington rolling stock, a 'Smoking Carriage' with first and second class accommodation.

to the M&L, remained forever at a disadvantage for the cross-Pennine traffic.

The three schemes authorized in 1836 were to give cohesive form to the railway system at the Yorkshire end of our territory. The North Midland extended from Rotherham to Leeds via Normanton from 1 July 1840 and, at the same time, the Y&NM completed a link from the latter point to its line south from York. That city now had a railway route to London, it was connected to Hull and Leeds and, when the M&L settled for Normanton as its way of reaching Leeds, York was linked to Manchester and East Lancashire from 1 March 1841. At the end of the same month, passenger trains began running north to Darlington over the Great North of England Railway.

North of York, real signs of competition to come emerged when the Clarence Railway opened its 1833 line from Shildon on the S&D to Port Clarence near the mouth of the Tees. This was designed to shorten the haul for West Durham coal going for shipment and produced strong competition between the Clarence and S&D companies. The former opened a branch to Ferryhill in 1834, and this was later extended west to Byers Green and east towards Hartlepool.

A significant mineral line was opened by the Stanhope & Tyne concern in 1834 and, like most of these early routes, it was soon conveying passengers in addition to the primary coal business. Coal produced a line from the Thornley and Haswell areas to the embryo docks at Hartlepool in 1835, and the Durham & Sunderland started carrying both coal and passengers in the following year, despite a route made up almost entirely of inclines. The 1830s also saw the completion of the Newcastle & Carlisle scheme, including its crossing to the north bank of the Tyne at Scotswood, a link between the N&C and the 1839 Brandling Junction Railway's South Tyneside route and a North Tyneside line from Manors to North Shields. Further south, the Whitby & Pickering line opened throughout on 26 May 1836 in anticipation of later connection with the York & North Midland Railway.

The next decade was a period of even greater expansion. Like those of the first generation, the lines opened in this second generation of railway building have mostly withstood the ravages of the contraction years to which many later enterprises fell victim. In the south the most important openings after those of the 1840–41 period were:

York-Scarborough—7 July 1845
Wakefield-Pontefract-Goole—1 April 1846
Leeds-Bradford—1 July 1846
Seamer-Hull—5 October 1846 and 20 October 1847
Shipley-Keighley—16 March 1847
Heaton Lodge-Huddersfield-Stalybridge—3 August 1847 and 1 August 1849
Askern Junction-Knottingley—6 June 1848
Dewsbury-Leeds—18 September 1848

with lines like Church Fenton-Harrogate and York/Selby-Market Weighton among those which have failed to survive.

In the north of the area, significant openings of the 1840s, other than those of the future East Coast Main Line, included:

Shildon-Bishop Auckland—19 April 1842
Belmont Junction-Durham—15 April 1844
Middlesbrough-Redcar—4 June 1846
Blyth-Northumberland Dock—3 March 1847

However, the North was still a fragmented area so far as railways were concerned, with many small independent concerns, some more substantial ones like the Brandling Junction and its Stanhope & Tyne/Pontop & South Shields neighbour, and a few strong medium-sized companies. The latter included the Newcastle & Carlisle, the Stockton & Darlington and the emerging Blyth & Tyne. At the same time, a main line situation was developing which was to act as a catalyst for the creation of the North Eastern Railway.

The East Coast Main Line is, of course, the backbone of the whole surviving railway system east of the Pennines, the Yorkshire Dales and the Cheviot Hills. Once the Great Northern had reached Doncaster, it was inevitable that the longer route via the North Midland/Midland lines would decline, and from 1850–52 the London-York traffic utilized the L&Y line from Doncaster to Knottingley and on via Burton Salmon and the York & North Midland line into York.

Over the Plain of York to Darlington, the Great North of England Railway opened its flat, straight line for goods on 4 January 1841 and for passengers on 30 March of that year, when a new joint station with the Y&NM was brought into use at York. All this construction had exhausted the GNE resources and on 11 April 1843 the company surrendered its northern powers to a new Newcastle & Darlington Junction concern which extended north to Rainton Crossing, near Durham from April/June 1844. From there, the route to the Tyne ran over earlier Durham Junction, Pontop & South Shields and Brandling Junction metals through Washington, Brockley Whins and Pelaw.

North of the Tyne, the Newcastle & Berwick Railway fulfilled the promise of its title with three openings in 1847. Then, on 1 September 1848, a link from Manors into Newcastle and a temporary bridge over the Tyne brought into being continuous rail connections between London and Berwick-upon-Tweed. By 10 October a temporary viaduct there carried the route on to meet the North British Railway's line from Edinburgh.

Between 1848 and 1850 the Tyne and Tweed crossings became permanent and the journey was shortened by a cut-off line between Washington and Pelaw, but the course of the ECML did not become the one we now know until 1872. Then, in the year following the opening of the new Doncaster-York route via Selby, the present course through Durham was established based on:

Croft Branch, Parkgate Junction to Tursdale Junction, Ferryhill	Opened 19 June 1844 under the N&DJ's take-over of former GNE powers
Relly Mill Junction to Newton Hall Junction at Durham	Opened 1 April 1857 as part of the N&DJ's Bishop Auckland branch
Newton Hall Junction to Gateshead	Opened 2 March 1868 by NER (passengers 1 December 1868)

This was then to remain the route of the main line until the Selby Diversion of 1983.

One other major railway needs to be mentioned to complete this outline picture of the formative years, viz the Leeds Northern. Authorized originally as the Leeds & Thirsk, it opened its first section, from Thirsk to Ripon, for goods traffic on 5 January 1848 and for passengers on 1 June 1848. Quickly extending south towards Leeds, it reached there on 10 July 1849 when the section south of Weeton

The North Eastern Railway pioneered the use of high-capacity wagons for its extensive flows of mineral traffic.

was opened. Three years later, on 2 June 1852, the Leeds Northern reached the Tees by opening a line from Melmerby through Northallerton to the Stockton & Darlington at Eaglescliffe. Although overshadowed by the East Coast Main Line, the Leeds Northern route remained important for over a century, and the end sections still survive as the Leeds-Harrogate passenger line and the Northallerton-Eaglescliffe freight route.

The railway melting pot of the 1840s had clearly shown the advantages of larger systems, and by the middle of the century the pre-1923 giants had already been born. The pioneer North Midland had become part of the Midland Railway, the Manchester & Leeds was part of the Lancashire & Yorkshire, and the London & North Western had acquired the Colne valley route constituents. The Great Central name had not emerged, but its basic system existed in the hands of the Manchester, Sheffield & Lincolnshire Railway. The time was ripe for the birth of the North Eastern giant.

The principal partners in the East Coast Main Line had come together as the York, Newcastle & Berwick Railway and this grouping, together with the York & North Midland and Leeds Northern empires (plus the smaller Malton & Driffield), became the North Eastern Railway with effect from 31 July 1854. The new railway was the largest of the period and operated in an area of buoyant traffic, so that the prospect of other railway companies in the North East remaining independent was not likely. Some bitter and often senseless competition ensued, but one by one the independents were taken over—the Newcastle & Carlisle in 1862, the Stockton & Darlington and the West Hartlepool in 1865, and the Blyth & Tyne in 1874—to lift the NER route mileage from 720 to nearly twice that figure and give it virtual domination of its home territory.

At the beginning of this new era, the North Eastern spent some time sorting out its financial affairs and then began to remedy the defects of the fragmentary evolution of the lines in its area. It took over floundering schemes like the Whitby, Redcar & Middlesbrough Union, filled in territorial gaps like the one in mid-Durham, and built important cut-off lines like those from Thorne to Goole and Hartlepool to Seaham. A significant number of connecting spurs were put in to create new routes, stations were rebuilt and remodelled, Sunderland got a bridge across the Wear, and Newcastle even got a second one.

Although some of its east-west lines carried only modest volumes of traffic, those serving the ports and industries of the four great rivers of the area kept the

NER wealthy by railway standards, except in times of national depression. It used its wealth wisely, building up its ports into the largest of the railway docks undertakings, constantly improving the system and constantly experimenting with new techniques, especially with powered signalling, various forms of railcars and with automatic warning systems. All these things helped the NER better to withstand the railway pressures of the twentieth century and, at the outbreak of the First World War, it was a strong, active undertaking with around 1,750 route miles of railway under its control.

The North Eastern Railway entertained a positive attitude towards electric traction right from the beginning of the century, when it used electrification to respond to the threat posed by urban tramways. The expanding Tyneside tramways made some serious inroads into local rail travel and by 1902 had cut the volume of suburban rail travel by half. In the same year, the NER approved a £250,000 conversion programme to provide a circular electrified route from Newcastle to New Bridge Street via Tynemouth. By 1903, trial running had commenced and public services began a year later, on 29 March 1904. This rapid response to the competition earned its reward, the reduced operating costs permitting a much improved service and quickly winning back half the traffic which had been lost. Electric services continued until 1967, and although then replaced by diesel multiple units, they were soon to be back in a modernized form as part of the Tyneside PTA's Tyne & Wear Metro scheme.

Encouraged by the success of its 1904 electrification, the NER looked at the lines south of the Tyne in 1907, but did not take any action, conversion of the South Shields line being shelved until the LNER revived the project in the 1930s. However, in 1913 construction work began on a 1,500 volt DC overhead electrification of the line from Shildon to Newport Yards at Middlesbrough. The objective was to reduce the operating costs of moving the substantial flow of coal traffic passing from the South Durham coalfield for export shipment and to use the scheme as a trial for future electrification decisions. One of the 13 locomotives built was a passenger prototype which might have gone into main line passenger service had it not been for the war and subsequent changes in the coal business. As it was, the route was worked electrically for only 19 years from 1915 to 1934.

Flying Scotsman *in the first year of the century, needing double-heading for its long and rather mixed train.*

The first quarter of the century produced a host of light railways authorized under the various Acts of the 1896–1912 period. A few, like the Derwent Valley, the Easingwold and the Cawood, Wistow & Selby, lay within NER 'territory' but, by and large, that company had a fairly easy time of it so far as competition from other railways was concerned. The exception was the Hull & Barnsley Railway which opened in 1885 and did rob the NER of some of its coal traffic before finally being absorbed into the larger company just before grouping.

The Hull & Barnsley had cherished ambitions to extend north-west through Barnsley and made some useful alliances, but it never really recovered from its high construction costs. In any event, Yorkshire was already rather full of railways. Every major valley—and many minor ones—had a rail route, often two, and all the major towns had a choice of goods depots with a full range of shed, cranage, warehousing and dock facilities. The Great Northern, in particular, showed a determination to penetrate the whole of the West Riding by either its own lines or by the use of running powers, and no traffic flows were safe from the sales efforts of the Midland canvassers.

The worst side of the competition showed itself in the sort of problems that attended the establishment of Leeds Central station and in the exactly parallel routes such as those between Barnsley and Sheffield, but the same spirit of competition provided excellent passenger services to London, great hotels, good docks and shipping, new rolling stock and a steady stream of other improvements. The rail users of the period could get from coast to coast by L&Y, from Leeds to Glasgow by Midland, from Liverpool/Manchester to Leeds by LNW, to all the coastal resorts of Lincolnshire and Yorkshire, and to Europe from Hull or Newcastle. This was an area full of activity and complexity, more than ripe for the rationalization that came with the 1921 Railways Act and its subsequent 'grouping'.

The heavy industries of the North East had made the North Eastern Railway relatively prosperous, regularly paying a dividend of 7½ per cent on the NE Consols which were its lowest ranking stock. With 1,758 route miles, it was the largest

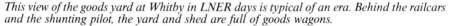

This view of the goods yard at Whitby in LNER days is typical of an era. Behind the railcars and the shunting pilot, the yard and shed are full of goods wagons.

Sentinel steam railcar Defiance, *pictured near Prospect Hill signal box at Whitby.*

of the seven railways which became the London & North Eastern Railway from 1 January 1923, and it contributed its General Manager, Ralph (later Sir Ralph) Wedgwood to become Chief General Manager of the new concern. The Great Central contributed 1,191 of the new railway's 6,590 route miles, the Great Northern 1,051, with 107 coming from the Hull & Barnsley system. Of the new LNER's 7,383 locomotives, 2,141 came from the North Eastern Railway, 752 of them 0-6-0 goods engines.

The new LNER company started off bravely, making decisions to build Gresley 'Pacifics' and to introduce Pullman services, but the 1920s were not good years for the nation. The 1926 General Strike was followed by further lean years while, in addition, the railways had to combat an increasing amount of competition from lorries and buses. In 1928 they obtained powers to invest in bus companies, building on a tradition the North Eastern had first begun with Beverley district services in 1903. Another reaction to the hard times was to prune some unprofitable passenger services, major closures of the 1929–31 period including South Gosforth to Darras Hall, Border Counties Junction to Allendale, Alnwick to Coldstream, Scarborough Road Junction to Gilling, Melmerby to Masham, and Carlton East Junction to Wellfield.

Things began to look up for Britain in the 1930s. In 1933, the year that saw the introduction of the LNER's *Northern Belle* cruise train, the railways also obtained significant protection against competition from the Road & Rail Traffic Act, and two years later came the dramatic introduction of the country's first streamlined train, *Silver Jubilee*. A maximum speed of 112½ mph was achieved during trials and then, in service, the much-publicized new train produced a four-hour timing between King's Cross and Newcastle. Two years later came the equally prestigious *Coronation* and *West Riding Limited* services. The LNER was taking a leading position in the drive for passengers, with excellent main line stock, finished in varnished teak, headed by Gresley's locomotives and producing impressive timings despite loads of 600 tons or more. The special stock for the streamlined trains included such innovations as a cocktail bar, hairdressing salon and cinema coach.

In 1938, the year that the South Shields line was electrified, *Mallard* took the world speed record with 126 mph on Stoke Bank. The motive power of the East

Pride of the LNER, a streamlined A4 'Pacific' and the Silver Jubilee *coach set.*

Coast Main Line had come a long way from 1903 when the era of the NER 4–4–0s gave way to the emergence of Worsdell's first 'Atlantic' design from Gateshead. Now 'Pacifics' were standard, many with special tenders to permit a change of crew without stopping, and the result was some excellent main line running. The 10 am *Flying Scotsman*, for example, was at Edinburgh by 5.25 pm, the noon Saturday *Norseman* arrived at Tyne Commission Quay five hours later, and the 5.30 pm *Silver Jubilee* reached Newcastle Central exactly four hours later.

Backing its 'Top Link', the LNER had many other fine engines, from the supporting 'V2' class and the Raven, Robinson and other designs inherited from its constituents, down to its coal train engines and the railcars and push and pull sets used on lightly-trafficked branch lines. Water troughs enabled water to be taken on at speed and huge coaling towers hoisted and tipped the wagons supplying them. The LNER was the first British railway to lay 90 ft rails and it was also in the van of new signalling and train control equipment and techniques. A considerable effort was put into upgrading stations, docks and other facilities and publicity was of prime importance. But the LNER also cared for its heritage and maintained the museum which the North Eastern had begun in the old station at York.

The LNER was to make a major contribution to the war effort in the years 1939–45. By the outbreak of hostilities, the company's workshops were already producing armaments and munitions. Its trains were then called upon to haul coal, steel and foodstuffs in previously unheard of quantities, and to carry forces personnel to bases, ports, aerodromes and leave destinations. The ships of the LNER were requisitioned for war service and many of its staff fought and died for their country. The location of the LNER railways in relation to Europe and Scandinavia brought it under heavy air attack, but it was also able to retaliate by supplying the nation's airfields, some three-quarters of which lay within the LNER territory.

Emerging from the war years near exhausted, but quickly producing a 'Five Year

Above *Major operators of road transport for goods collection and delivery, the railways used this 3 ton, three-wheel 'mechanical horse' for its versatility and manoeuvrability.*

Below *A reminder of the Deltic era on the East Coast Main Line, as D9008* The Green Howards *stands at Gateshead MPD in October 1966.*

Above *Coal is the Eastern Region's main freight commodity, with such trainloads of hopper wagons a commonplace sight.*

Left *A solitary locomotive in the shed at York captures the atmosphere of the steam traction era. The date is 1947, the last year before nationalisation.*

Below *Near the end of the dmu era, a two-car set at Hexham in 1988 on the Down line, but waiting to leave in the Up direction.*

Above *An InterCity HST set gets a high-speed clean.*

Below *Tyne & Wear Metro train.*

The Pacers arrive; a Darlington area set in service in April 1986.

Plan' for rehabilitation and improvement, the system quickly got its services back to something like normal. However, the separate identity of the London & North Eastern Railway survived only until the last day of 1947, when the Transport Act of that year ushered in the new nationalized railway system. The mantle of the old North Eastern Railway was to fall on the North Eastern Region of the new organization.

The 1950s were to bring a period of great change to the traditional railway system. In the year that the Sheffield-Woodhead-Manchester electrification scheme was finally completed, the 1954 Modernization Plan offered a massive capital injection but, at the same time, the hounds of competition were being freed from traditional fetters. The new funds brought diesel multiple units to the branch lines, colour light multiple aspect signalling and a host of other improvements. A fleet of $22 \times 3,300$ hp 'Deltics' came into service on the East Coast Main Line in 1962 and increasingly capitalized upon the track improvements which had lifted it up to a capacity for 100 mph running. By 1973 the journey time between King's Cross and Newcastle had been reduced to 3½ hours but the increased activity on the trunk routes had to be matched by a wholesale pruning of branch and secondary lines begun in earnest in the '50s and completed under the Beeching era Reshaping Plan in the '60s. Major losses included the central section of the Leeds Northern line and the whole of the Hull & Barnsley system.

On the slimmed-down Eastern Region railway system, the 1970s saw the second half of the railway revolution. Resources concentrated on the most productive routes led to the introduction of the InterCity 125s in 1978–9, High Speed Trains running on high grade track, under modern mas signalling and supported by equally dramatic changes in timetabling, control and passenger traffic servicing. On the freight side the traditional wagonload business finally bowed out, as steam had done in 1968. The new freight age was one of block trains for coal, fuel, aggregates and other dedicated products, Freightliners for container traffic, and high speed, air-braked services for other longer distance or specialized business, all computer planned and monitored. The system had come a long way from its A and B containers delivered by mechanical horse, its hump marshalling yards and its constant search for improvement with devices like the Roadrailer.

The 1980s saw the Eastern Region (as the North Eastern had become) and its Northern Operating Area capitalizing on the years of physical and technological change. Main line passenger business had responded to the service provided by the HSTs and the introduction of Sprinter units helped to attract further passengers to the important North Wales/Liverpool/Manchester-Leeds/Hull/York/Scarborough and the NE/SW routes. Despite financial constraints, the involvement in local railway services of the South and West Yorkshire PTEs produced a new era for local rail travel, especially in the West Riding, and the Tyne & Wear Metro system was attracting interest from all over the world. As Pacers slowly ousted the life-expired dmus, local routes, like those from Hull and Newcastle, also enjoyed increasing levels of patronage. A sign of the times was the acquisition of the world long-distance start-to-stop diesel speed record on 27 September 1985 when a pre-view run for a new Tees-Tyne Pullman service produced an average speed of 115.4 mph for the 268.6 miles between Newcastle and London, with intermediate section averages of up to 140.1 mph.

As this book is being written, electrification works are showing increasing progress on the East Coast Main Line and the connecting route to Leeds. The massive scheme, involving an investment of over £300 million, was planned to give, in successive years from 1987, electrification to Peterborough, trial-running to Grantham and then Leeds, and the full service to Leeds from late 1989. With all works, including the new Class '91' 'Electra' locomotives, ready early, the scheme has been put forward to give Leeds electric trains ahead of the target date, with electrification then reaching Edinburgh by 1991.

Part of the preparation work for the electrification of the East Coast Main Line.

Abbreviations used

AHB	Automatic half barriers
AOCL	Open crossing with road warning lights monitored by train crew
AOCR	Open crossing with road warning lights monitored by signalman
CCTV	Closed circuit television
ch	Chains
DGL	Down Goods Loop
dmu	Diesel multiple unit
DPL	Down Passenger Loop
DRS	Down Refuge Siding
emu	Electric multiple unit
ET	Electric Token
HST	High Speed Train
LC	Level crossing
m	Miles
mas	Multiple Aspect Signalling
mgr	Merry-go-round
OT	One Train
PTE	Passenger Transport Executive
RC	Remotely-controlled
R/G	Red/Green
TCB	Track Circuit Block
TMO	Trainmen-operated
UGL	Up Goods Loop
UPL	Up Passenger Loop
URS	Up Refuge Siding
X	Crossing works automatically in the wrong direction

Key to maps

Open line and station

Freight and non-passenger line

Closed line and station

Tunnel

Tyne & Wear Metro

Gazetteer

Note During the period 1988–92 a number of new, simple stations are likely to come into service in the PTE areas. The following, although not included in the gazetteer, are either newly opened, under construction or planned: Cottingley (Leeds), Outwood (Wakefield), Steeton & Silsden (Keighley), Cononley (Skipton), Thurnscoe, (Sheffield-Leeds line), Goldthorpe (Sheffield-Leeds line), Burley Park (Leeds), Berry Brow (Huddersfield), Hawksworth (Leeds), Thornhill (Dewsbury), Armley (Leeds), Milnsbridge (Huddersfield) and Salterhebble (Halifax).

A.1 Adwick Junction—see Stainforth-Adwick Line

A.2 Acklington

East Coast Main Line, between Morpeth and Alnmouth. 28 m 43 ch from Newcastle

Lying on the line opened by the Newcastle & Berwick Railway on 1 July 1847, Acklington today retains many of its period features whilst filling a modern role for passengers catching the Newcastle-Alnmouth/Berwick trains there. The station consists of two conventional platforms with a long shelter on the Up side and elaborate, gabled stone buildings on the Down. Even the stone goods shed is stylish.

This stretch of the East Coast Main Line is controlled by Chevington signal box (25 m 49 ch) where there is a barrier crossing and cottage, and Up and Down Passenger Loops. There was a station at Chevington which lost its passenger service on 15 September 1958, and just beyond it the old Amble branch began its 5¾ mile journey to the coast. Lying on the northern edge of the Northumberland coalfield area, this line had opened for coal conveyance on 5 September 1849 and started carrying passengers on 2 June 1879. In its later years there were six trains each way daily between Chevington and Amble, calling at Broomhill (3¼ m), and taking 15 minutes for the journey. The passenger service ended as early as 7 July 1930, but the route remained open for goods until the end of the 1960s.

Beyond Acklington the ECML crosses the River Coquet by a high viaduct and then passes near the ruins of Warkworth Castle. There is a trailing crossover at Southside Crossover (30 m 55 ch) and an AHB LC at Warkworth (31 m 67 ch), which also had a station at one time. A little further on the trackbed of the former line to Newton-on-the-Moor can be seen on the Down side.

A.3 Allens West

Darlington-Saltburn line, between Darlington and Eaglescliffe. 3 m 65 ch from Darlington.

Allens West was opened during the Second World War to meet the needs of workpeople vital to the war effort. It remains Ministry of Defence property and carries a disclaimer notice to its users. The station, which lies on a section of the line opened back in 1825 by the Stockton & Darlington Railway, consists of platforms, shelters and an AHB LC and it is served by the Saltburn and Hartlepool route trains.

Urlay Nook signal box and level crossing (7 m 39 ch) lies to the west of Allens West station, and a Down Goods Loop survives near the once-extensive Down side siding network.

A.4 Allerton Main Branch—see Castleford

A.5 Alnmouth

East Coast Main Line, between Morpeth and Berwick. 34 m 69 ch from Newcastle

The East Coast Main Line drops gently to Alnmouth before a climb of nearly four miles at 1 in 170 north of the town. Alnmouth itself is a very pleasant Northumberland resort beside the estuary of the River Aln, once a port and now a yachting centre. A few miles up river lies the ancient town of Alnwick which had a rail link to Alnmouth and the main line until 1968, some 16 trains a day performing the 3 mile, seven minute journey in each direction.

From Alnwick, a meandering rural route north to Coldstream had been opened in 1887 (2 May for goods and 5 September for passengers). Noted for its elegant station buildings more than its traffic levels—three trains each way seems to have been standard—the route ran via Edlingham (7m), Whittingham (10 m), Glanton (11½ m), Hedgeley (13½ m), Wooperton (15¾ m), Ilderton (18½ m), Wooler (22¼ m), Akeld (24¾ m), Kirknewton (27¾ m) and Mindrum (35¾ m). Trains took just over one and a half hours for the 35¾ mile through journey to Coldstream until their withdrawal on 22 September 1930. After storms destroyed a bridge in 1948, the section between Ilderton and Wooler was closed, freight activity surviving on the two truncated parts for another five years.

Alnmouth today enjoys a local train service to and from Newcastle, plus calls by Berwick and some King's Cross-Edinburgh services. It has recently been provided with new station buildings on the Up side in a scheme costing £77,000, part of which was contributed by Alnwick District Council. The project involved a purpose-designed building embracing booking, parcels and waiting facilities, together with improved car parking and bus turning areas in the station forecourt. The main structure, on the Up side, is to an attractive, modern design enhanced by a bright colour scheme. A footbridge leads to the Down side where the platform was formerly an island.

The Down direction approach to Alnmouth is via Warkworth AHB LC (31 m 67 ch) where a superb Up side house survives in the former station area. Then comes Wooden Gate CCTV LC (33 m 71 ch) with its loops, refuge sidings and trailing crossover. After Alnmouth station the trackbed of the Alnwick line is visible on the Down side, followed by a viaduct with a view of Lesbury advance warning radar station, Longhoughton station site, and another at Little Mill CCTV LC (39 m 34 ch), where a trailing crossover remains operational. Alnmouth signal box covers from 30 m 55 ch to 40 m 39 ch.

A.6   Altofts
Sheffield-Leeds line, between Normanton and Leeds. 186 m 34 ch from St Pancras

Altofts station is really rather a functional affair of wooden platforms perched high above the road and served by the Sheffield-Leeds trains. By the time the first Altofts station opened in 1870, the location had had a railway for 30 years, and memories of the momentous linking of the North Midland and York & North Midland lines to provide the first through route to York would have been forgotten.

Altofts Junction (185 m 73 ch), where the Leeds and York routes separate, lies south of the station and is controlled by the wooden Altofts Junction signal box (186 m) on the Down side. North of the station the railway passes close to the union of the Aire & Calder Canal and the Calder river, crossing both these waterways in turn.

A.7   Anlaby Road Junction—see Hull

A.8   Apperley   Junction—see   Ilkley Branch

A.9   Applehurst Junction—see Stainforth-Adwick Line

A.10   Ardsley
Wakefield-Leeds line. 180 m 61 ch from King's Cross

The 297 yard Ardsley Tunnel (180 m 61 ch) lies midway between Wakefield and Leeds and is one of the few remaining features of what was once a crossroads of the Great Northern Railway. Just five days after the main line had opened from Wakefield to Leeds on 5 October 1857, another GNR satellite (the Leeds, Bradford & Halifax Junction Railway) completed its link through to Laisterdyke, near Bradford. By means of the Methley Joint line eastwards and the westward links via Gildersome and Dudley Hill to Low Moor, Bradford and Shipley, the Great Northern was able to penetrate the whole area.

The original Great Northern plans to penetrate the West Riding had been rejected by Parliament and these routes via Ardsley were part of the company's response to the earlier disappointments. With the 1866 West Riding & Grimsby scheme, now the main line to Doncaster, the Ardsley routes enabled the GNR to tap the vast freight potential of this part of Yorkshire, and to create a network of local passenger services to feed its mainline trains.

Some of the Wakefield-Bradford local trains ran via Dewsbury and Batley, but others served Lofthouse (3¾ m), Ardsley (5¾ m) and then turned west through Tingley (6¾ m), Morley (8 m) and Gildersome (9½ m) to Drighlington. This route left today's line south of the tunnel. North of it, traces remain of the connections south of Beeston which were used by the Leeds-Bradford trains. Some of these crossed above the main line near the northern mouth of the tunnel; others reversed at Ardsley.

A.11   Arram—see Hull-Scarborough Line

A.12   Ashington—see Lynemouth Colliery and Butterwell

A.13   Askern   Colliery   Branch—see Shaftholme Junction-Knottingley Line

A.14   Austin & Pickersgill's Shipyard—see Monkwearmouth

B.1   Baildon—see Ilkley Branch

B.2   Bardon   Mill—see   Newcastle-Carlisle

B.3   Barnsley
Wincobank Junction, Sheffield to Horbury Junction line, junction with Huddersfield line. 6 m 54 ch from Penistone

Like most of South Yorkshire, the coal, glass and clothing-based town of Barnsley has a complex railway history, featuring in a variety of trunk route and local schemes as railway promoters succumbed to the lure of coal and other traffics, and local commercial worthies demanded for their products the transport facilities afforded to their neighbours and competitors. In fact, Barnsley joined Britain's growing railway network on the first day of the second half of the nineteenth century when it was reached from Horbury by a line promoted by the Sheffield, Rotherham, Barnsley, Wakefield, Huddersfield & Goole Railway, later to become part of the Lancashire & Yorkshire Railway system. The North Midland's line to Leeds had been serving Barnsley by coach links up to that time.

Following the arrival of the first trains at Barnsley proper, there came a round of railway development by the South Yorkshire and Manchester, Sheffield & Lincolnshire companies that was eventually to mark Barnsley as Great Central territory. Just one year and one month after the advent of the SRBWH&G, on 1 July 1851, the

South Yorkshire's route from Doncaster via Mexborough reached Barnsley. Then, in 1854, the first section of the line to Penistone was opened (completed in 1859) and a link to Sheffield was established, from 4 September, over the new SRBWH&G line from Aldam Junction through Chapeltown to Wincobank Junction. Finally the Midland, who were now calling the NM Barnsley station Cudworth, built a short branch across the valley to Barnsley proper which it reached on 2 May 1870 (goods 28 June 1869).

Today, Barnsley still retains its first railway, that north through Darton to Horbury (and Wakefield), but the GC route down the eastern side of the Dearne Valley has gone and trains from Barnsley to Sheffield switch to the former Midland route at Quarry Junction. The Barnsley-Penistone line closed on 5 January 1970 but then re-opened on 16 May 1983 when the Sheffield-Huddersfield services were re-routed via Barnsley. The once-complicated railway network of the area, detailed in outline on the map, has thus become much simplified. The last train to use the GC and Midland joint station at Court House left on 15 April 1960, leaving the present station—formerly called Exchange—to handle the remaining services.

Prior to the closure period, Barnsley's single-platform Exchange station provided services to Wakefield and Leeds via the L&Y route and south to Sheffield (Victoria) over the GCR Chapeltown line. From Court House, Barnsley folk had the alternative of going to Leeds via Nostell and Sheffield by the Midland route, and could also catch the Penistone-Doncaster trains or the nine minute push and pull service to Cudworth. During the week of Barnsley Feast, holiday excursions would run to such resorts as Blackpool, Scarborough, Skegness and Yarmouth. Both the Barnsley stations had substantial goods yards (although there was no fixed crane at Court House) and the area had several private sidings, for wood, beer, glass and Corporation traffic as well as coal.

On the approach to Barnsley from Wombwell, the mileage changes from the Midland's 173 m 48 ch to the GC's 7 m 50 ch from Penistone at the former Quarry Junction. About a mile earlier, the line from Sheffield dips below the route of the former GC line and then makes a viaduct crossing of the River Dove. The old Moor End branch used to follow the valley floor below. There are also signs of former colliery connections and of the line towards the Court House station.

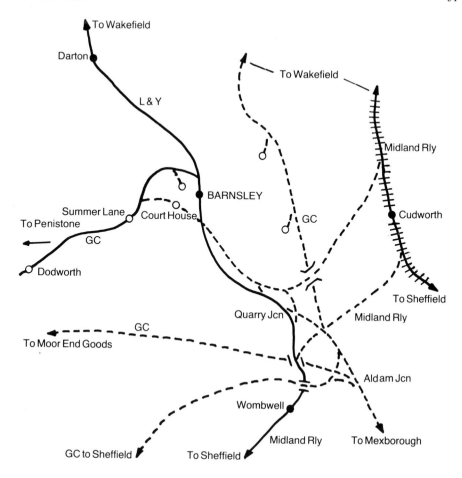

Today's Sheffield-Huddersfield and Sheffield-Wakefield trains approach Barnsley's main Down platform via a crossover, a barrier crossing and the small, square and low Jumble Lane signal box (6 m 59 ch) which stands at the south end of the station (6 m 54 ch). They depart via the much taller wooden box at Barnsley Station Junction (6 m 43 ch), where the two routes divide. Between the two boxes the station consists of the short Up platform, added in 1960 when Court House closed, and the long Down platform, which houses the main station building. This consists of a long block in red brick with a more decorative centre section and with a supplementary retaining wall at the south end.

The station building at Barnsley Court House station was actually built as a court house in 1861, nine years before its adoption by the Midland Railway for use as a station. It survived the closure of its rail route to join other notable Barnsley buildings such as the Town Hall at the top of Regent Street and the headquarters building of the National Union of Mineworkers which lies beyond.

B.4   Barnsley-Huddersfield Line

From Barnsley Station Junction, with the Sheffield to Horbury Junction line, to Springwood Junction, Huddersfield. 19 m 69 ch

This route took over from the direct Sheffield-Deepcar-Penistone-Huddersfield line as recently as 1983 and now carries a Sheffield-Barnsley-Penistone-Huddersfield service. The change arose from difficulties over the PTE support funding for the direct route which culminated in the closure of the section between Sheffield and Penistone (via Neepsend, Wadsley Bridge, Oughty Bridge, Deepcar and Wortley) from 16

May 1983. In its place a service was introduced over the former Midland route to Barnsley and then on to Penistone over the Barnsley-Penistone line.

Local services between Barnsley and Penistone had been withdrawn on 29 June 1959 and the intermediate stations at Silkstone, Dodworth and Summer Lane closed. The remaining through passenger train was then rerouted on 5 January 1970, at the same time as the closure of the western section of the old Great Central main line through Woodhead Tunnel. Finally, the Penistone-Dodworth section was closed completely on 20 July 1981.

Following an agreement between BR and the South and West Yorkshire PTEs, the Barnsley-Penistone line was reinstated to passenger train standards in just 75 days, but doubts over the continuation of financial support produced closure proposals in late 1983 as a precaution against the withdrawal of funding. Closure authority already existed for the Denby Dale to Penistone section, but fortunately this gap between the two territories and the South Yorkshire end of the route were reprieved.

The ex-L&Y route to Wakefield and the reopened line to Penistone separate at Barnsley Station Junction (6 m 43 ch), under the control of the wooden signal box there. To the east, Barnsley housing slopes down to the River Dearne, but our line curves sharply round the north side of the town, climbing at 1 in 50/67 through a cutting to the site of the old Summer Lane station and then becoming single at 5 m 72 ch. On this, the last section to be opened, the junction from the old GC goods depot and from the Midland line (at Court House Junction) used to join, and traces of former activities can still be spotted.

The curving and climbing continues to a summit on the steel girder bridge straddling the M1, with traces of Old Silkstone and Silkstone Fall colliery connections either side of Dodworth barrier crossing and brick signal box (3 m 67 ch). The line then continues through rolling upland landscape as it heads for Silkstone Common which was reopened in 1984 and has a simple wooden platform on the Down side of the line. Traces of the former platform and goods yard are still visible.

Just beyond Silkstone Common an old tramway route is crossed, followed by the trackbed of the former connection from the Aldam Junction to Moor End goods branch. Then comes the 558 yard Oxspring Tunnel (63 ch to 38 ch), a brick-lined single bore leading to the former Barnsley Junction with the Don Valley route to Sheffield, and where the mileage changes from zero to 29 m 13 ch (from Manchester). Our line has crossed the River Don by means of Oxspring Viaduct, just before the surviving tunnel.

Penistone, detailed in a separate entry, retains the substantial station where the Woodhead and Huddersfield routes joined, the latter beginning its distances at the tall Huddersfield Junction signal box (13 m 42 ch). This line was authorized to the Huddersfield & Sheffield Junction Railway in 1845 and opened throughout on 1 July 1850, nine years before the completion of the Penistone-Barnsley line, which took the MS&L from 15 May 1854 to 1 December 1859 to complete.

Leaving the H&SJ/L&Y platforms at Penistone station (13 m 36 ch), the single line heads for the high, 29-arch Penistone Viaduct which carries it over the broad valley of the Don and affords superb views over the town to the rolling hills beyond. From the 415 yd Wellhouse Tunnel (12 m 48 ch to 12 m 29 ch), the route begins to drop gently, but still maintains its propensity to curve. Another viaduct heralds the approach to Denby Dale (9 m 31 ch) and its short platform, simple stone shelter and adjacent former goods shed. Denby Dale is a centre for walkers and noted also for its giant meat and potato pies.

More curves precede the 906 yd Cumberworth Tunnel (9 m 5 ch to 8 m 44 ch) which links the Dearne and Fenay Beck valleys. Then the route comes to the wooden signal box at Clayton West Junction (7 m 67 ch) which marks the change back to a double track status that will continue all the way to Huddersfield. The box also used to control the modest branch out via Skelmanthorpe (9½ m from Huddersfield) to Clayton West (11¼ m). Opened by the L&Y on 1 September 1879, the branch had once had hopes of becoming a through route to Barnsley but had to settle instead for a quite reasonable 1930s service of 10 daily trains each way. The Clayton West branch closed on 24 January 1983 but the trackbed and junction site are still evident.

Shepley station (7 m 14 ch) has staggered platforms linked by an overbridge. Although they are only provided with waiting shelters, the station house and goods shed are still in existence and provide reminders of a period when forwardings of stone and munitions traffics were quite substantial. A rare level section ends near the next station, Stocksmoor (6 m 26 ch), where the short platforms are provided with traditional stone shelters. A heather-covered embankment then leads to the 1,631 yd Thurstonland Tunnel (5 m 58 ch to 4 m 63 ch) which carries the route through to the valley of the River Holme. The tree-covered tunnel is largely on a down gradient of 1 in 100 with a significant curve at the Huddersfield end.

Brockholes (4 m 25 ch) is a pleasant station in a traditional style, with station house and buildings in Yorkshire stone. It was formerly Holmfirth Junction where trains veered south from the main route to follow the eastern side of the Holme Valley to Thongs Bridge (5¼ m from Huddersfield) and Holmfirth. The 1 m 65 ch branch had opened with the 'main line' on 1 July 1850 and enjoyed an excellent service of 15–20 trains each way daily in its best years, finally closing on 2 November 1959 to passengers and on 3 May 1965 for goods.

Towards Huddersfield, the gradient continues to fall at 1 in 100/97/107/100. On this stretch, which gives impressive views of nestling villages and dramatic rock outcrops across the valley, lies Honley station (3 m 28 ch) still sporting some period sign boards, and the short but curving 228 yd of Robin Hood's Tunnel (2 m 70 ch to 2 m 60 ch).

There was a station at Berry Brow until 4 July 1966, but today's trains just continue their descent to Lockwood (1 m 18 ch) where the station has been simplified, although some traditional wood and brick buildings remain on the Up side. The location is preceded by the 476 yd 122 ft high Lockwood Viaduct over the River Holme, at the Huddersfield end of which a retaining wall marks the former junction with the branch to Netherton (3 m from Huddersfield), Healey House (3¾ m) and Meltham (5 m). This had a number of false starts before substantive opening on 5 July 1869, with setbacks ranging from a tunnel collapse to the subsidence of an embankment. Passenger services on the single line branch lasted for 80 years, ending on 23 May 1949, with complete closure from 5 April 1965.

Lockwood station is followed by the 205 yd Lockwood Tunnel (1 m 16 ch to 1 m 7 ch) and then a dramatic curve across the River Colne to Springwood Junction (40 ch) with the Manchester line, and the final tunnel approach to the grandeur of Huddersfield station. The river crossing is effected by Paddock Viaduct which rises 70 ft above ground level and uses 11 stone arches and five metal ones to curve the Penistone route round to its junction with the main Manchester lines.

Counting the early morning turn round working out from Huddersfield to Denby Dale and back, the route now has some ten daily trains in each direction, thanks to PTE support. Perhaps they do not quite carry the prestige of the one-time 'Thro Corr Exp' which left Bradford and Marylebone each morning at 10 o'clock with a five hour journey ahead, including some request stops between Huddersfield and Penistone, but they do make an important contribution to local travel needs.

B.5 Batley—see Manchester-Leeds Line

B.6 Battersby—see Middlesbrough-Whitby Line

B.7 Beacon Hill Tunnel—see Halifax

B.8 Beam Mill Junction—see Middlesbrough-Saltburn Line

B.9 Bedlington—see Benton-Morpeth Line

B.10 Belasis Lane—see Billingham-Seal Sands Storage Line

B.11 Belford

East Coast Main Line, between Alnmouth and Berwick. 51 m 45 ch from Newcastle

Belford signal box controls a stretch of the East Coast Main Line from No 174 R/G LC (50 m 37 ch) through Belford loops and crossovers, Crag Mill CCTV LC (52 m 48 ch), No 179 R/G LC (54 m 68 ch) and Smeafield CCTV LC (54 m 79 ch) to Fenham Low Moor LC (55 m 31 ch). Belford station lost its passenger service on 29 January 1968, but although Smeafield had gone much earlier—on 1 May 1930–it had continued for a while as a private station.

The station buildings at Belford, still standing on the Down side, were built in 1847 for the original Newcastle & Berwick Railway. Using local grey stone and with tall gables and chimneys, steeply-pitched roofs, and decorative canopies and finials, they represent a lasting tribute to the work of the N&B's architect Benjamin Green.

North of Belford a siding connection on the Up side leads to the Tilcon works.

B.12 Bempton—see Hull-Scarborough Line

B.13 Ben Rhydding—see Ilkley Branch

B.14 Bensham—see Newcastle

B.15   Benton

East Coast Main Line, junction with Morpeth via Bedlington and Callerton lines. 4 m 26 ch from Newcastle

Although the Newcastle & Berwick Railway's main line was opened on 1 March 1847, the second (Blyth & Tyne) line at Benton did not come into use until 27 June 1864 and the two were not connected until early this century. Now the ex-B&T east-west route is primarily a Tyne & Wear Metro activity, with BR freight trains using the same metals on their way west to Callerton and taking a parallel course eastwards as far as Earsdon Junction.

The Benton site lies in a cutting with the double line connection for Callerton departing at South Junction (4 m 20 ch) and run-

ning behind Benton signal box (6 ch) to join the Metro route at Benton Station Junction (27 ch). The other double line spur leaves Benton North Junction and heads east for 64 chains before becoming single. The former BR station at Benton is now a Metro stopping point.

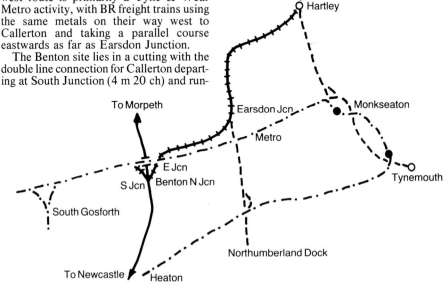

A clean piece of civil engineering, Benton Hall Bridge on the main line north of Newcastle.

B.16 Benton-Morpeth Line

East Coast Main Line, from Benton North Junction to Morpeth North Junction via Bedlington. 16 m 11 ch

This freight-only route originally formed the backbone of the Blyth & Tyne Railway, itself derived from individual wagonways with roots back in the eighteenth century or earlier. A cohesive coal route from the Blyth area to the larger shipping available on the Tyne first emerged in 1846 based on a connection to the Seghill Railway's 1840/1 line south to Northumberland Dock. Passengers were carried from 3 March 1847 and the enterprise became the Blyth & Tyne Railway as a result of an Act of 30 June 1852.

The system subsequently expanded to serve the collieries and resorts along the coast—

> Newsham-Morpeth — 1 April 1858 (goods 1 October 1857)
> Hartley-Tynemouth — 1 April 1861 (goods 31 October 1860)
> Newcastle-South Gosforth — 27 June 1864 (goods 1 May 1863)
> Monkseaton-South Gosforth — 27 June 1864 (goods 1 May 1863) —

before passing to the North Eastern Railway in 1874. The main subsequent extensions were the Quayside (1870) and Riverside (1871) branches at Newcastle, a new route between Monkseaton and Tynemouth (1882), spurs at Benton and South Gosforth (1903–5) and the connection to the main line at Manors (1 January 1909).

The main passenger service over the B&T system was that from Newcastle via Jesmond (½ m), West Jesmond (1¼ m), South Gosforth (2¼ m), Benton (4 m), Backworth (6½ m), Seghill (8¾ m), Seaton Delaval (9¾ m), Hartley (11 m), Newsham (12¾ m), Bebside (14½ m), Bedlington (15½ m), North Seaton (17½ m) and Ashington (18½ m) to Newbiggin (21 m). A shuttle service operated over the one and a half mile link between Newsham and Blyth, which then had a further service inland via Newsham (1½ m), Bebside (3¼ m), Bedlington (4¼ m), Choppington (5½ m) and Hepscott (7¾ m) to Morpeth (9¼ m). Blyth also had a good service south along the coast through Newsham (1½ m) and Hartley (3½ m) to Monkseaton (7 m) where passengers could connect with the circular service serving North Tyneside.

The northern section of the B&T lost its passenger trains on 2 November 1964, but, thanks to improvements at Blyth harbour begun by the NER in 1881 and continued over some 50 years, BR still handles ship-ment coal there. Additionally, inland coal movements pass over the B&T route from the Ashington area collieries to longer distance destinations.

From Benton North Junction, the ex-B&T route takes the 1904 curve and passes below what is now the Metro line, becoming single after 64 chains and changing to the B&T main line mileages at what used to be Earsdon Junction (2 m 53 ch/7 m 8 ch). After the AOCL crossing at Holywell (7 m 41 ch), the single line passes through the former Seghill station where there is an AHB LC (9 m 6 ch) and continues via a similar situation at Hartley (11 m 12 ch) to Newsham (12 m 45 ch). Beyond Newsham level crossing the line reverts to double track and at Newsham North Junction (12m 74 ch) sheds a 36 chain, OT single line running via Isabella TMO LC (25 ch) to the exchange point with the colliery.

The 'main line' continues via Plessey Road CCTV LC (13 m 16 ch) and Bebside LC (14 m 67 ch) to the signal box and barrier crossing combination at Bedlington South (15 m 60 ch) and then Bedlington North (15 m 71 ch). The Lynemouth Colliery branch continues north from here (see separate entry) leaving the Morpeth line to continue as a Tokenless Block single line through AHB crossings at Choppington (17 m 6 ch) and Hepscott (19 m 21 ch) to Hepscott Junction (19 m 44 ch). The triangular connection with the main line is made here, comprising a single line to the south via Morpeth signal box and level crossing (20 m 40 ch) to Morpeth Junction (20 m 46 ch) and one of similar length north via a 25 chain double line section to Morpeth North Junction (20 m 46 ch).

B.17 Berwick-upon-Tweed

East Coast Main Line. 67 m from Newcastle

This attractive and historic border town was for many years a key centre in the intermittent warfare between the English and Scottish nations. The arrival of the North British Railway in 1843 maintained a link with history by using the site of the twelfth century castle for Berwick's first station, and today's rail travellers can still get a taste of the past from a station plaque recording:

The station stands on the site of a great wall of Berwick Castle. Here on 17 November 1292 the claim of Robert Bruce to the crown of Scotland was declined and the decision in favour of John Baliol was given by King Edward I before the Parliament of England and a great gathering of the nobility and populace of England and Scotland.

The principal obvious remains of the old castle are the West Wall, which used to be the goods yard boundary, and its semi-circular gun tower. Little else remains visible and it is not easy to imagine the Great Hall and King's Chamber where express trains now run, or the deep defensive ditch which used to occupy the car park area. Because the castle walls and vaults are scheduled monuments, pre-electrification work has required the approval of the Secretary of State, and BR has provided facilities for archaeological observation and recording during the progress of the work.

The Newcastle & Berwick Railway's line from the south reached the banks of the Tweed on 29 March 1847, with a temporary viaduct then linking it with the NBR to create a through route to Scotland from 10 October 1848. In due course, the temporary structure was replaced by the Royal Border Bridge which started carrying goods traffic from 20 July 1850 and passengers from the 29th of the following month.

The magnificent bridge across the Tweed is the work of Robert Stephenson and its construction was of such significance that Queen Victoria herself attended the opening ritual. Stone was used for the piers and to face the 28 arches in order to give the bridge a mellow appearance, as it passes over the houses of Tweedmouth and then 126 ft above high water in the Tweed to the

high north bank and then Berwick station.

The present Berwick station was built by the LNER in 1927 and consists of rather grand Up side main buildings with footbridge access to the two island platforms beyond. The former has an imposing two-storey stone frontage with iron balustrades flanking the central clock housing, while the Down island has a long wooden building on a brick base and with an overall canopy. A number of Anglo-Scottish services call at Berwick-on-Tweed and the station also has a local service to and from Newcastle; but the route to Coldstream and Kelso via Tweedmouth is no more.

Beyond the Berwick station platforms, goods loops and down side sidings, the ECML heads for R/G LC No 23 (68 m 52 ch) and a long climb northwards at 1 in 190. At the Regional Boundary the mileage changes from 69 m 67 ch from Newcastle to 54 m 49 ch from Edinburgh.

B.18   Beverley
Hull-Scarborough line, between Hull and Driffield. 8 m 20 ch from Hull

The railway from Hull to Bridlington was opened on 6 October 1846, and Beverley would have been linked with York via Market Weighton soon afterwards, if the York & North Midland company had completed its 1846 Parliamentary authoriza-

The Royal Border Bridge seen from the north bank of the Tweed at Berwick and with the remnants of a wall of Berwick Castle in the foreground.

Beverley station, complete with overall roof and all the station paraphernalia of the 1960 period.

tions. As it was, only the York-Market Weighton section was constructed and Beverley had to wait until 1 May 1865 when the North Eastern Railway filled the gap.

The Beverley-York line ran via Cherry Burton (12 miles from Hull), Kipling Cotes (16¼ m), Market Weighton (19¾ m), Londesborough (21½ m), Nunburnholme (23½ m), Pocklington (26 m), Fangfoss (30¼ m), Stamford Bridge (32¾ m), Holtby (34 m), Warthill (36 m) and Earswick (39½ m). In later years it carried some non-stop and semi-fast as well as all-stations services, the fastest time for the former being around 52 minutes for the 42 miles. The route was closed on 29 November 1965, but the section between Beverley and Market Weighton has now come back into useful public service as a walkway. Humberside County Council have named this after George Hudson who lived in the area for a time.

Today Beverley has an excellent local service to and from Hull, plus trains north to Bridlington and Scarborough. The original station by G.T. Andrews, currently being refurbished, retains its overall roof and distinctive foot-bridge. The signal box and adjacent barrier crossing lie at the south end, with the former yard area and coal drops at the north.

The approach to Beverley provides a fine view of the Minster on the Down side. Dating from the thirteenth century and succeeding an earlier Saxon church, this fine example of Gothic architecture is dominated by the two great west towers. Both the Minster and the surrounding town hold much of interest, and the Museum of Army Transport is situated nearby. On the route out of Beverley are the CCTV crossings at Cherry Tree (8 m 39 ch) and Beverley North (8 m 62 ch), followed by the departure of the trackbed of the old Market Weighton line.

The North Eastern Railway was only just behind the Great Western in introducing local bus services, and Beverley has the distinction of being on one of the first routes.

B.19 Billingham

Northallerton-Newcastle line, junction with freight line to Seal Sands Storage. 64 m 47 ch from Leeds

Billingham lies to the north of the River Tees and its tributary, the Billingham Beck. The area, which has a mixture of industry and housing, received its first trains when the Clarence Railway extended its west-east line from Norton Junction to new coal staiths at Haverton Hill and Port Clarence. This began to carry mineral traffic from 29 October 1833 and later had a modest local passenger train service of about five trains each way daily.

Today the Darlington-Hartlepool and Middlesbrough-Newcastle trains call at Billingham station, the present location dating from 1966 and consisting of an island with brick shelter and steps to the former ticket office, now used by a taxi firm. The previous station lay west of the junction with the Seal Sands line, where the tall Billingham-on-Tees signal box now controls a barrier crossing (63 m 60 ch), Billingham Junction (63 m 69 ch) and the new Billingham station (64 m 47 ch). Beyond the latter comes Cowpen Lane AHB-X level crossing (65 m 44 ch).

B.20 Billingham–Seal Sands Storage Line

Northallerton-Newcastle line, branch from Billingham Junction. 7 m 49 ch

This line, surviving as the freight access to the industrial activity of the north bank of the Tees, dates back to the extension of the Clarence Railway from Norton Junction to Port Clarence on 29 October 1933. It later came to carry a modest passenger service which ran between Billingham-on-Tees and Port Clarence (3½ m) calling at Belasis Lane (¾ m) and Haverton Hill (2 m). Cut back to Haverton Hill from 11 September 1939, the service ended altogether on 14 June 1954 except for a few workmen's trains.

From Billingham Junction (0 m) the line is double track to the signal box at Belasis Lane (1 m 4 ch) where the OT single line Haverton South Branch heads off towards the ICI works. It runs from 0 to 75 chains and then from 64 m 42 ch to 63 m 34 ch, the latter section being the surviving part of a route along the Tees to the Leeds Northern main line at Stockton. The Haverton Hill end of this was installed to serve the works in 1901, with the extension to Stockton and a west-south curve at Haverton Hill following 19 years later. The Stockton end also survives to serve the Freightliner terminal there, although the latter is to move to Wilton.

Back on the Clarence Railway route at Belasis Lane box, an Electric Token single line runs without interruption to the ground frame at Port Clarence (3 m 5 ch) and another serves Philips Siding (3 m 25 ch). The operation changes to OT as the single line turns away from the river and passes via AOCL crossings at North Tees (4 m 19 ch) and Seal Sands (4 m 71 ch) to Seal Sands Branch Junction (5 m 1 ch). It then reverses direction east and completes its journey back to the river via a variety of level crossings and works connections, viz ICI Brinefield (12 ch), NEEB (39 ch), Philips (62 ch), Rohm Haas (1 m 42 ch), Monsanto Siding Junction (1 m 43 ch), Monsanto (1 m 46 ch), Rohm Haas No 2 (1 m 49 ch), SS Chemicals (2 m 11 ch), Philips No 2 (2 m 14 ch), Philips No 3 (2 m 22 ch), the end of BR maintenance (2 m 42 ch), and a 6 chain siding section to Seal Sands Storage.

The beginning of the block train era. Two immaculate B1 locomotives prepare to leave ICI Billingham for King George V Dock, London with 300 tons of iso-octanol.

All the elements of a period passenger station are present in this evocative scene at North Road station, Darlington.

B.21   Bingley

Leeds-Skipton line, between Shipley and Keighley. 208 m 68 ch from St Pancras

The Leeds & Bradford Railway opened the section of line from Shipley to Keighley on 16 March 1847, subsequent extensions putting Bingley on a major cross-country route carrying trains from the south to Scotland and the Lancashire coast. This century, Bingley received calls from some of the *Isle of Man Boat Expresses* in addition to its 70 or so local and semi-local trains. The goods yard and its 10 ton crane were also kept pretty busy.

Various improvements at Bingley culminated in a new station in 1892, executed in stone to the designs of Charles Trubshaw and recently cleaned to show its elegant lines to better advantage. The canopied platforms are linked by bridge and this is approached by a double stairway on either side.

From the Leeds direction a cutting precedes the 151 yd Bingley Tunnel (208 m 56 ch to 208 m 63 ch) and the station is followed by an 'overhang' signal box (209 m 7 ch) on the Up side. Nearby is the impressive Damart mill and the 'Five Rise' locks of the Leeds & Liverpool Canal. Bingley Tunnel is labelled by a rather nice example of traditionally-lettered notice board on the station platform.

Bingley is served by the through Leeds-Morecambe trains and by the Leeds/Bradford-Keighley/Skipton locals.

B.22   Bishop Auckland Branch

East Coast Main Line, branch from Parkgate Junction, Darlington. 14 m 47 ch

This modest but well-used branch from the East Coast Main Line, together with its freight extension into Weardale, is all that remains of the once-extensive rail network of West Durham. Apart from its value to the large numbers travelling to and from work or going shopping in Darlington, the survival of part of the route of the 1825 Stockton & Darlington Railway represents a positive memorial to the promoters and builders of that pioneer line. The original S&D line dropped from Witton Park Colliery to West Auckland and then to Shildon with two intermediate inclines. From there to North Road Station, Darlington, its course was much that of today's railway, apart from the tunnel section at Shildon.

The hourly trains between Saltburn and Bishop Auckland use Platform 4 at Darlington and then run the short distance to Parkgate Junction (44 m 58 ch) on a bi-directional single line parallel to the East Coast Main Line. Just 6 chains further on, the single line curves away west and picks up the east-west course of the S&D route to pass via Albert Hill (32 ch) to Darlington North Road station (49 ch). This section between the main Darlington station, formerly Bank Top, and Albert Hill was originally the S&D's Croft branch opened

on 27 October 1829 and later to carry a connecting service between Bank Top and North Road. Only a little-used goods line, a few rusting sidings and some abandoned bridge abutments survive of the once-extensive infrastructure on this section.

North Road station, which replaced the first S&D station in 1842 and is dealt with in the main Darlington entry, retains much of its original appearance, but the main station area is now a museum and the Bishop Auckland trains use only the outer face of the Down island platform. The additional goods line continues to Hopetown Junction (75 ch) where a 15 mph connection bet-

ween the two lines is controlled from a ground frame before the 34 chain OT single line departs to serve the UKF depot. On this section, the 1909 Railway Hotel stands on the Down side and a large brick shed on the Up but, apart from the UKF line, there are but few traces of the triangular junction which led to the Barnard Castle line, of the old North Road Locomotive Works or of the 1825 S&D branch to the Northgate coal depots.

The Barnard Castle line was the work of the Darlington & Barnard Castle Railway,

Typical of the clean, simple lines of many new or modernized stations, this is Newton Aycliffe on the Darlington-Bishop Auckland line.

authorized on 3 July 1854 and opened two years and five days later. It later connected at Barnard Castle with the South Durham & Lancashire Union Railway, which was authorized to construct a route from the S&D at Spring Gardens Junction (west of West Auckland) through Barnard Castle to Tebay (on the Lancaster & Carlisle Railway). After receiving its Act on 17 July 1857, this new railway opened the Tebay-Barnard Castle section on 7 August 1861, with the section on to Spring Gardens Junction coming into use on 1 August 1863. A new through station at Barnard Castle replaced the former D&BC terminus.

Several branches were built from the Darlington-Tebay line, viz the Eden Valley line (opened from Kirkby Stephen to Penrith on 9 June 1862), the Tees Valley line (opened from Barnard Castle to Middleton-in-Teesdale on 12 May 1868) and two freight lines, the 1866 branch to Forcett

and the 1870 one to Barton. The service west of Kirkby Stephen ended on 1 December 1952, in 1962 the Penrith line closed on 22 January and that between Barnard Castle and Bishop Auckland on 12 June, and on 30 November 1964 the Darlington-Barnard Castle-Middleton route 'lost its passenger trains. With the withdrawal of goods facilities from 5 April 1965 came the final demise of a once-significant system which had many dramatic stretches and called for considerable operational skill in the worst winters.

In pre-war days there were five through trains daily between Darlington and Penrith, most with connections to Tebay and with one through Newcastle-Blackpool service running that way. On the one and a half hour journey, the stopping trains called at Piercebridge (2¼ m), Gainford (9 m), Winston (11 m), Barnard Castle (16¾ m), Lartington (19 m), Bowes (22¾ m), Barras

A product of Shildon Works, a 30 ton NER ironstone wagon built in 1905.

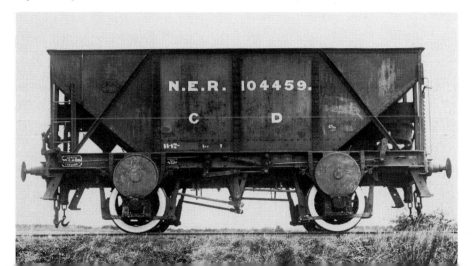

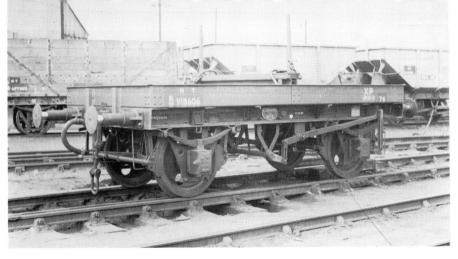

A single bolster wagon, normally used for the overhang of long loads of steel, pictured outside Shildon Wagon Works.

(33 m), Kirkby Stephen (38½ m), Musgrave (43¾ m), Warcop (45½ m), Appleby (50¼ m), Kirkby Thore (54¾ m), Temple Sowerby (56½ m), Cliburn (58¼ m), Clifton More (61 m) and then Penrith (64¾ m). On the Tebay portion the stations were Smardale (2¼ m), Ravenstonedale (5¾ m), Gaisgill (9¼ m) and then Tebay (11¾ m).

There were about seven trains each way daily on the Middleton branch, with one early and one later service through from/to Darlington. The stations were at Cotherstone (2¾ m), Romaldkirk (5¼ m), Mickleton (7 m) and Middleton-in-Teesdale (8¾ m). On the 15 mile route between Bishop Auckland and Barnard Castle there were intermediate stations at West Auckland (2¾ m), Evenwood (5¼ m) and Cockfield Fell (7¾ m).

Back on the BR line to Bishop Auckland, the Faverdale suburb of Darlington—where the LNER had a training school—gives way to a landscape of flat grassland and the route rises to cross the A1(M) and pass through Whiley Hill AHB level crossing (3 m 57 ch). Just over a mile further on, some railway cottages herald the approach to Heighington (5 m 8 ch) where a double track portion begins. Originally Aycliffe Lane, Heighington comprises staggered platforms either side of a barrier crossing and Down side signal box. Its low platform and former station building date back quite a long way as befits the point at which *Locomotion No. 1* began its career, whereas Newton Aycliffe (6 m 30 ch), the next station, is a simple, modern affair with short wooden platforms, brick shelters and a footbridge.

The Clarence Railway joined the S&D route near Newton Aycliffe and its trackbed is still visible on the Up side. Named after the Duke of Clarence, the railway was

The pattern for local services – modern units and signalling plus simple track and station infrastructure – seen in this case at Bishop Auckland.

intended to cut down the distance for coal shipments to the Tees by taking a course across the neck of the great loop south taken by the S&D line. It was opened during 1833 and was chosen by the North Eastern for experimental electrification which became operative from 1 July 1915. Ten electric locomotives were used to haul coal trains between Shildon and Newport Yard, near Middlesbrough, but by the time their renewal was required 20 years later the level of the business was not sufficient to justify further capital expenditure. Shildon marshalling yards and engine shed were closed in 1935, although the line from Simpasture Junction to Stillington Junction on the Ferryhill line was to remain open for another 28 years.

The former yard area is still apparent on the journey from Newton Aycliffe to Shildon, especially where a long overbridge crosses the route. The original course of the S&D turned off west just before Shildon station, and was subsequently met by the Barnard Castle-Bishop Auckland line at Spring Gardens Junction. Shildon wagon works lay along here, with Shildon station on the stretch of line opened on 19 April 1842 to a temporary terminus on the south eastern outskirts of Bishop Auckland. Shildon is also the home of the Timothy Hackworth Museum with its working replica of the *Sanspareil* locomotive which competed in the Rainhill Trials.

Shildon station (8 m 28 ch) is on a curve and comprises platforms, shelters and an Up side signal box. Soon after, at 8 m 57 ch, the line becomes single again, enters a cutting and passes between the stone retaining walls that precede the 1,220 yd Shildon Tunnel (8 m 66 ch to 9 m 42 ch). No less than four lines connected with our route along the next stretch which leads to embankments preparatory to crossing the valley of the Gaunless River. These give train passengers a view of the far dales away to the west.

Bishop Auckland is the traditional seat of the Bishop of Durham and was the home of the former Prince Bishops who exercised great power in religious, secular and even military affairs. Its first trains were provided by the Bishop Auckland & Weardale Railway which opened from the S&D Shildon-South Church extension to Crook on 8 November 1843. The North Eastern Railway then arrived at a separate station with its line from Durham on 1 April 1857, a triangular joint station being provided ten years later.

The present Bishop Auckland station (11 m 23 ch) was opened in June 1986, freeing the Durham line site of the old station for development as a supermarket. The new location, controlled by Shildon signal box, consists of a modern, single-storey Up building leading to a single platform and adjoining platform line. Beyond this is the single freight line which continues for 19¼ miles to Eastgate. This is part of the former Wearhead line and has its own separate entry. In addition to its passenger services to Wearhead, Barnard Castle and via Durham to Sunderland, Bishop Auckland also had a modest service to Ferryhill, as well as trains on the Darlington-Blackhill route. A small revival of the routes beyond Bishop Auckland came with the introduction of an experimental Sunday service to Stanhope in the summer of 1988.

In addition to its transport utility, this now modest line holds a great deal of interest. Its Quaker originators overcame their natural caution to launch a whole new transport era and the route became part of a busy and substantial network. The same proper caution led the S&D proprietors to encourage extensions by subsidiaries, and even Shildon Tunnel was the work of a separate company. The tunnel, built to replace the inclines over Black Boy Ridge, was the site of an early electric telegraph instrument which was such a novelty at the time that its use code included a signal for 'I am demonstrating the instrument to a friend'. Prior to singling, the tunnel was laid with gauntletted track.

B.23   Blaydon—see Newcastle-Carlisle Line

B.24   Boldon

Northallerton-Newcastle line, between Sunderland and Gateshead. 94 m to 95 m 16 ch from Leeds

Two venerable railway routes intersect at Boldon, those of the 1834 Stanhope & Tyne Railway and the 1839 Brandling Junction Railway. The latter now forms part of the important coastal railway linking the Tees, Wear and Tyne areas and is crossed on the level by the remnant of the S&T system, which links Boldon coal stockyard with the Tyne.

On the BR main line an open stretch of countryside between the settlements of the Wear and those of the Tyne is followed by East Boldon station (93 m 17 ch) consisting of platforms, signal box and barrier crossing. A little way beyond the station the trackbed of the line north to Harton and

South Shields is still visible together with a signal box at an angle to both routes. Although this was part of the original BJR line, it was abandoned soon after opening but later came to carry an intensive Sunderland-South Shields passenger service. Tile Shed barrier crossing (93 m 64 ch) marks the site of the former junction.

The east-south spur towards Boldon has gone, although its course is still visible, and the east-north link between the two lines (formerly from Tile Shed Junction to Harton Junction) is now effected by a 20 chain single line spur following Boldon AHB LC (94 m) and running from Boldon East Junction (94 m 63 ch) to Boldon North Junction. At the latter point it meets the S&T route which has come from the coal stocking area, over the main line via the right angle Pontop Crossing and then on north to the junction and, eventually, the Tyne Coal Terminal.

Reverting to the main line, Boldon East Junction is followed by the staggered platforms of Boldon Colliery station and its signal box (95 m 12 ch) and then by Boldon West Junction (95 m 16 ch) which provides the west-north access to the ex-S&T route. It runs to North Junction (32 ch), Green Lane Junction (52 ch) and then Tyne Coal Terminal. Ahead along the widening Tyne lay the course of the original Stanhope & Tyne route and its Pontop & South Shields successor, extended by the NER into South Shields proper on 2 June 1879. The South Shields routes have changed over the years but still include National Coal's extension of the Boldon line from Dean Road exchange sidings to Harton Staiths and the modern Metro route which runs alongside.

As Brockley Whins, Boldon Colliery station lay on the course of the original main line until this was shortened to run via Pelaw.

B.25 Bolton-on-Dearne—see Swinton-Milford Line

B.26 Boulby Potash Mine Branch
Darlington-Saltburn line, branch from Saltburn West Junction. 11 m 45 ch

A section at the north end of the former coastal route from Saltburn to Whitby survives as a freight-only line serving British Steel, Skinningrove and the Cleveland Mining complex at Boulby. It was reopened in 1973 and potash traffic has now risen to the level of 700,000 tonnes a year, including 420 tonne trainloads passing to a special distribution terminal opened in the goods yard at Middlesbrough.

The original Whitby, Redcar & Middlesbrough Union Railway had a difficult route to contend with because of the number of valleys which interrupted its cliff top course. The company took a long time to get construction started, and even then made such a poor job of it that when the North Eastern Railway took over in 1875 it had to rebuild some of the works. Not that the NER found construction easy, because it took that concern eight years to complete the 34 mile succession of cuttings, embankments, tunnels and viaducts. However, the railway that had been authorized on 16 July 1866 eventually opened for traffic on 3 December 1883. It closed to passengers south of Loftus on 5 May 1958 and between Loftus and Guisborough on 2 May 1960.

A high viaduct at Whitby linked the two coastal lines north and south of that resort and most trains ran between Scarborough and Middlesbrough (or beyond), with shuttle links from Whitby's high level West Cliff station down to the Esk Valley terminus in the town and over the 4¼ mile link

The viaduct between Carlin How and Loftus as it was in 1866.

between Saltburn and Brotton via North Skelton. Beyond Brotton there were stations at Skinningrove (20½ miles from Middlesbrough), Loftus (21½ m), Grinkle (22¾ m), Staithes (26¼ m), Hinderwell (28 m), Kettleness (31½ m), Sandsend (34 m) and then Whitby West Cliff (36½ m).

The area served by the WR&MU line has long-standing mining links and Kilton Embankment, near Skinningrove, was converted from a viaduct by using mining spoil. There was a complicated incline to the Loftus mines and another down from Staithes to the Grinkle Park Ironstone mine.

Today, the branch leaves the Saltburn line at Saltburn West Junction (27 m 5 ch from Darlington) and is double for the first 74 chain rising section. There is then a Tokenless Block section as far as Crag Hall signal box (33 m 69 ch) followed by Electric Token working on through the 992 yd Grinkle Tunnel (36 m 77 ch to 37 m 42 ch) to Boulby Potash Mine (38 m 50 ch). The route, which has a line speed maximum of 30 mph, is controlled by Longbeck signal box south of Redcar. Access to the Skinningrove sidings is under the control of a Chargeman at Crag Hall and the signal box there also releases the tokens for the section on to Boulby, either direct or through an intermediate instrument. Movements at the potash sidings are under the authority of the Cleveland Potash Shunter.

B.27   Bowesfield

Darlington-Saltburn line, junction with Hartburn Curve from Stockton. 10 m 76 ch from Darlington

On the Up side of the line at Bowesfield a standard brick and wood signal box controls the section from Bowesfield to Eaglescliffe South, together with the 44 chain double line curve from Hartburn Junction. The Middlesbrough-Newcastle trains use the latter and the Darlington-Saltburn services the former.

The first line through this location was the original 1825 route of the Stockton & Darlington, with Bowesfield then becoming a junction on 27 December 1830 with the extension of the S&D to Middlesbrough, and the Hartburn Curve opening on 1 May 1863. The other line in the area was that opened on 1 May 1877 (goods 1 July 1877 and passengers 1 March 1880) by the North Eastern Railway as a route completion exercise and running from Castle Eden Junction to join up with the Clarence Railway. There was also a short-lived curve between the Leeds Northern route

and the 1877 line, joining the latter at Bowesfield West Junction.

B.28   Bowling—see Bradford

B.29   Bradford

Bradford Forster Square is the terminus of the line via Shipley, 208 m 55 ch from St Pancras; Bradford Interchange is the terminus of the lines from Leeds and Manchester Victoria, 40 m 27 ch from the latter

Laid waste and then revived by the Normans, Bradford became first an important market town and then a major woollen centre. Its nineteenth-century worthies were as keen to join the railway age as their contemporaries in other northern manufacturing districts and originally, like Leeds, wanted a link to the vessels trading up the Yorkshire Ouse to Selby. Early plans of the 1830s failed to prosper, however, and Bradford's first trains eventually began running on 30 May 1846. These goods services were followed by the first passenger services on 1 July, running from Market Street station, effectively today's Forster Square, and taking a slightly roundabout route to Leeds via Shipley in order to achieve an easy course out of the city and then capitalize upon the valley of the River Aire.

This first Bradford railway enterprise was achieved by the Leeds & Bradford Railway. Later, in conjunction with the Manchester & Leeds Railway, the L&B was involved in plans to build a route through the centre of Bradford. This came to nothing at the time but the idea has been revived several times since. As it was, the second railway to reach Bradford was the Manchester & Leeds company's successor, the Lancashire & Yorkshire Railway, which reached Low Moor from Mirfield by its West Riding Union scheme in 1848 and then pushed on to reach Bradford on 9 May 1850. This last section involved the steeply-graded Bowling Tunnel and then a combination of tunnels and cuttings on the final approach to a simple, but central, station at Drake Street (later Exchange).

Another aspirant for Bradford's high passenger and goods traffic potential arrived from the east in 1854. This was the Great Northern Railway, in the guise of the Leeds, Bradford & Halifax Junction company, which opened on 1 August of that year to admit trains from the GN system via Laisterdyke to a third Bradford station, Adolphus Street. Inconvenient both in location and elevation, the GNR sought to replace Adolphus Street with a new connection to the L&Y's approach to Exchange and was successful at the second attempt. Great Northern trains ran into an expanded Exchange from 7 January 1867 with its own terminus then becoming a goods depot.

The next round of major change came in the 1880s when the through line concept was again revived but allowed to lapse in favour of individual reconstruction. The Midland Railway, as successors to the Leeds & Bradford, rebuilt Market Street into an attractive six-platform terminus with an imposing hotel on the west side. At Exchange a major demolition and reconstruction scheme produced an impressive new 10-platform station beneath a double-span roof, and capable of handling all the L&Y and GN services, including those from the latter's extensions via Queensbury and to Shipley.

Much has changed since the early Bradford railway development crystallized in the 1880s. The two major termini are still functioning although Forster Square has become but a shadow of its former self and Exchange, slightly west of its pre-1977 location, is now part of the purpose-built Interchange complex, linking train, bus and coach services.

In the process of rail rationalization, Bradford has lost a number of lines and services over the years:

The GN route via St Dunstan's (¾ m), Laister Dyke (2 m), Eccleshill (4¾ m), Idle (6 m) and Thackley (6½ m) to Shipley Bridge Street (8¼ m); from 2 February 1931.

The routes west via Queensbury serving St Dunstan's Horton Park (1¾ m), Great Horton (2¼ m), Clayton (3½ m), Queensbury (4½ m), Holmfield (6¾ m), Ovenden (7¾ m), Halifax North Bridge (8¾ m) and Halifax Old (9½ m), plus the Keighley line; from 23 May 1955.

The circuitous route via Otley to Harrogate; from 25 February 1957.

The services to Leeds (10½ m) via Laister Dyke and then Stanningley (4½ m), Pudsey Greenside (4¾ m), Pudsey Lowtown (5½ m), Bramley (6¾ m), Armley & Wortley (8½ m) and Holbeck; from 15 June 1964.

To Wakefield Kirkgate (18½ m) via Laister Dyke and Dudley Hill (4 m), Birkenshaw & Tong (5¾ m), Drighlington (6¾ m), Howden Clough (8¼ m), Upper Batley (9 m), Batley (9¾ m), Batley Carr (10¾ m), Dewsbury (11¼ m), Earlsheaton (12¼ m), Ossett (13¼ m), Flushdyke (14½ m), Alverthorpe (16¼ m) and Wakefield Westgate (17½ m); from 7 September 1964.

To Huddersfield via Bowling Junction (1¼ m), Low Moor (3 m), Cleckheaton (5½ m), Liversedge Central (6¾ m), Heckmondwike Central (7¾ m), Northorpe North Road (9¼ m) and Mirfield (10¾ m); from 14 June 1965.

To Wakefield Westgate via Drighlington and then Gildersome (8 m), Morley (9¾ m), Ardsley (12¾ m) and Lofthouse (14½ m); from 4 July 1966.

The streamlining process affected mainly the later Great Northern lines and left much of the LMS system intact, but Bradford did lose many of its smaller local stations and dozens of private sidings closed down. Even the great goods depots like Adolphus Street (LNER) and Valley (LMS), with their 20 ton cranes, were to close and now many of the great activity centres of the past, like Manningham loco shed, are barely discernible.

The run into Bradford on the orginal Shipley line is through semi-industrial scenery, past the premises of Worsted Spinners and Fellmongers. Although the intermediate stations at Frizinghall and Manningham were closed in March 1965, the former has been reinstated by the PTE with a simplified modern calling point (206 m 67 ch) operational from 1987. Only two

The two Bradford stations handle a substantial local Metrotrain service, plus London, York and cross-Pennine trains.

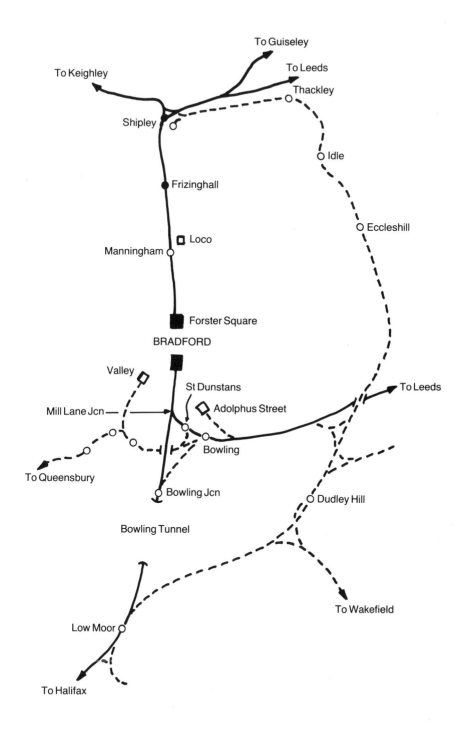

To Guiseley

To Keighley

To Leeds

Thackley

Shipley

Idle

Frizinghall

Eccleshill

Loco

Manningham

Forster Square

BRADFORD

Valley

St Dunstans

Mill Lane Jcn

Adolphus Street

To Leeds

Bowling

To Queensbury

Bowling Jcn

Dudley Hill

Bowling Tunnel

To Wakefield

Low Moor

To Halifax

running lines remain, worked as a single section from Shipley Bradford Junction, and Forster Square itself has only two working lines between the six long platform faces.

The exterior of Forster Square station must have been quite impressive when it was rebuilt in the 1880s, but by 1987 the classical arcade frontage, tower, balustrades and tall chimneys had fallen into neglect. The adjoining Midland Hotel, dating from the same mid-1880s rebuilding of the square, is by Charles Trubshaw and is also in a rather flamboyant style. Hopes of a return to former glories then came early in 1988 with the announcement of a £38 million shopping development scheme which would include refurbishment of the station area.

Meanwhile, the route down Market Street, past the Town Hall, keeps the mood set at Forster Square, but at the site of the former GN/L&Y Exchange station only the Victoria Hotel preserves past architectural fashions. Nearby, in the place of the old Exchange station, stands Bradford Interchange, efficient and modern but also pleasing, thanks to the floral displays and painted buffer sets. From the frontage road circulating area an escalator rises to the ticketing and information centre beyond which lie the four platform lines and a parcels line. The rest of the site is occupied by a huge bus station with coach pick-up and setting down points.

Apart from the Interchange and Forster Square stations themselves, so much of Bradford's railway past has disappeared that it is quite difficult to visualize earlier eras of constant train movements, of thousands of wagons of coal, metals, woollens and 'general merchandise', of three major locomotive depots, and all the other paraphernalia of past railway systems. Just a few clues remain, like the blocked up mini-tunnel on the Down side as the New Pudsey line curves round from Wakefield Road Tunnel to Mill Lane Junction and which marks the old Great Northern route ahead to City Road Goods and the Queensbury route. As today's trains continue into Interchange, stone retaining walls mark the lines of approach to Bridge Street yard on which the new bus and rail complex was built. When this was opened in 1973, Exchange was to be relegated to a car parking site.

The approach to Interchange station from the Halifax direction is via the 1,648 yd Bowling Tunnel (38 m 18 ch to 39 m 13 ch) leading to Bowling Junction (39 m 20 ch) and Mill Lane Junction (39 m 79 ch). Some sidings remain from the former Springmill Street activity on the Down side and on the Up the course of the GN connection from Bowling Junction, round through Bowling station to Laisterdyke is still visible.

Although much has changed at Bradford, not least the image of the city itself, it still enjoys excellent rail services ranging from local Metrotrains to the HST service to and from King's Cross. There is a frequent York-Leeds-Bradford-Manchester service via Halifax and the Calder Valley, with some trains taking the Preston/Blackpool line instead. Forster Square has an hourly service to and from Ilkley and another to Keighley/Skipton, with links at Shipley into the Leeds-Morecambe trains. The *Bradford Executive* service puts London within a three-hour journey time and now serves Forster Square and Shipley.

B.30   Bradley   Wood   Junction—see Milner Royd-Mirfield Line

B.31   Bramhope Tunnel

Leeds-York line, between Leeds and Harrogate. 5 m 65 ch from Wortley Junction, Leeds

Lying just to the east of the market town of Otley, Bramhope Tunnel was one of the major engineering works on the Leeds & Thirsk Railway. The 2 mile 247 yd bore (5 m 65 ch to 7 m 76 ch) descends into Wharfedale with a 1 in 94 gradient which not only added to the construction problems of water inundation, but also represented something of a challenge for the Up trains of the steam era. The tunnel was built between 1845 and 1849 and the casualties of its construction period are remembered by a monument erected by the contractor, James Bray, in the graveyard of Otley's parish church. In the form of a miniaturized replica of the tunnel, the monument reproduces the castellated northern portal which is one of the tunnel's most striking features. That portal also carries the Leeds & Thirsk coat of arms and, in addition, a face is carved in stone at each end. Four air shafts now survive from the nineteen shafts used in the original construction.

B.32   Bramley—see Leeds-Bradford Line

B.33   Brampton—see Newcastle-Carlisle Line

The northern portal of Bramhope Tunnel, complete with castellated turrets and a coat of arms above the running lines.

B.34   Bridlington

Hull-Scarborough line. 30 m 72 ch from Hull

Bridlington has a long history as a market town and fishing port, owed in part to its position south of Flamborough Head and to the Gypsey Race river which ends its journey from the Wolds to the sea there. The growth of Bridlington as a resort owed much to the coming of the railway, the first trains arriving over the line from Hull on 16 October 1846, and the town then being linked with Scarborough via Seamer from 20 October 1847.

Rail visitors to Bridlington increased steadily as the seaside holiday became part of the British way of life. The original station was expanded to cope with the influx, which reached its peak on summer Saturdays when there were through services, not only from King's Cross and York, but also from places like Leicester, Nottingham and Bradford. Handling these workings would tax the limits of the stabling sidings and give the small loco depot quite a cosmopolitan look. In addition to the longer distance services there were local trains between Selby and Bridlington and along the coast route.

Today's station is much simplified, although still of considerable interest. Approached from the south via an ornate gatehouse, overbridge and the Down side Bridlington South signal box (30 m 58 ch), the two platform areas are staggered and at a slight angle to the line of the site. There are extensive buildings on either side of the two lines still in use, with the ticket and main administrative offices beyond the Up side bays and canopy. The route north of Bridlington station leaves via Bridlington Quay signal box and barrier crossing (31 m 6 ch), which provides a reminder of the short-lived branch to the harbour. This section on to Hunmanby is single and worked on the Electric Token System.

Bridlington enjoys a service of some 20 trains each way on weekdays, about half of them operating between Hull and Bridlington and turning round at the latter point.

B.35   British Steel Redcar—see Middlesbrough-Saltburn Line

B.36   Brockholes—see Barnsley-Huddersfield Line

B.37   Brodsworth   Colliery Branch

Doncaster-Wakefield line, branch from Castle Hills Junctions. 1 m 49 ch

This is a long-standing colliery line, authorized to serve Brodsworth Main Colliery on 26 July 1907. The 24 chain northern curve of the triangular junction at Castle Hills, between Castle Hills North Junction and Castle Hills West Junction, was opened in May 1908 and the 16 chain southern spur from South Junction in September 1969. From West Junction the Track Circuit Block, 15 mph single line runs for a further 1 m 25 ch to the exchange point with the colliery.

B.38   Broomfleet

Doncaster/Leeds-Hull   lines,   between Gilberdyke Junction and Brough. 14 m 33 ch from Hull

The volume of freight to and from Hull used to warrant four tracks on much of the Gilberdyke Junction-Hull section but now the two extra Slow lines have been removed. The station itself now consists of new timber platforms, a signal box and a barrier crossing, and the train service is provided by the Hull to Doncaster, Sheffield and York workings.

On the approach to Broomfleet the route passes Oxmardyke barrier crossing (16 m 22 ch) and former signal box, and then over the Market Weighton Canal. Beyond the station the route comes alongside the Humber estuary, with a barrier crossing and cabin at Cave Crossing (13 m 60 ch) and then the crossing and Down side signal box at Crabley Creek (12 m 57 ch).

B.39   Brough

Leeds/Doncaster-Hull line, between Gilberdyke Junction and Hull. 10 m 38 ch from Hull

Brough stands on the north bank of the Humber, on the railway route opened by the Hull & Selby Railway on 2 July 1840. It is served by the trains from Hull to Doncaster and beyond and by the services to and from Leeds, Chester and North Wales. There is also a local Hull working which turns round at Brough.

The route here was formerly four-track, but the course of the Slow lines outside the two island platforms is now used as Hull end bays. The various changes to the station layout have isolated the small Down side ticket office and the quite stylish station house, now a DIY centre.

B.40   Burley-in-Wharfedale—see Ilkley Branch

B.41   Butterwell Junction

East Coast Main line, between Morpeth and Alnmouth. 20 m 63 ch from Newcastle

From the Up side at Butterwell Junction a short, 15 mph TCB single line leads to National Coal's opencast colliery. The latter is also connected to the Bedlington-Lynemouth branch by a 3 mile 43 chain line from the site of the old Ashington station. This second access route, to Butter-

well Colliery South, is double between the station and Ashington West Junction (8 ch)—where the 49 chain double line connection to Ashington Colliery departs—and on to the signal box at Ashington No 1 loop. It is then a TCB single line for the rest of its course through AOCL crossings at NCB (66 ch), New Moor (68 ch), Potland (1 m 47 ch) and Linton Lane (2 m 47 ch) to the exchange point at Signal B6 (3 m 43 ch).

C.1   Callerton Branch

East Coast Main Line, branch from Benton South Junction. 7 m

Once a North Eastern Railway branch line and then partly absorbed into the Tyneside rapid transit system, this route is still used by BR freight services to gain access to the ICI works at Callerton. In doing so trainmen have to recognize some variations in working practices to fit in with the slightly different equipment used by the Tyne & Wear Metro system.

The Metro route is double throughout and is reached by a double line curve from the main line at Benton South Junction, past Benton signal box (6 ch) to Benton Station Junction (27 ch) where the Metro's South Gosforth Control Centre takes over and a simplified form of Track Circuit Block commences. The spur between the main line and the Metro route was installed in 1903 for access to the depot at Gosforth.

On this section (originally Blyth & Tyne Railway), the Metro has stations at Benton (34 ch), Four Lane Ends (71 ch) and Long Benton (1 m 37 ch). It is followed by a bi-directional, single line, 10 mph portion of independent line from Gosforth East Junction (2 m 47 ch) and round the northern edge of Gosforth depot. When the Metro is then rejoined at Regents Centre East Junction, the route is that of the NER's Ponteland branch, opened for goods and mineral traffic on 1 March 1905 and for passengers on 1 June of the same year.

In North Eastern days the train service on the branch ran from South Gosforth via West Gosforth (¾ m), Coxlodge (2 m), Kenton (3½ m) and Callerton (4¾ m) to Ponteland (7 m). A 1¼ mile extension south-west to Darras Hall was opened on 27 September 1913 and three of the nine daily trains on the branch reversed at the Ponteland terminus and then continued to Darras Hall. From 1921 until 1929 the Wallridge Extension mineral line had

Beyond the present end of the Metro system at Bank Foot, a single BR freight line continues north west to serve ICI Callerton.

lengthened the route some eight miles north-west from Darras Hall to serve Kirkheaton Colliery. The passenger service between South Gosforth and Darras Hall ended on 17 June 1929, the latter closing entirely on 2 August 1954 and Ponteland losing all but some residual siding traffic from 14 August 1967.

From Regent Centre East Junction, today's modern Metro cars nip along where the old NER auto-cars would have huffed and puffed. There are stations at Regents Centre (2 m 54 ch), Wansbeck Road (3 m 21 ch), Fawdon (3 m 43 ch) and, more recently, Kingston Park and Bank Foot. On the approach to the latter there is a 20 chain section of bi-directional single line parallel to the Metro's platform line, with the BR freight line then continuing under OT regulations through the TMO crossings at Bank Foot (5 m) and Callerton (6 m 34 ch) to Callerton Run-Round Loop (7 m) where BR jurisdiction ends.

C.2 Carcroft Junction—see Doncaster-Wakefield Line

C.3 Cargo Fleet—see Middlesbrough-Saltburn Line

C.4 Castleford
Normanton-Colton North Junction line, between Altofts Junction and Milford Junction. 20 m 79 ch from York

Castleford's first station was opened on 1 July 1840 when the York & North Midland Railway completed its line from York to meet the North Midland's Rotherham-Leeds line at Altofts Junction and give York its first railway route to London. There were then no significant developments for 20 years when the L&Y gave the town a second station on the Wakefield, Pontefract & Goole Railway's Methley-Pontefract line. This was later to be called Castleford Cutsyke and the one on the Y&NM/NER route—moved ¼ mile west of its original location in 1871—Central.

Another round of change took place at the end of the 1870s, starting with the completion of the Leeds, Castleford & Pontefract Junction Railway which the North Eastern Railway had backed from its incorporation in 1873 and then taken over three years later. Opening from Garforth to a junction near the old station took place on 8 April 1878, and then an east-south curve linking the NER and L&Y (ie the original) routes was brought into use on 1 April two years later. After a chequered history, including two closure periods, the latter is once again in use—by today's Leeds-Goole trains which reverse at the former Central station.

Trains from Leeds join the ex-Y&NM route at Whitwood (22 m 4 ch) signal box and junction and then run via Castleford West Junction where the 1880 curve from the Cutsyke line joins in advance of Castleford station (20 m 79 ch). Former sidings and a surviving Down side goods shed are a reminder that there used to be considerable freight activity at Castleford, including coal, oil, chemicals, bricks and glass.

Castleford station itself has a brick signal box on the Up side at the Leeds end, and comprises single-storey traditional station buildings in brick plus a modern shelter and canopy opposite. In 1988 the whole property was rejoicing in a fresh coat of green paint. From the station, the trains to Goole reverse back to West Junction, but the ex-Y&NM line does continue eastwards, albeit for freight only since 5 January 1970.

The double freight line beyond Castleford runs via Castleford East Junction (20 m 39 ch), Fryston signal box (19 m 4 ch), the 65 yd Fairburn Tunnel (17 m 52 ch to 17 m 49 ch) and Hillam Gates CCTV LC (15 m 57 ch). Although passenger services on the Garforth line ceased on 22 January 1951, a portion of the route survives at the Castleford end to serve local collieries. This amounts to 2 m 75 ch of single line running north from Castleford East Junction (6 m 17 ch from Garforth) to Ledston signal box (4 m 43 ch) and then on as a OT

Hownes Gill Viaduct on the Waskerley line. It took over from two inclines in 1858.

route via Leeds Road (Wood End) NCB level crossing to the Stop Board at Allerton Main (Bowers Opencast), 3 miles 22 chains from Garforth.

About a third of the Castleford trains turn round there and return to Leeds, with another third doing the same at Knottingley and the rest going through to Goole. Those that go on leave the Y&NM line at West Junction and traverse the 61 chain curve through a cutting to Cutsyke Junction. Here the trackbed of the L&Y line from Methley joins, there is a small modern signal panel, and the mileage becomes 59 m 2 ch from Manchester. The section on to Prince of Wales signal box and barrier crossing (56 m 65 ch) and then to Pontefract West Junction (56 m 42 ch) passes beside the racecourse and then through a vast mining and quarrying area.

There was a separate NE/LNER/ER goods depot at Castleford Moss Street, reached from Whitwood, but this closed for public traffic in 1970.

C.5 Castle Hills Junctions — see Doncaster-Wakefield Line

C.6 Castleton Moor—see Middlesbrough-Whitby Line

C.7 Cattal—see Leeds-York Line

C.8 Chapeltown—see Sheffield-Barnsley Line

C.9 Chathill
East Coast Main Line, between Alnmouth and Berwick. 45 m 78 ch from Newcastle

This section of the East Coast Main Line originally opened on 29 March 1847 with the branch from Chathill to the coast at Seahouses being opened on 1 August 1898 for goods and 14 December 1898 for passengers. The station at Chathill remains open and still has its incredible Down side buildings, among the most attractive in Britain and another example of the delightful neo-Tudor style adopted by the Newcastle & Berwick Railway's architect Benjamin Green. The location is served by the Newcastle-Berwick trains.

The ECML climbs at 1 in 70 for 3½ miles north of Alnmouth, through the former stations at Longhoughton and Little Mill, and then drops at 1 in 150 through Christon Bank CCTV LC (43 m) and Fallodon Bank AHB LC (43 m 45 ch). These, too, used to have stations although the latter was a private one. After the station, signal box and (facing and trailing) crossovers at Chathill the route continues north through Newham crossing (47 m 9 ch) and Lucker CCTV LC (49 m 17 ch), again sites of former stations. A number of former station buildings survive on this section, together with the old coal staiths at Little Mill and the goods shed at Christon Bank. There used to be water troughs between Newham and Lucker.

The branch to the fishing port of Seahouses, an independent project of the North Sunderland Railway, was closed on 29 October 1951. In the '30s, the standard train service used to be five trains each way daily, including Sundays. They took 15 minutes for the 4 mile journey with one stop, at North Sunderland.

C.10 Chester-le-Street
East Coast Main Line, between Durham and Newcastle. 71 m 72 ch from York

Chester-le-Street got its first station when the present course of the East Coast Main Line was opened in 1868 and it is today served mainly by the Newcastle-Durham local trains. The main station buildings, a substantial block in red brick, are on the Up side where the goods shed survives, albeit in private hands.

North of the station, beyond the site of former private sidings, the trackbed of the old Stanhope & Tyne route can be seen. This was one of the early railways of the North East, opening at the Consett end on 15 May 1834 and between Annfield and South Shields on 10 September of that year. A passenger service began on 16 April 1835, but six years later financial problems led to the enterprise being reformed, with the Pontop & South Shields Railway taking the eastern end and the Derwent Iron Company the western. The route west of Chester-le-Street was the more complex and difficult to work because of the gradients called for by the terrain it traversed and because of the inclines needed to overcome them, but the postion was improved by NER deviations of 1886 and 1893.

As part of the 1893 alterations, a west-north curve was put in between South Pelaw Junction on the old S&T route and Ouston Junction on the main line. This was used for passenger traffic from 1 February 1894 to 23 May 1955, the trains from Newcastle serving Gateshead West (½ m), Bensham (1¾ m), Low Fell (3 m), Lamesley (4¼ m) and Birtley (5¾ m) on the main line and then Pelton (8¾ m), Beamish (11 m), Shield Row (12¾ m), Annfield Plain (15 m), Consett (19½ m) and Blackhill (22 m).

At the western end of the S&T, the 1834 route continued into Weardale via Hownes Gill, Rowley and Waskerley, connecting at Consett with the 1862–7 Durham-Blackhill-

Newcastle route and at Burnhill with the 1845 line to Crook. In addition to the limestone from Stanhope, the route came to carry coal traffic and, of course, the great Tyne Dock-Consett iron ore trains. It was also notable for the outstanding Hownes Gill Viaduct west of Consett. One of the works of the ill-fated Thomas Bouch, the 243 yd viaduct with its 12 arches rising to a height of 150 ft was opened for the Stockton & Darlington successors to the S&T on 1 July 1858.

Back on the ECML, the section north of Chester-le-Street was also crossed by several private coal lines, including the Bowes Railway whose Kibblesworth-Black Fell engine-powered incline passed beneath the NER route, followed by another between Park Drift and Allerdene.

C.11   Church Fenton

Junction of Leeds-York and Sheffield-Normanton-York lines. Church Fenton North Junction is 10 m 31 ch and the station 10 m 58 ch from York

Church Fenton lies on the original York & North Midland Railway line which was opened south from York to Milford on 29 May 1839 and on to a connection with the North Midland Railway at Normanton in 1840, to give York its first through railway route to London. Seven years later, Church Fenton became a junction when the Y&NM opened the first portion of its line to Harrogate, reaching Spofforth on 10 August 1847 and Harrogate proper on 20 July 1848.

From 1 April 1869, the 5 mile connection with the Leeds-Hull line at Mickleford put Church Fenton on a direct route between York and Leeds. It lost its East Coast Main Line trains to Selby in 1871 but became part of a new route between the North Eastern and Midland railways when

Up side view of Church Fenton where the Leeds and Sheffield lines join for the final section on to York.

The rather spartan-looking Wetherby Racecourse station.

the Swinton & Knottingley line was opened between Swinton and Ferrybridge from 1 July 1879.

The line north-east from Church Fenton carried a bit of a mixture of services ranging from a 1.40 pm through train from King's Cross to York-Leeds locals. Some trains ran through to Harrogate, others had a connection at Wetherby. There were stations at Tadcaster (4¾ m), Newton Kyme (6¾ m), Thorp Arch (8¼ m), Wetherby (14¼ m), Spofforth (17 m) and then Harrogate (22 m), with the Leeds line departing south at Wetherby. In the second part of the last war a 6½ mile single line loop was constructed from Thorp Arch to serve a local munitions complex. Operated in one direction only, the loop carried workers to stations on the site. It stayed in partial use until the late '50s, but from 6 January 1964 the routes from Cross Gates and Church Fenton to Wetherby and Harrogate both closed.

The two double-track routes from Leeds via Mickleford Junction (15 m 62 ch) and from Normanton become parallel at Church Fenton South Junction (10 m 77 ch) and then pass through the three-platform station with its wooden buildings, canopies and stairs to the Up side main buildings. The two routes are linked at Church Fenton North Junction (10 m 31 ch) but continue northwards as Up and Down Normanton and Up and Down Leeds pairs.

Church Fenton is served by the hourly Manchester-York/Scarborough and the local Sheffield-York trains.

C.12 Clayton West Junction—see Barnsley-Huddersfield Line

C.13 Cliff House
Northallerton-Newcastle line, between Stockton and Hartlepool. 70 m 6 ch from Leeds

The Up side signal box at Cliff House on the 1840 Stockton & Hartlepool line controls Up and Down Goods Loops, although these are now rarely used. It also used to control a connection to the Cliff House branch which, in turn, had linked with the line to Burn Road goods depot. Latterly the 67 chain One Train branch to Cliff House had served scrapyard premises, but by early 1988 it was out of use.

C.14 Colton Junctions
East Coast Main Line, junctions with Leeds and Sheffield lines. Colton Junction is 182 m 79 ch and Colton North Junction 183 m 65 ch from King's Cross; Colton South Junction is 6 m 25 ch from York

Controlled by York panel, this junction links the Leeds and Sheffield lines, which have arrived as two parallel pairs of tracks from Church Fenton, with the East Coast Main Line at the northern end of the Selby Diversion. The Sheffield lines are still known as the Up and Down Normanton, a reminder of the original route from York to London. They are linked to the Leeds lines at Colton South Junction, the combined routes then being joined with the ECML at Colton Junction. The latter then has crossovers to the Leeds line at Colton North Junction, with the two pairs of tracks then continuing on to York.

Although the York & North Midland Railway opened its line south from York to connect up with the Leeds & Selby Railway on 29 May 1839, Colton only received its present status when the ECML junction changed from Chaloners Whin in 1983. Between the two locations there are R/G crossings at Earfit Lane (184 m 5 ch) and Copmanthorpe No 2 (185 m 22 ch), the latter marking the remains of the former Copmanthorpe station which closed to passengers on 5 January 1959.

Colton is also notable as the first BR junction to be designed for use at 125 mph.

C.15 Commondale—see Middlesbrough-Whitby Line

C.16 Corbridge—see Newcastle-Carlisle Line

C.17 Cottingham—see Hull-Scarborough Line

C.18 Cramlington
East Coast Main Line, between Newcastle and Morpeth. 9 m 74 ch from Newcastle

The Newcastle-Morpeth local trains serve Cramlington which lies just north of the boundary between Tyne & Wear and Northumberland. The station follows CCTV crossings at Killingworth (5 m 76 ch) and Dam Dykes (8 m 46 ch) and comprises platforms with shelters and connected by an overbridge. There are old gradient boards on the Down platform.

North of Cramlington the main line crosses a viaduct and then continues via Stannington signal box and level crossing (13 m 74 ch) and a further CCTV crossing at Clifton (14 m 56 ch).

C.19 Crigglestone—see Horbury Junction

C.20 Crimple Viaduct
Leeds-York line, between Pannal and Harrogate

The first railway to reach Harrogate was the York & North Midland company's branch up from Church Fenton which opened on 20 July 1848. To reach Harrogate the line had to cross the wide Crimple Valley and did so by means of a 1,873 ft long viaduct with 31 arches. The 1848–9 Leeds & Thirsk route to the north chose to bypass Harrogate in favour of a line along the valley floor, 110 feet beneath the viaduct of its rival.

The formation of the North Eastern Railway provided great scope for rationalization and improvement, and part of a scheme to provide better access to Harrogate led to a connecting line between the lower and upper routes at Crimple. Operational from 1 August 1862, this connection and the portion over the viaduct and into Harrogate survived the 6 January 1964 closure of the Church Fenton line and today provides excellent views of the valley from the trains of the Leeds-Harrogate-York service. Crossing the viaduct, the Leeds & Thirsk trackbed can be seen below, while at the former Crimple Junction, at the east end of the viaduct, the Church Fenton line trackbed is now straddled by a garden as it heads for the old Crimple Tunnel.

C.21 Crofton—see Doncaster-Wakefield and Wakefield-Pontefract Lines

West Yorkshire PTE Class 144 Metrotrain at Crossflatts station.

C.22   Crossflatts
Leeds-Skipton line, between Shipley and Keighley. 209 m 45 ch from St Pancras

Crossflatts station, on the 1847 Leeds & Bradford Railway's Shipley-Colne Extension, dates from 17 May 1982. It is served by Leeds/Bradford-Keighley/Skipton locals and comprises Up and Down platforms with shelters.

C.23   Cross Gates
Leeds-Hull line, between Leeds and Micklefield. 16 m 11 ch from Selby South Junction

Lying on the line opened in 1834 by the pioneer Leeds & Selby Railway, Cross Gates is served by the hourly Manchester-York/Scarborough trains and by a number of local Leeds-Selby/Hull workings. The centre through lines have now been lifted and the station just consists of the two outer platforms with shelters, a high Down side retaining wall, and the overbridge and footbridge at the Leeds end. To the south lies Temple Newsam House, a period mansion standing in a vast park and currently housing the civic treasures of Leeds.

East of Cross Gates station lies the site of the former Cross Gates Junction, where a stone retaining wall still identifies the departure point of the line to Wetherby and Harrogate. This opened as a single line branch on 1 May 1876 but was doubled in 1902 as part of a scheme to route trains from Newcastle to Liverpool this way. In the process Wetherby got a new station south of the triangular connection with the Church Fenton-Harrogate line.

In addition to its Leeds-Harrogate trains, the line to Wetherby also had some services through to Church Fenton, with connections between Harrogate and Wetherby. Beyond Cross Gates there were stations at Scholes (6½ m from Leeds), Thorner (8¾ m), Bardsey (10¾ m), Collingham Bridge (13 m) and then the re-sited Wetherby (14¼ m). The route was quite steeply graded, with a summit just north of Scholes, and this was to lead to the diversion of its through trains, and then to complete closure from 6 January 1964.

At one period, Cross Gates enjoyed an intensive service of Leeds-Micklefield trains which also called at Marsh Lane and Osmondthorpe on their way from Leeds City station.

C.24   Cudworth—see Normanton

D.1   Danby—see Middlesbrough-Whitby Line

D.2   Darlington
East Coast Main Line, junction with Bishop Auckland and Stockton/Saltburn lines. 44 m 10 ch from York

At one time the Stockton & Darlington Railway's pioneer engine *Locomotion No. 1* stood on a plinth on the main platform at Darlington, a reminder of the achievements of that early railway which had formally opened its original line on 27 September 1825 and had gone on to develop a major rail network east and west of Darlington. The route of the S&D passed across today's East Coast Main Line just north of Bank Top station, its course marked by a sign board, and the S&D's early history is also recorded by a series of display panels at the end of the Darlington bay platforms.

Following the 1825 west-east line, the S&D built a mineral branch from Albert Hill Junction, near North Road station, to Croft and opened this on 27 October 1829. This branch was later purchased by the Great North of England Railway for incorporation in its projected north-south main line. The portion which now passes through Bank Top station was, in fact, so used, the Darlington-York line opening to passengers on 30 March 1841 and to goods five days later. The section of the ECML north from Darlington was opened by the Newcastle & Darlington Junction Railway, from Parkgate Junction and its right-angle crossing of the S&D, which came to be a well-known and much photographed railway location. Opening northwards was on 15 April 1844 for goods and 19 June 1844 for passengers.

Under NER auspices, a new route was opened from the main line south of Bank Top station and then east to join the original course of the S&D at Oak Tree Junction. The section between that point and the main line at Polam Junction opened on 1 July 1887 and is the course now taken by the Saltburn line trains. Despite the diversion of traffic to this new routing, the old S&D line continued to handle east-west freight trains until 21 May 1967.

The other main route from Darlington was that to Barnard Castle, opened on 8 July 1856 and covered in the Bishop Auckland entry. Two goods branches ran south from that line, serving Barton Goods and Forcett Depot. The S&D also built a short branch south from its North Road station to carry coal nearer to the centre of Darlington.

The town of Darlington goes back to Saxon times and at one time had a flourishing textile industry. The railway age ac-

Above *A train with less-than-efficient steam heating at Darlington in November 1961.*

Below *The huge signal gantry just south of Darlington station. The through lines pass to the right of the station and, of course, the whole appearance has now changed.*

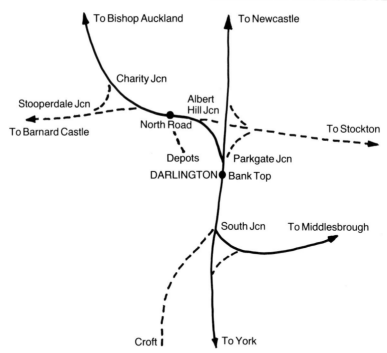

celerated and altered its development, bringing an increase in heavy industry including the railway workshops. These had begun life in 1863 when the NER took over the S&D and had developed considerably after the original overall control gave way to full integration of the two companies. At one time the works employed over 2,000 people, but they were closed down in 1966.

Darlington lost its trains to Barnard Castle and Middleton-in-Teesdale on 30 November 1964. Its services beyond Bishop Auckland and to Richmond have also gone but it still has some excellent rail facilities including trains to London in under three hours, a regular service on the Bishop Auckland-Darlington-Middlesbrough-Saltburn line, and links to Hartlepool and the Whitby branch.

On the approach to Darlington from the south, the Saltburn line joins what was originally the Croft branch at South Junction (43 m 61 ch), where the Up Goods line from Parkgate Junction ends. Croft Depot closed on 27 April 1964. Darlington panel box (43 m 70 ch) stands on the Down side near the small loco and engineers depot. It marks the point at which the platform lines separate from the Up and Down main which pass east of the station, outside its three-span overall roof area. The single

island platform beneath the one main plus two subsidiary spans has two London end bays and a duplicate Down line, the latter with crossovers to permit the use of either end of No 4 platform. There is also an extra Up line.

The main station facilities are on the island platform, with car parking at the country end and a decorated subway exit on the Down side. The high tower there used to house a large bell, now recovered and mounted on the platform. Beyond Bank Top station, at Darlington North Junction (44 m 36 ch), the platform lines become one Bishop Auckland line and one bidirectional line as they pass the former locomotive depot, come to Parkgate Junction (44 m 58 ch) where the Bishop Auckland line leaves, and then pass the sign marking the 1825 S&D route. On the section on to Aycliffe (49 m 36 ch), the ECML passes beneath the route of the 1833 Clarence Railway, marked by the abutments of a former overbridge.

Darlington's other station at North Road is detailed in the entry for Bishop Auckland. It is the 1842 successor to the S&D original and its period main buildings are now part of a museum project which embraces *Locomotion No. 1*.

The 1841 station on the Bank Top site was rebuilt in 1860 and then replaced with

Above *Croft Ground Frame used to control the reception lines south of Darlington and was electrically released from Darlington South signal box.*

Below *Even LNER A3 'Pacifics' like 2570* Tranquil *could find themselves on freight trains, as this view of Croft Viaduct shows.*

the present station which was brought into use on 1 July 1887 after an 18-month construction process which had cost £81,000. The 100th anniversary was celebrated in 1987 with a variety of events, including a ceremony to mark the planting of the 13,000th mast of the East Coast electrification scheme.

D.3   Darton
Wincobank Junction, Sheffield to Horbury Junction line, between Barnsley and Horbury Junction. 49 m 29 ch from Manchester Victoria

Although the line was a project of the Sheffield, Rotherham, Barnsley, Wakefield, Huddersfield & Goole Railway, opened between Horbury Junction and Barnsley on 1 January 1850, the Manchester-based distances reflect the fact that it was leased to the Manchester & Leeds before opening and then later became part of the substantial Lancashire & Yorkshire network. After separating from the Huddersfield line just north of Barnsley, the Horbury line drops down to the floor of the Dearne valley to reach Darton station, which is a very modest affair with simple wooden platforms and a couple of small wooden buildings on the Down side. An Up side retaining wall and some former railway cottages opposite are a reminder of more elaborate times, but the location is now just a functional one to provide access to the local Sheffield-Leeds trains.

Just south of Darton there are signs of the trackbed and embankment which used to carry the rail connection to the colliery at North Gawber. On the opposite, Down, side there used to be an earlier 2 mile line out to Silkstone and the colliery there. This had been opened a few days after the main line to join a complex of basic lines serving the Silkstone area and there was a fair volume of traffic over the line until the GC connection from Moor End started to tap the Silkstone output from the beginning of the 1880s. Although both lines were still in the 1938 edition of the *RCH Handbook of Stations*, the ex-L&Y line was virtually closed by then.

North of Darton the Horbury Junction line transfers from the South Yorkshire PTE area to that of West Yorkshire as it continues its course along the valley.

D.4   Dawdon
Northallerton-Newcastle line, between Hartlepool and Seaham. 84 m 22 ch from Leeds

The signal box at Dawdon controls the passenger and freight movements on the 1905 coast line, and also Dawdon Junction (84 m 11 ch) which gives access to Seabanks over a double track freight route via Bone Mill open crossing. The latter is part of the rail links with Dawdon Colliery and Seaham Harbour, and to the collieries west of the BR main line. These include South Hetton whose coal output played a big part in the initial development of Seaham from fishing port to industrial harbour.

D.5   Deighton—see Manchester-Leeds Line

D.6   Denby Dale—see Barnsley-Huddersfield Line

D.7   Dewsbury
Manchester-Huddersfield-Leeds line, between Bradley Junction and Leeds. 33 m 62 ch from Manchester Victoria

Dewsbury, noted for its mills and markets, lies on the section of the main trans-Pennine route originally opened by the Leeds, Dewsbury & Manchester Railway on 18 September 1848. It later came to be served by the L&Y, GN and Midland companies but, apart from a freight link from Dewsbury East Junction to Railway Street goods depot, only the original line survives. However, it provides Dewsbury with an excellent local service to and from Huddersfield and Leeds, plus stops by many of the longer distance cross-country services.

Dewsbury's first railway facilities were provided by Thornhill station on the 1840-41 Manchester & Leeds Railway, but these were neither adequate nor near enough to satisfy the town's needs—particularly for a link with Leeds. Matters improved considerably with the opening of the LD&M line in 1848 but commercial activity in the locality went on growing, particularly the 'shoddy' trade (which separates wool from rags), and other railways began to cast envious eyes on the town's traffic. The L&Y, successors to the M&L, got nearer to Dewsbury from 1 April 1867 (goods 27 August 1866) with a 1½ mile branch from the Normanton line to a new station at Dewsbury Market Place.

The next company to want a share of the Dewsbury traffic was the Great Northern. Through the agency of the Bradford, Wakefield & Leeds Railway it had reached Batley from Wrenthorpe Junction, Wakefield in 1864 and in 1871 had obtained an Act for a 2½ mile branch from that line, near Ossett, into Dewsbury. This was opened to passengers on 9 September 1874 and extended north to rejoin the 1864 line at Batley from 12 April 1880. The new GNR station later became Dewsbury Central and in LNER days carried a few Leeds 'circular' trains, a Wakefield-Leeds service and a Wakefield-Bradford service.

The Midland Railway only had a goods presence in Dewsbury although it included the full range of cranage, livestock and other facilities. The line had arrived on 1 March 1906 as a branch from the Royston Junction to Thornhill Junction line and had descended to a depot at Savile Town through a short tunnel. In addition to this depot, the GN and GC had goods facilities at Central, the L&Y at Market Place and the LNW at Wellington Road.

The later arrivals at Dewsbury did not survive the rationalization period. Market Place had lost its passenger trains as early as 1 December 1930 and Savile Town closed on 18 December 1950. The remaining facilities were altered again in 1964–5 and now consist just of the so-called Headfield Branch which was retained primarily for APCM and Gas Works traffic. Now little used, it is made up of 27 chains of double line from Dewsbury East Junction and then a 49 chain OT section on to Railway Street Goods.

D.8   Dinsdale

Darlington-Saltburn line, between Darlington and Eaglescliffe. 3 m 65 ch from Darlington

After leaving the East Coast Main Line south of Darlington station, the double track route of the Saltburn line passes through Maidenhead (1 m 72 ch) and comes to the modest station at Dinsdale. This is reached from the overbridge at the east end with the platforms and shelters below then served by the Darlington-Hartlepool workings and by the two trains an hour on the Saltburn line.

Beyond the present Dinsdale station is Oak Tree Junction (4 m 28 ch) which marks the beginning of a stretch of the original Stockton & Darlington Railway route. The junction now only functions as the connection to Dinsdale permanent way depot, which lies just along the S&D route towards Darlington. There was an S&D station on this section at Fighting Cocks, but when the new line from Darlington to Oak Tree Junction opened on 1 July 1887 this became a goods depot, lasting then until 9 March 1964.

D.9   Doncaster-Wakefield Line

Doncaster, Marshgate Junction to Wakefield Westgate. 19 m 37 ch

Although it originated as a small, independent railway, intent on linking the West Riding with the Humber, this line is now part of the trunk route from King's Cross to Leeds and thus part of the new East Coast electrification. At the beginning of 1988 it was being used by the London-Leeds HSTs, which called at Doncaster and Wakefield, and by an hourly Scunthorpe-Leeds service which, with a few peak additions, catered for the three intermediate stations at South Elmsall, Fitzwilliam and Sandal & Agbrigg.

Opened on 1 February 1866, the line was a project of the South Yorkshire Railway & River Dun Navigation. Labelled the West Riding, Hull & Grimsby Railway, it had been authorized on 7 August 1862 for a line from just south of Wakefield Westgate to Stainforth where it would use the SYR's line to Thorne and then on to Hull. A branch from Adwick to Doncaster North Junction created a direct link with that town. In the 1866 opening year the route was vested in the Great Northern and MS&L companies as the West Riding & Grimsby Joint Railway.

After Marshgate Junction (156 m 28 ch) at Doncaster, the route passes under that of the Doncaster avoiding line as it heads north west via CCTV crossings at Dock Hills (156 m 63 ch) and Bentley (157 m 52 ch) to the triangular Down side junction with the single line to Brodsworth Colliery. The connections at Castle Hills South Junction (158 m 40 ch) and Castle Hills North Junction (158 m 67 ch) are both on the Doncaster panel.

Traditional stone buildings on the Up side mark the site of the station which opened as Adwick in 1866 and closed as Carcroft & Adwick-le-Street on 6 November 1967. On the same side the 1909 southern curve of the triangular connection with the Stainforth line—from Carcroft Junction to Skellow Junction—is followed by the much less severe northern curve from Adwick Junction to Skellow Junction. The Adwick-Stainforth line, which has its own entry, dates from 1866 but lost its passenger trains on 14 May 1979.

Cereals and root crops are a feature of the countryside on the next section, through the closed station at Hampole. The WR&G passes beneath the former Hull & Barnsley Railway lines to Denaby and Wath on this section, and the route of the connection to the latter is still visible. Then comes South Elmsall (164 m 48 ch) which, although simplified, retains many features of the original station. In addition to the main Down side buildings, there are also railway cottages and a brick goods shed.

The Doncaster-Wakefield line passes under and then meets the connection from the S&K line at South Kirby Junction (165 m 74 ch). The connection from South Kirby Colliery is also made here, but the Kinsley Colliery loading point on the Up side is now out of use and the area is dominated by the Hemsworth Reclamation Scheme which demonstrates the degree of rehabilitation achievable on former mining sites.

Fitzwilliam (169 m 15 ch) got its station on 1 June 1937 and now comprises simple modern platforms with shelters and with ramps to the London end overbridge. Beyond it is the site of the Nostell Colliery siding, where a crossover survives (170 m 50 ch), and then Hare Park Junction (171 m 73 ch) where the 1 m 29 ch link from Wakefield Westgate via Crofton West Junction joins. On the final stretch to Wakefield Westgate the route passes beneath the Midland's Cudworth line (to which it was formerly connected on the Down side) and then makes its dramatic, high, curving approach to the single line connection—at Wakefield Westgate South Junction (175 m 38 ch)—from Kirkgate, and on into Westgate station (175 m 65 ch).

On the section north from Fitzwilliam there were formerly stations at Hemsworth, Nostell, Hare Park & Crofton, and Sandal, the latter having now been brought back into use. The former link to the Midland line, between Sandal and West Riding junctions, was opened on 1 September 1866 and that from Hare Park Junction to the L&Y at Crofton Junction on 8 November of the same year.

D.10 Drax Power Station Branch

Wakefield-Goole line, branch from Drax Branch Junction. 4 m 16 ch

This double, freight-only line is the longest surviving stretch of the former Hull & Barnsley Railway which opened in 1880 (20 July for goods and one week later for passengers). The venture was hardly a success because the intermediate areas along its route were predominantly rural and the passenger service west of Howden ended as early as 1 January 1932. The mainstay of the line was coal traffic and this continued until 1958.

The present section of line has remained in service to supply fuel to the massive Drax power station. Access is controlled by Hensall signal box, with the branch commencing at Drax Branch Junction and running via West Bank Hall AHB LC (1 m 49 ch), Jacky Duffin Wood R/G LC (2 m 18 ch) and Linwith Lane AHB LC (2 m 46 ch) to the power station reception lines (4 m 16 ch). Track Circuit Block applies and the line speed is limited to 35 mph.

The main line of the H&B passed over the ex-L&Y line between Hensall and Snaith and the connection between the two then ran from Gowdall Junction to Hensall Junction. At Aire Junction, near the former, the 1916 GC & H&B Joint line headed off south to Doncaster.

D.11 Driffield

Hull-Scarborough line. 19 m 38 ch from Hull

The centre of an important agricultural area, Driffield got its first railway services on 6 October 1846 when today's line was opened between Hull and Bridlington. In that same year, the modest Malton & Driffield Railway obtained powers for the line mentioned in its title and for a branch from Driffield westwards to Frodingham Bridge. Only the former was built, opening on 19 May 1853 and then lasting until 5 June 1950 for passenger traffic and eight years more for freight.

The second half of the nineteenth century was halfway through before Driffield's third railway route was authorized. This was for a line to Market Weighton which, along with a shorter route between Nafferton and Cayton, was to enable the Scarborough, Bridlington & West Riding Junction Railway to live up to its title. Based on an Act of 6 August 1885, this company opened the Driffield-Market Weighton part of its enterprise in 1890 (freight 18 April, passengers 1 May). It was worked by the North Eastern Railway, to which it passed in 1913 with its other ambitions unfulfilled.

From soon after its opening, the Market Weighton line was used by the through services from the West Riding to the East Yorkshire coastal resorts. Most of these called at Driffield to give the town good links with Leeds and beyond until the 1960s, when the rerouting of the through traffic and a general decline in local traffic led to closure between Selby and Driffield on 14 June 1965.

Above *The NER introduced a motor bus service to the east of its railway line between Beverley and Driffield in 1903. Two vehicles are pictured here outside the saddlers at Driffield.*

Below *The surviving section of the Hull & Barnsley Railway handles very different quantities of goods from those represented by this wagon, built by Pickering & Co and fitted with their patent brake.*

The train service on the Driffield-Malton line was never lavish. A typical 1930s pattern provided departures from Malton at 7.10 am, 10.37 am, and 5.50 pm, with return workings at 9 am, 12.35 pm, and 7.30 pm. The latter called at Garton (3 m), Wetwang (6¾ m), Sledmere & Fimber (8½ m), Burdale (11 m), Wharram (13 m), North Grimston (15¼ m) and Settrington (16½ m) on the 20 mile journey to Malton and took 43 minutes over its none-too-easy course.

The now-closed routes joined where the A164 road enters Driffield, then linking with the Hull line near the Driffield signal box and level crossing (19 m 38 ch). All three routes crossed the River Hull and tributaries on the approach and the station is not far from the town's earlier transport route, that of the 1770 Driffield Canal.

Driffield station maintains the pattern of Beverley and Filey, with its main buildings on the Down side. A large brick goods shed still stands near Wansford Road box and crossing (19 m 54 ch) at the country end. The station also has a modest arcade in addition to its canopy, and an original signal box, in the same style as the one at Seamer, is still in existence near the former junction for Selby and Malton.

All Hull-Scarborough line trains call at Driffield to give the town nearly 40 trains a day, Monday to Saturday.

D.12　Dryclough Junction—see Halifax

D.13　Dunston—see Newcastle-Carlisle Line

D.14　Durham

East Coast Main Line. 66 m 13 ch from York

The heart of Durham City lies in a loop of the River Wear, a site chosen by the former monks of Lindisfarne when they arrived in 995 AD bearing the body of St Cuthbert and seeking to create a new home for their order. The building they erected was succeeded by the present great cathedral on which work was started in 1093 as soon as the masons had finished their work on Durham Castle. This was the beginning of the era of the powerful bishop-nobles, charged with the task of protecting the border with Scotland, and bringing riches to themselves and their city in the process. Today the castle is part of the university complex and is just one of many locations of interest in what has become a thriving modern city, owing not a little to the

coalfields which surround it.

Travellers on the East Coast Main Line get a good view of Durham as they approach the city over the high viaduct which carries trains across the Wear just south of the station. Both station and viaduct were first brought into full operation on 1 April 1857 with the opening of what was then just a branch line to Bishop Auckland. During this period the main line from London to the Tyne passed east of Durham. The present ECML route was not completed until 1 October 1871 when the section south to Ferryhill and the 1868 line north to Gateshead were both joined to a section of the 1857 Bishop Auckland branch to produce a new main line.

Durham's first trains had been moved by stationary engines and Durham travellers had to go a mile and a half out of the city to the terminus of the Durham & Sunderland Railway, which had been authorized on 13 August 1834 and had opened to Sherburn House on 6 November 1837. This line was extended into Elvet station Durham in 1893 but regular passenger service ceased on 1 January 1931. A station at Gilesgate, Durham had started handling trains on 15 April 1844, giving a connection to the 'Old Main Line' at Belmont Junction north east of the city. This branch became redundant when the Bishop Auckland route was opened, losing its passenger trains from that date but continuing to find an employment for goods at the Gilesgate site until 7 November 1966.

On the 'new' main line, the approach from Ferryhill makes a viaduct crossing of the Deerness river. Beyond this is the site of Relly Mill Junction where three routes came to join that of the ECML, ie, the 1857 Bishop Auckland branch, the 1858 Dearness Valley Railway and the 1862 Lanchester Valley route to Consett.

The line from Bishop Auckland, opened for goods on 19 August 1856 and then for passengers on 1 April 1857, is covered in the Bishop Auckland entry. The Dearness Valley Railway left it about a mile outside Durham and then hugged the small River Deerness for its 5¾ mile westerly journey to Waterhouses, where a private line along the edge of Stanley Wood connected it with the colliery at East Hedleyhope. Another connection led south via Stanley Incline to Crook.

The DVR was originally built to serve the mines at Ushaw Moor and Waterhouses. It had strong NER support and was absorbed by that company in 1857, but did not get a passenger service until 1 Novem-

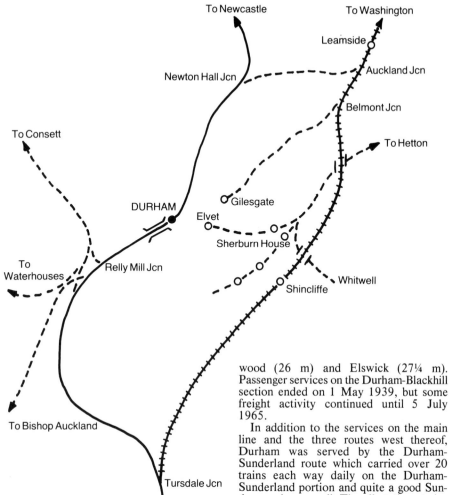

To Newcastle

To Washington

Leamside

Auckland Jcn

Newton Hall Jcn

Belmont Jcn

To Consett

To Hetton

DURHAM

Gilesgate

Elvet

Sherburn House

To
Waterhouses

Relly Mill Jcn

Whitwell

Shincliffe

To Bishop Auckland

Tursdale Jcn

To Ferryhill

wood (26 m) and Elswick (27¼ m). Passenger services on the Durham-Blackhill section ended on 1 May 1939, but some freight activity continued until 5 July 1965.

In addition to the services on the main line and the three routes west thereof, Durham was served by the Durham-Sunderland route which carried over 20 trains each way daily on the Durham-Sunderland portion and quite a good Sunday service as well. The all-stations trains called at Leamside, Fencehouses, Penshaw, Cox Green, Hylton, Pallion, Millfield and then Sunderland. By changing at Leamside, Durham passengers had access to the stations on the 'Old Main Line' to Newcastle, but the Durham-Sunderland trains via Penshaw ceased on 5 May 1964.

On the approach to Durham today the former route and junction complex at Relly Mill is still apparent, and is followed by a cutting with a stone retaining wall and then the high, 10-arch viaduct which leads to the station. The station buildings date from 1857 and are in local stone. The main entrance has a five-arch portico with castellation above, while behind this imposing introduction the main buildings are gabled at each end and topped with tall, elegant chimneys. The main platform canopies

ber 1877, nor an intermediate station until 1884. In the good years Waterhouses had nine trains each way daily, but in the bad ones there were as few as two. Passenger traffic ceased on 29 October 1951 and mineral traffic 13 years later.

The service from Durham north-west through Lanchester used the valley of the River Downey at the start of its journey. The seven trains a day between Durham and Blackhill called at Bearpark (2 m), Witton Gilbert (4¼ m), Lanchester (8 m) and then Blackhill (14 m) from whence some continued on to Newcastle (29 m) via Shotley Bridge (15¼ m), Ebchester (16¼ m), High Westwood (17¼ m), Lintz Green (19¾ m), Rowlands Gill (21¼ m), Scots-

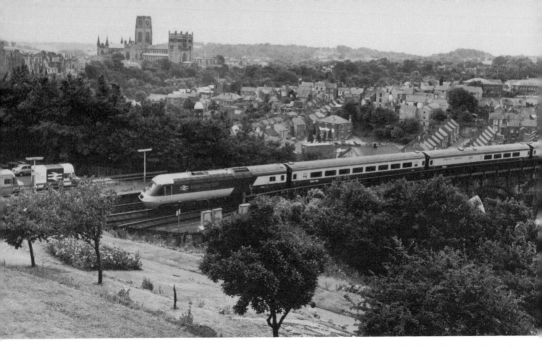

A Down HST makes a viaduct crossing into Durham station, with the city, castle and cathedral in the background.

have a wealth of fussy ironwork and a former dock lies at the country end. The two platforms are served by the Slow lines, but only the Up and Down Fast continue after the emergency crossover (66 m 40 ch) and Signal TY354.

Durham today, albeit without former Newcastle service permutations, nevertheless has a good service to that point over the main line. The local services turn round at Durham which also has calls by Newcastle-Liverpool and North East/South West trains. London trains take about three hours for the 254¾ mile journey.

E.1   Eaglescliffe

Darlington-Saltburn line, junction with Northallerton-Stockton line. 8 m 63 ch from Darlington, 57 m 1 ch from Leeds

Although the S&D's pioneer line was opened through Eaglescliffe on 28 September 1825 with a short branch to Yarm following, the town did not get its first station until 25 January 1853. The Leeds Northern's line up from Northallerton to Stockton had been opened on 2 June of the previous year, and the new station resulted from a piece of early rationalization that relaid the S&D route alongside that of the Leeds Northern to facilitate interchange between the two. There was also a curve between the Darlington and Northallerton lines as they converged, the latter being

crossed by the Yarm branch which was only to last a short time longer.

The two double line routes now join at Eaglescliffe West Junction (8 m 58 ch/56 m 76 ch) and then come to the station's single island platform with its simple brick shelters. On the Down side a now cleared yard area is a reminder of the considerable interchange traffic of former days. The two routes subsequently separate at Eaglescliffe North Junction (9 m 2 ch/57 m 20 ch) and then run parallel for a short distance before the Saltburn line turns off east towards Middlesbrough. The 1925 Stockton & Darlington centenary celebrations took place near here.

Eaglescliffe enjoys a good service from the Darlington-Hartlepool and Middlesbrough line trains.

E.2   Easington

Northallerton-Newcastle line, between Hartlepool and Seaham. 80 m 35 ch from Leeds

The tall Down side signal box at Easington controls the access to the sidings of Easington Colliery which has its own locomotive for internal shunting. The location has a Down Refuge Siding but the Down Goods Loop and colliery connection near the Up side Horden box (78 m 58 ch) is now out of use.

E.3   East Boldon—see Boldon

The Bishop Auckland branch ends at the buffer stops beyond the platform, but a single line freight route, the line on the left, continues on to Eastgate.

E.4   Eastgate Branch

East Coast Main Line, extension of the Bishop Auckland branch. 19 m 23 ch

Passenger services from Darlington terminate at Bishop Auckland but the route continues into Weardale as a OT single line serving the APCM works at Eastgate. Beyond Bishop Auckland (11 m 23 ch from Parkgate Junction, Darlington) it turns west to pick up the same direction as the River Wear over a section via Etherley Ground Frame (13 m 31 ch) to the former Wear Valley Junction. Here the line for Crook and on to Stanley Colliery and Waskerley used to depart, a fact still recognized by a change of mileage to the zero distance of the original Wear Valley Railway.

Along the Wear Valley proper, the Eastgate branch runs even closer to the river, passing Witton-le-Wear LC (1 m 14 ch), Wiserley Hall R/G LC (7 m 15 ch), Broadwood AOCL LC (9 m 77 ch) and Unthank TMO LC (13 m 30 ch), before finally coming to Eastgate (15 m 79 ch) where a ground frame gives access to the cement works sidings. Fed by a quarry on the hillside above, the APCM plant loads to bulk cement wagons which are then forwarded in trainloads to APCM terminals in the North East and Scotland.

The original railway scheme promoted by the Wear Valley Railway was leased to its backers, the Stockton & Darlington Railway, in 1847 shortly after the opening

of the line on 3 August of that year. The Bishop Auckland-Crook line had already been opened by that time (19 April 1842 for goods and 8 November 1843 for passengers) and had been extended to Waskerley (16 May 1845 for goods and 1 September 1845 for passengers).

The passenger service over the Wear Valley line used to run via stations at Etherley (2¼ m), Witton-le-Wear (4¼ m), Harperley (7½ m), Wolsingham (10½ m), Frosterley (13¾ m), Stanhope (15¾ m), Eastgate (18½ m), Westgate-in-Weardale (21½ m) and St John's Chapel (23 m) to Wearhead (25 m). There were visions of extending the line further but nothing came of them and contraction started instead, with the end of passenger services on 29 June 1953. Local goods traffic ceased at various dates in the 1960s.

At one time the line had a short quarry branch on the Down side from Frosterley to Bishopsley and also carried coal, sand and steel traffics.

E.5   Eastrington—see Leeds-Hull Line

E.6   Eggborough Power Station—see Wakefield-Goole Line

E.7   Egton—see Middlesbrough-Whitby Line

E.8   Elland—see Milner Royd-Mirfield Line

E.9   Elsecar—see Sheffield-Barnsley Line

E.10   Eryholme
East Coast Main Line. 38 m 72 ch from York

Today Eryholme is notable only for the crossovers between the Up and Down main lines but, then named Dalton, it had become a junction as early as 10 September 1846 when the Great North of England Railway, newly part of the York & Newcastle Railway, opened a branch from its main line to the ancient town of Richmond. Eryholme itself lost its passenger service on 1 October 1911, but the train service between Darlington and Richmond continued until 3 March 1969, calling at Croft Spa (2¾ m) on the main line and Moulton (7½ m), Scorton (9¾ m) and Catterick Bridge (11½ m) on the branch and taking 30 minutes for the 15 mile journey.

The double line Richmond branch has a place in railway history as the test bed for the NER's electric fog signalling apparatus, but it will be remembered by many as the rail access route to Catterick Camp. This dates from the First World War and was linked to the NER branch by the 5 mile Catterick Military Railway which had a station in the camp and another at Brompton Road, adjacent to Catterick Bridge.

Over the years the Catterick Military Railway carried various forms of passenger service for servicemen going on leave plus special and freight workings, trains over the steeply-graded route being provided by the main line company. The passenger services ceased in 1964 and freight ended when the Richmond branch lost its trains in 1970.

F.1   Farnley Branch—see Leeds

F.2   Ferriby
Doncaster/Leeds-Hull line, between Gilberdyke Junction and Hull. 7 m 42 ch from Hull

There is an additional Up Slow line from Melton to just east of Ferriby creating a three-track section through the station which has platforms to the Up Slow and Down Fast lines. The main buildings are on the Down platform and consist of a single-storey block constructed in wood to an LNER country station formula. Painted in grey and fronted by flowers and shrubs, they look very attractive.

Hull-York, Doncaster and Sheffield trains provide the service and the route east of Ferriby affords excellent views of the bird life on the Humber foreshore.

F.3   Ferrybridge
Swinton Junction-Milford line, between Pontefract Baghill and Milford Junction. 2 m 10 ch from Burton Salmon

Ferrybridge, part of the Knottingley conurbation, is important in railway terms for the large power station which is fed by merry-go-round trains of coal from the Yorkshire pits. To facilitate the movement of these there are freight spurs from the east-west

The signal box at Eryholme was provided with a mechanical frame for operating local points and a control panel for colour light signals and remote electrically operated points.

This two-cylinder compound Worsdell locomotive type would have often been seen at Ferryhill. Locomotive 1324 is photographed as exhibited at Newcastle in 1887.

Wakefield/Leeds-Goole line to the north-south Sheffield-York line, one of which is used by coal trains from the Doncaster direction via Knottingley.

The line from Doncaster was the first to serve Ferrybridge, reaching Knottingley in 1848 and being extended on through Ferrybridge to Burton Salmon two years later. From 8 August 1850, Great Northern services linked London and York this way with the line then remaining part of the East Coast route to the north until rerouting via Selby took place in 1871. Ferrybridge station never had ECML status for it was opened on 1 May 1882 after the Swinton & Knottingley route had been brought into use for goods on 19 May 1879 and for passengers on 1 July following.

Ferrybridge eventually lost its passenger services on 11 July 1947, but subsequently acquired the power station rail connection which forms a continuous loop from the S&K line north of the spurs from the L&Y. The latter run from Pontefract Monkhill Goods Junction (3 m 6 ch from Burton Salmon) round to Ferryhill South Junction (2 m 38 ch) and from Knottingley West Junction (2 m 71 ch) to Ferrybridge North Junction (2 m 27 ch), the former a single line and the latter double. Then comes the Up side Ferrybridge signal box (2 m 10 ch) and the Down side access to the power station where special regulations exist for the movement of coal and oil trains.

Some station buildings survive on the Down side.

F.4 Ferryhill
East Coast Main Line, junction with Norton-on-Tees, Pelaw and Kelloe Bank Foot lines. 56 m 17 ch from York

The Clarence Railway was the first to reach Ferryhill with a line north from Stillington Junction on the 1833 west-east route between Shildon and Port Clarence. This opened on 16 January 1834 for mineral traffic and on 17 July 1835 for passengers, the line terminating at a goods depot at Coxhoe. In 1837, on 31 March, the system was extended westwards through Spennymoor to tap the coal traffic around Byers Green, further extension following on 19 October 1840, and an east-west connection being made with the Kelloe Bank Foot line east of Ferryhill in 1846.

Whereas the east-west lines existed mainly to carry mineral traffic, the north-south railways derived from much grander ambitions, particularly those of the Great North of England Railway which was concerned with linking York and the Tyne. However, the financial strains of building the section south of Darlington resulted in the GNE handing over the northern end of its enterprise to the Newcastle & Darlington Junction Railway by an Act of 11 April 1843. That company then put Ferryhill on the East Coast Main Line from 19 June 1844 when it opened a line from Parkgate Junction, Darlington to join the Durham Junction Railway north of its Rainton Meadows terminus, thus providing a through route to the Tyne via Washington and Brockley Whins. The present course of the ECML dates from 1 October 1871 (15 January 1872 for passengers) when a link was brought into use from Tursdale Junction, north of Ferryhill, to Relly Mill near Durham.

Ferryhill passenger station closed on 6 March 1967, but the location had at one time four local routes in addition to its main line services. On the line from Middlesbrough the trains served Thornaby (3¼ m), Stockton (5½ m), Redmarshall (9 m), Stillington (10¾ m), Sedgefield (15¼ m) and then Ferryhill. This service ended on 31 March 1952, with the Hartlepool service following on 9 June of that year. The

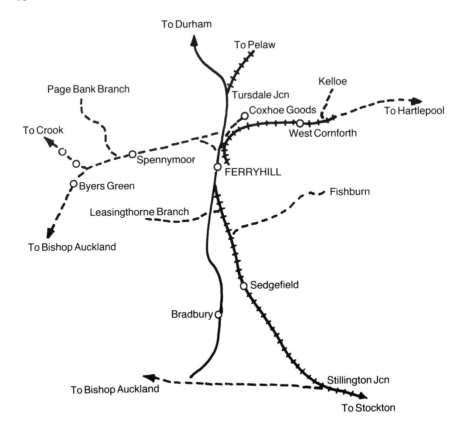

modest passenger service out to Spennymoor (4 m), Byers Green (6 m), Coundon
(7¾ m) and Bishop Auckland (9½ m) had
already ended by the outbreak of war (4
September 1939) and Ferryhill was also to
lose, from 28 July 1941, the link via Shincliffe (4½ m) and Sherburn Colliery (6¾ m)
to Leamside and on to Newcastle through
Washington and Pelaw.

From the south the freight line from
Stockton and Norton draws steadily nearer
the ECML as the two approach Ferryhill,
the connection finally being made from
Ferryhill South Junction (56 m 17 ch). The
four tracks then continue north as Fast and
Slow pairs—at first with an Up Goods
Loop and sidings parallel—past Ferryhill
box (56 m 70 ch) to Kelloe Bank Foot
Junction (57 m 50 ch) and then Tursdale
Junction (58 m 71 ch). At the former the
Steetley quarry connection is made, where
the stub of the former Hartlepool line rises
for its 3 mile surviving section's course, and
at the latter the 'new' and 'old' main lines
part company. Ferryhill box covers these
locations and, indeed, the whole area from

Aycliffe as far as Hett Mill CCTV LC (60
m 21 ch).

There is still some evidence of the 1837
route to Byers Green where the Kelloe
Bank Foot line departs on the Up side of the
main line. Byers Green itself had three stations at various periods, the second on the
extension to Crook and the third along the 1
December 1885 line from Burnhouse Junction to Bishop Auckland. Between Spennymoor and Byers Green there was a
connection to the 1856 Page Bank colliery
branch.

F.5   Ferryhill-Norton-on-Tees Line

East Coast Main Line, link to Tees-side.
10 m 72 ch

After opening its east-west cut-off route
from Simpasture Junction, Shildon to
Stockton and Port Clarence in 1833, the
Clarence Railway added a line from that
route to Ferryhill in the following year.
This was opened for mineral traffic on 16
January 1834 and ran from Stillington

Junction northwards to Coxhoe Depot at Ferryhill. A passenger service began on 11 July 1835 and eventually became a Middlesbrough-Ferryhill service which lasted until 31 March 1952.

Today the line remains in use as a cut-off route between the Tees and the North, carrying a significant volume of freight over its double, Absolute Block lines. From Ferryhill South Junction (10 m 32 ch) these gradually veer away from the course of the East Coast Main Line and then turn east to Stillington signal box (3 m 71 ch) and the Stockton-Hartlepool line. They join the latter via Norton-on-Tees West signal box and LC where one leg of the triangular junction turns east towards Billingham and the other south to Stockton.

The route used to have a colliery branch from Bishop Middleham Junction, just south of Ferryhill, to the coking plant at Fishburn. It also connected at Carlton with the route north from Murton Junction to Sunderland. This at one time was seen as an important north-south main line despite its piecemeal origins—Wellfield to Haswell in 1835, Sunderland to Haswell 1836, a connecting line there in 1877, and the Carlton-Wellfield section in 1878 (passengers 1 March 1880). Although some through passenger and freight services did use the route it never achieved major significance. Its local service was sparse and ran from Stockton via Thorpe Thewles (4¾ m), Wynyard (7¼ m), Hurworth Burn (10¼ m) and then Wellfield (13½ m), where passengers could change and pick up the West Hartlepool-Wellfield-Sunderland trains. The service ended on 2 November 1931.

There were intermediate stations on the Ferryhill-Norton-Stockton line at Sedgefield (3 m), Stillington (7½ m) and Redmarshall (9¼ m).

F.6   Ferryhill-Pelaw line
East Coast Main Line, branch from Tursdale Junction. 18 m 26 ch

Two miles north of Ferryhill the 'Old Main Line' turns away from the 'new' one to take up a parallel course a few miles to the east. It was used by early services linking the capital and the Tyne until the present route via Durham was brought into use in 1871/2.

The first route to Gateshead was completed by the Newcastle & Darlington Junction Railway which had added lines north and south of the one opened by the Durham Junction Railway between Rainton Crossing and Washington on 24 August 1838 (passengers 9 March 1840). The N&D then opened the southern portion from Shincliffe, Ferryhill to Rainton on 19 June 1844 which created a through route of sorts via Brockley Whins and the Brandling Junction line. This was then shortened from 1 September 1849 (passengers 1 October 1850) when the northern link was completed between Washington and Pelaw.

After the ECML trains had been diverted via Durham, the original main line settled down to carrying a Durham/Ferryhill to Newcastle local service. The all-stations trains from Ferryhill called at Shincliffe (4½ m), Sherburn Colliery (6¾ m), Leamside (9¼ m), Fencehouse (11¾ m), Penshaw (13¾ m), Washington (15½ m), Usworth (16¾ m), Pelaw (20¼ m), Felling (21½ m), Gateshead East (23¼ m) and then Newcastle Central (23¾ m). The through journey took just over an hour.

Today the 'Old Main Line' remains open for freight and diversionary purposes. From Tursdale Junction (2 m 49 ch) it is double to Penshaw via Whitwell LC and signal box (6 m 29 ch) and the crossing and box at Fencehouses (12 m 43 ch). Between these two the former rail network east of Durham included the Sherburn junctions with the Durham & Sunderland route, the Leamside junctions for Durham (Gilesgate) and Bishop Auckland and, further north, the links with the original DJR terminus at Rainton Meadows and with North Hetton Colliery.

North of Fencehouses the BR route connected with the Lambton, Herrington, Houghton-le-Spring and Philadelphia colliery systems. It is single from Penshaw (14 m 76 ch) over the Victoria Bridge across the Wear to join the former Stanhope & Tyne route at Washington (16 m 5 ch) which also had a connection to local mines. The route continues under its course under the control of Usworth signal box (17 m 45 ch) and with level crossings there and at Follingsby (19 m 9 ch). Finally it comes to Wardley signal box (19 m 76 ch) and the junction at Pelaw (20 m 75 ch).

F.7   Filey
Hull-Scarborough Line. 44 m 30 ch from Hull

Trains first reached Filey on 5 October 1846 with the opening of the York & North Midland Railway's line from Seamer, the through route south to Bridlington and on to Hull coming into use a year later, on 20 October 1847. The other major development at Filey was then to wait for another hundred years until 1947 when, among its final achievements, the LNER opened Filey Holiday Camp station on 10 May to serve the Butlin's holiday camp south of the town.

The new station had four platforms and its own road access to the camp. The rail access involved a double line spur from each direction on the Hunmanby-Filey section of the main line with three small signal boxes at each corner of the triangle. These were switched in specially for the campers' trains which were numerous and heavily loaded on peak summer Saturdays. An unexpected arrival occurred in 1956 when a K3 locomotive and empty coach train ran through the buffers and finished up on the platform. Apparently the vacuum brake had not been coupled up and the locomotive brake proved inadequate against the falling gradient of 1 in 106/228 from Hunmanby.

On this descent the embankments of the access lines to the camp are still visible today, although the station was formally closed on 26 November 1977. Then the main line crosses the A165 at Royal Oak AHB crossing (43 m 4 ch) and comes to the resort of Filey, another traditional fishing port whose long, fine sands have attracted the holidaymakers.

Filey station still retains its original form and is to a design of G.T. Andrews. An overall roof spans the two platforms which are linked by a decorated footbridge and the main buildings, behind whitewashed walls, are on the Up side. A gated level crossing

and traditional signal box stand at the country end.

F.8   Fitzwilliam—see Doncaster-Wakefield Line

F.9   Foss Islands Branch—see York

G.1   Garforth
Leeds-Hull line, between Leeds and Micklefield. 13 m 23 ch from Selby South Junction.

Today Garforth is served by the Manchester-York/Scarborough trains plus some extra services to cater for commuter traffic to and from Leeds. The station retains its old buildings plus the former dock and goods yard and is crossed by a decorative footbridge and a skew road bridge.

The line was opened on 22 September 1834 by the Leeds & Selby Railway, and was supplemented on 12 August 1878 by a branch south through Kippax, Bowers and Ledston to Castleford. The latter had originated in 1873 as a project of the Leeds, Castleford & Pontefract Junction Railway, but it had been absorbed by the North Eastern two years before opening. The line carried some coal traffic as well as its seven passenger trains each way daily but was closed to passengers on 22 January 1951.

G.2   Gascoigne Wood
Leeds-Hull line, junction with Normanton/ Sheffield/York line. 6 m 27 ch from Selby

Although the date is 1947, the trains in Filey Holiday Camp station include some pretty old and varied stock.

Commuters detraining at Garforth in 1978. The volume of local West Riding/West Yorkshire traffic has grown significantly since then.

Gascoigne Wood has been of significance as a railway junction for many years and its strategic location led to the establishment of a marshalling yard south of the Leeds-Hull line. After this was closed in 1959 a few sidings were retained for wagon storage, but the area seemed to have lost forever the railway status it had first acquired when it became the site of an early junction.

That was until 1983 when Gascoigne Wood became the loading point for rail traffic from the new Selby drift mine, Europe's largest and most modern coalfield. Rail forwardings are based on a loading complex where two large bunkers can load a 1,000 tonne block train with coal in around 15 minutes. Train despatches can be made every half hour to achieve a planned movement of 50,000 tonnes of coal to local power stations every working day. The BR facilities, which include 12 extra sidings in the adjacent Milford Yard to maintain the supply of empties for loading, cost just over £4 million. British Coal and the EEC contributed £1.5 million towards the new track and signalling work involved in setting up the facility.

The area got its first trains when the Leeds & Selby Railway opened its pioneer line on 22 September 1834. Five years later a north-to-east spur from the York & North Midland line produced a station at York Junction, which later became Old Junction and later still Milford Old Junction. From 1879 to 1902 the station was known as Gascoigne Wood but after that it only remained open to serve the yards. The east-to-south curve dates from 1840 and linked the former York Junction with Milford Junction station.

Today the traditional Up side signal box at Gascoigne Wood controls the movement of the busy passenger service on the Leeds-Hull line and also movements into and out of the coal loading area. It deals with Milford box in offering and accepting trains over the 1 m 8 ch double line freight spur from Sherburn Junction to the north and for movements to and from the Normanton and Sheffield lines to the south.

G.3 Gateshead—see Newcastle

G.4 Gilberdyke
Junction of Leeds-Hull and Doncaster-Hull lines. Station 16 m 76 ch and junction 17 m 7 ch from Hull

Gilberdyke was known as Staddlethorpe until 1974 and had become a junction in 1869 when the North Eastern Railway's link from Thorne to join the 1840 Hull & Selby line created a major new approach route to the port of Hull. Today trains on both routes serve the station to give it excellent links to York, Doncaster, Sheffield, Leeds and Chester, as well as into the city and port of Kingston-upon-Hull.

The Doncaster and Leeds routes join at Gilberdyke Junction west of the station and under the control of a conventional signal box there. The two running lines then continue through the station, over the 1782–1971 Market Weighton Canal and on to Broomfleet. Gilberdyke station itself has long wooden buildings with a glazed mini-arcade on the Down side and just a wooden shelter on the Up. The latter houses a NER 17 milepost.

G.5 Glaisdale—see Middlesbrough-Whitby Line

G.6 Gledholt Tunnels—see Huddersfield

G.7 Goldthorpe Colliery Branch—see Swinton Junction-Milford Line

G.8 Goole
Doncaster-Hull line, junction with Pontefract line. 6 m 46 ch from Gilberdyke Junction.

Goole began to develop as a port when the Knottingley & Goole Canal came into use in 1826. The expansion accelerated when the line, prompted by the Wakefield, Pontefract & Goole Railway and then absorbed by the Lancashire & Yorkshire Railway, reached there in 1848. For years L&Y steamers sailed between Goole and Europe and the port dealt with a large amount of railway business, especially export coal.

The L&Y line ran directly into the port area but its passenger station was closed on 1 October 1869 as the result of an agreement between the L&Y, MS&L and NER companies which led to the opening of the latter's connecting link from the Doncaster-Scunthorpe line at Thorne to the Leeds-Hull line at Staddlethorpe (now Gilberdyke Junction). Under the revised arrangements the L&Y trains connected with the new line where the two crossed, but a second connection was established in 1910 when the Selby to Goole line opened.

The train service pattern of the later 1930s gave Goole trains from London and Doncaster, plus cross-Pennine services via Penistone and Wakefield. Local services linked the port with Leeds and Wakefield and there were some five trains each way daily over the 12 miles to Selby via Airmyn & Rawcliffe (3½ m), Drax Hales (6 m), and Barlow (8½ m). The latter ended on 15 June 1964.

The line from Doncaster makes a level approach to Goole over two waterways, first the Dutch River which takes its name from the nationality of its drainage engineer constructors, and then the Knottingley & Goole section of the Aire & Calder Navigation. Next the Hull line passes over the docks access lines, the latter marking the course of the original L&Y approach to Goole. The Leeds line now runs parallel with the ex-NER route before rising to join it at Potters Grange Junction (7 m 5 ch) and then passing via Goole barrier crossing and

signal box (6 m 51 ch) into the station (6 m 46 ch). On this section there is an Up side link with the docks and, on the Down side, a loading compound and ramp for imported Renault cars.

Goole station is typical of its period, constructed in red brick with the main buildings on the Up side and canopies on both. The Up side block incorporates the former station house, with a bay looking out on to the platform, and a brick goods shed still stands at the end of the former goods yard.

A mile and a half beyond the station the route crosses the River Ouse by means of Goole Swing Bridge (5 m 6 ch), an impressive structure with approach spans and a signal box above the movable section. Passing through the latter can be difficult owing to the tidal river conditions and regular collisions between shipping and the timbers protecting the central jetty and its hydraulic machinery nearly brought closure in 1983. Had this come about, Goole would have got a new station west of the level crossing, with the line being closed from the latter to Gilberdyke Junction.

On the main line Goole has services to Sheffield, Doncaster and King's Cross in one direction and to Hull in the other. The services over the old L&Y route to Leeds give the town further connectional permutations.

G.9   Goose Hill Junction—see Normanton

G.10   Grangetown—see Middlesbrough-Saltburn line

G.11   Great Ayton—see Middlesbrough-Whitby Line

G.12   Greatham

Northallerton-Newcastle line, between Stockton and Hartlepool. 67 m 28 ch from Leeds

Goole swing bridge in the open position. Buffeting of the bridge by passing ships almost brought closure of this section of the line.

This is a simple station on the 1840 Stockton & Hartlepool Railway line, with just two platforms and a peak period service. The Up side signal box controls a barrier crossing and access to the extensive sidings of the vast Hartlepool South Works of British Steel, which has its own signal box and internal motive power.

G.13 Greensfield Junction—see Newcastle

G.14 Greetland—see Milner Royd-Mirfield Line

G.15 Grosmont—see Middlesbrough-Whitby Line

G.16 Guisborough Junction—see Middlesbrough

G.17 Guiseley—see Ilkley Branch

G.18 Gypsy Lane—see Middlesbrough-Whitby Line

H.1 Halifax
Manchester Victoria-Bradford line, between Milner Royd Junction and Low Moor. 32 m 28 ch from Manchester

The ancient town of Halifax, crowded into the steep-sided Hebble Valley, can trace its involvement with the cloth trade right back to the fifteenth century. Although tools, textiles and toffees were added to the town's manufacturing activity, it still has some dramatic riverside mills as well as such notable buildings as Sir Charles Barry's 1863 town hall built in the Palladian style. The fifteenth-century Shibden Hall has become the home of the Folk Museum of West Yorkshire and the late eighteenth-century Piece Hall now houses an industrial museum, art gallery and craft shops.

Early rail travel to and from the area was catered for by the Manchester & Leeds Railway's main line which opened throughout on 1 March 1841 but ran some three miles to the south of Halifax proper. By the time this line was opened, work had already started on a branch link to Halifax and this was opened from North Dean (later Greetland Junction) to a terminus at Shaw Syke on 1 July 1844. This steeply-graded single line was hardly likely to satisfy the railway ambitions of the people of Halifax for long.

The first improvement in the rail facilities at Halifax came after six years when another L&Y enterprise, that of the West Yorkshire Union Railway for a link through to Low Moor and Bradford, came to fruition. The rail journey today still reveals how difficult an engineering task this was, and it is not surprising that opening from a temporary through station at Halifax via Low Moor via Hipperholme, Lightcliffe and Pickle Bridge (replaced by Wyke & Norwood Green) did not take place until 7 August 1850.

The 1850s brought more railway changes for Halifax. Following the opening of its route north east to Low Moor, the WYUR brought into service a new connection to the 1841 M&L route, but this time facing west towards Manchester. This 2¾ miles from Dryclough Junction to Milner Royd Junction, still used by today's Manchester-Bradford/Leeds trains, was opened on the first day of 1852 and had an intermediate station at Copley.

From 1854, the Great Northern Railway had access to Bradford via a new LB&HJ line, and its associations with the L&Y allowed it to begin services to and from Halifax. This additional work was part of the reason for providing a new station from 23 June of the following year.

Between 1876 and 1884 the Great Northern extended its penetration of the area west of Bradford by opening first to Thornton and then to Keighley. This provided the opportunity for a new, separate access to Halifax, although still in conjunction with the L&Y. The two companies, in the form of the Halifax and Ovenden Joint Railway, opened a line north from Halifax to North Bridge on 17 August 1874 and then extended it on to Holmfield on 1 September 1879 (passengers on 1 December). This came to carry a useful passenger service calling at Halifax North Bridge (¾ m), Ovenden (1¼ m), Holmfield (2¾ m), Queensbury (5 m), Clayton (6 m), Great Horton (7¼ m), Horton Park (7¾ m), St Dunstan's (9 m) and Bradford Exchange (9½ m). Passenger services ceased on 23 May 1955 and goods on 27 June 1960.

The final railway line to Halifax was a separate branch from Holmfield to a new station at St Pauls. This was a project of the

Halifax High Level & North & South Junction Railway which had been conceived as part of a trunk route link-up with the Hull & Barnsley. Like many railway hopes of the nineteenth century, the reality was much more modest, in fact just a very expensive 3 mile branch opened throughout on 5 September 1890, worked by the GN&L&Y Joint and lasting only until 1 January 1917 for passengers (27 July 1960 for freight).

In the 1930s Halifax enjoyed a good pattern of east-west services, albeit entailing a change at Sowerby Bridge on some occasions. It had through services from St Pancras and Euston and links with both Marylebone and King's Cross. There was a regular service on the Huddersfield-Elland-Bradford line and LNER trains on both the local Bradford service and further afield via Ardsley. Today the permutations have diminished to the services over the 'Summit' route, but they give Halifax an hourly Scarborough/York-Manchester interval service, Leeds-Preston/Blackpool trains and turnround 'locals' between Halifax and Leeds. The latter hardly have the character of the old locals to Clayton West and Holmfirth, but in total Halifax has over 30 trains each way daily and connectional access to considerably more.

West of Sowerby Bridge, the main line from Manchester and Rochdale runs on the south side of the River Calder and its Calder & Hebble Navigation companion. The Halifax line crosses both waterways after the two routes separate at Milner Royd Junction (29 m 21 ch). Copley station lay along this stretch and gave its name to the viaduct across the river, but now the trains just tackle the two miles of 1 in 118 gradient through the 214 yd Bank House Tunnel (30 m 57 ch to 30 m 67 ch) and out again to meet the 1 m 11 ch double freight line from Greetland at Dryclough Junction (31 m 36 ch). The combined routes are now in the crowded lower valley of the Hebble Brook and provide an interesting view of Halifax as they emerge from the rough-hewn stone of the approach cuttings.

Halifax station has a basic elegance which it owes to the L&Y's architect Thomas Butterworth. The location dates back to 1855, although it was substantially rebuilt in the 1880s with separate accommodation for its Great Northern and Lancashire & Yorkshire users. More recent years have brought some deterioration with only the Up island platform currently in use, but a restoration scheme is now breathing life back into the warm stone and decorative frontage of the main west-side building. Beyond this the Shaw Syke and South Parade areas relinquished by earlier stations grew into a vast goods complex, still with a stone shed extant. The higher level St Pauls station lay further west still, beyond the surviving traces of coal drops.

The long wooden Halifax signal box stands at the north end of the station. From here the trains on the steeply-graded H&O Joint route continued nearly straight ahead whereas those on the L&Y line turn east near the Rowntree factory and plunge into the 1,105 yds of Beacon Hill Tunnel (32 m 40 ch to 33 m 10 ch), named after the beacon which once stood high above as part of the early warning system set up to meet the threat from the Spanish Armada. On the section on to Low Moor traces remain of the three former stations which were located between the tunnels—the 388 yd Hipperholme Tunnel (34 m 5 ch to 34 m 32 ch), the 70 yd Lightcliffe Tunnel (34 m 67 ch to 34 m 70 ch), the 1,365 yd Wyke Tunnel (36 m 12 ch to 36 m 74 ch) and the 69 yd New Furnace Tunnel (37 m 7 ch to 37 m 10 ch). A 'Goods trains stop here' notice also survives.

H.2   Haltwhistle—see Newcastle-Carlisle Line

H.3   Hambleton Junctions
East Coast Main Line, junctions with Leeds-Hull line. Hambleton South Junction 174 m 10 ch and North Junction 174 m 75 ch from King's Cross; Hambleton East Junction 3 m 34 ch and West Junction 4 m 43 ch from Selby

From South Junction a double freight line route passes via Scalm Lane R/G crossing (174 m 56 ch) to West Junction (175 m 33 ch) to cater for Doncaster-Leeds route movements. Hull-York passenger services use the single line spur between East Junction and North Junction. Both spurs are on the York panel, but the sharper curve of the passenger route limits its line speed to 40 mph compared with 70 mph on the freight line.

In contrast with the 1983 newness of this stretch of the East Coast Main Line, the higher level line dates back to the pioneer Leeds & Selby concern and was opened in 1834. It had a station at Hambleton until 14 September 1959.

H.4   Hammerton—see Leeds-York Line

H.5   Hare Park Junction—see Doncaster-Wakefield Line

H.6   Harrogate
Leeds-York line. 17 m 24 ch from Wortley Junction, Leeds and 20 m 38 ch from Skelton Junction, York

Harrogate, with its spa, dales and conference centre, developed in the mid-nineteenth century when urban space was at less of a premium, and it remains a pleasant, open town with flowers much in evidence. The original Brunswick station, opened on 20 July 1848 with the York & North Midland Railway line from Church Fenton, lasted only until 1 August 1862 when the present site took over all passenger workings.

The Leeds & Thirsk Railway's route passed well to the east of Harrogate, but soon after the formation of the North Eastern Railway a connecting line was built from the L&T line at Pannal to give access to the town via the Y&NM approach from Church Fenton over Crimple Viaduct. As part of the same round of improvements, this new line into Harrogate was continued on to rejoin the Thirsk line at Bilton Road Junction, with a further connection from Dragon Junction to Starbeck North. The 1848 York-Knaresborough line had been extended to Starbeck South Junction in 1851 and this had a further connection to Stonefall Junction, which saw little use and was severed at the Knaresborough end around 1907. The new, more central station at Harrogate was part of the 1862 package of changes, Brunswick being relegated to a goods terminal.

In the 1930s Harrogate enjoyed a considerable variety of train services over its seven radiating lines. The longer distance, eg Liverpool-Newcastle, and prestige, eg *Harrogate Sunday Pullman*, services used the line from Leeds and north through Ripon, with local services running to Leeds via Thorner, to Church Fenton, to Bradford via Otley, to York, to Pilmoor and up the Nidd valley to Pateley Bridge. Opened on 1 May 1862, the single line of the latter carried a service of four or five trains a day serving Ripley Valley (4 m), Hampsthwaite (5½ m), Birstwith (6¾ m), Darley (9½ m), Dacre (11 m) and Pateley Bridge (14½ m). From 11 September 1907, the Nidd Valley Light Railway, constructed to serve Bradford Corporation's reservoirs, provided an onward service from its own station in Pateley Bridge to Wath-in-Nidderdale (1½ m), Ramsgill (4 m) and Lofthouse-in-Nidderdale (6 m). The steam railcar service on the Lofthouse section ended on 1 January 1930, although it continued to

Above *Harrogate North signal box. The exterior looks quite modern, but there is a traditional frame inside, as is apparent from the amount of signal wire and point rodding.*

NORTH EASTERN RAILWAY

NIDDERDALE FEAST.

CHEAP EXCURSION TO THE SEA-SIDE.

On TUESDAY, Sept. 20th, 1870,

A SPECIAL TRAIN will leave PATELEY BRIDGE, and Stations as under, for

SCARBRO

LEAVE		A.M.
Pateley Bridge	-	6 0
Dacre Banks	- - -	6 8
Darley	- - - -	6 12
Birstwith	- - - -	6 17
Hampsthwaite	- - -	6 21
Ripley	- - - -	6 30
Starbeck	- - - -	6 40
Knaresbro'	- - - -	6 50

FARE THERE AND BACK.

COVERED CARRIAGES.

3s.

Children under Twelve Years of Age, Half-fare.

The Return Train will leave Scarbro' at 5.30 p.m. same day.

NO LUGGAGE ALLOWED.

☞ The Tickets are only available for Scarbro' in going, and for the Stations at which they were issued on return.

As only a limited number of Carriages can be allotted to this Train, the following Regulations will be strictly observed, in order, as far as possible, to secure the comfort of the public, and to avoid delay :—The number of Tickets supplied for issue will only be equal to the amount of Carriage accommodation, and no persons except holders of Tickets for this Train will be permitted to travel by it, *and any person attempting to travel without a Ticket will be charged the full ordinary fare both ways. The Tickets are at the Stations ready for issue ;* and persons who intend to travel by this Train must apply early enough to enable the Station Clerks to procure any additional Tickets that may be required.

YORK, August, 1870.   **W. O'BRIEN, General Manager.**

EDWARD BAINES AND SONS, GENERAL PRINTERS, LEEDS.

Left *Scarborough was a popular excursion destination from all over Yorkshire, as this 1870 Harrogate poster shows.*

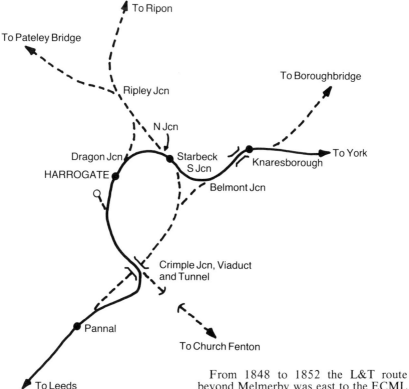

To Ripon

To Pateley Bridge

Ripley Jcn

To Boroughbridge

N Jcn

Dragon Jcn   Starbeck   Knaresborough   To York
HARROGATE   S Jcn

Belmont Jcn

Crimple Jcn, Viaduct
and Tunnel

Pannal

To Church Fenton

To Leeds

carry materials for another six years. On the Harrogate-Pateley Bridge portion the passenger service lasted until 2 April 1951, and freight services for another thirteen years.

The Leeds & Thirsk Railway had opened its southern section in stages in 1848/9 and was completed through to Stockton on 2 June 1852. It changed its name to Leeds Northern, but intending travellers from Harrogate still had to go out to Starbeck to catch LN trains until the new Harrogate station was opened under NER auspices 10 years later. North-bound trains then descended the 1 in 66 gradient to pick up the original route at Bilton Road Junction and head for the first station at Nidd Bridge (3½ m). A further descent at 1 in 357 to Wormald Green (6¾ m) was then followed by a drop of nearly 3 miles at 1 in 133 to complete the descent to the plain and run through the pleasant countryside around Newby Hall and Fountains Abbey into the cathedral city of Ripon (11½ m). There were then no gradients of any significance to the junction at Melmerby (11½ m).

From 1848 to 1852 the L&T route beyond Melmerby was east to the ECML at Thirsk, but on 2 June 1852 a single line was opened through Sinderby, Pickhill and Newby Wiske to Northallerton (and thence to Stockton). The North Eastern downgraded this to branch status and reverted to routing via Thirsk, but another change in 1901 resulted in the direct line being doubled. The Melmerby-Thirsk line lost its passenger trains first, from 14 September 1959, those over the Harrogate-Ripon-Northallerton line finishing from 6 March 1967.

The North Eastern Railway opened a branch west from the former Leeds Northern route at Melmerby. This was the 7¾ mile single line out to Masham which opened on 9 June 1875. It had one intermediate station at Tanfield and a modest train service to and from Ripon which ended on 1 January 1931 as one of the victims of the fairly extensive round of LNER closures of that period. Goods traffic continued until 11 November 1963.

The closures of the 1950s and 1960s reduced Harrogate's services and the need for its full range of station bays, centre lines and awnings. However, the spacious layout was constructively remodelled in the '60s and retains one centre line in addition to the platform lines. An oil siding also survives from the once-extensive freight complex at the York end.

Harrogate's main station buildings, in brick, are on the west side and merge into the commercial complex on the overbridge. The remaining signal box, formerly Harrogate North, is located at 20 m 30 ch from York. Nearby the mileage changes from 17 m 24 ch from Leeds to 20 m 38 ch from York and this is accompanied by a direction change—from Down ex Leeds to Up to York.

Today Harrogate has an excellent hourly service to York and a half-hourly one to Leeds. A few services originate there, including a through train to King's Cross.

H.7   Hartburn Junction—see Bowesfield

H.8   Hartlepool

Northallerton-Newcastle line, between Stockton and Sunderland. 71 m 55 ch from Leeds

The earliest Hartlepool settlement dates back to the seventh century but the site, at the northern point of Hartlepool Bay, was raided by successive Danish, Norman and Scottish invaders before it began to grow and prosper. From the development of the dock system in the nineteenth century the location spread along the Tees estuary, creating West Hartlepool and, today, the Hartlepool District.

The first railway to Hartlepool, that of

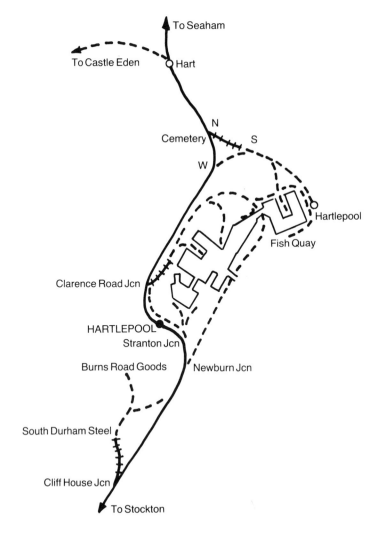

A conveyor in operation for shipment coal at Hartlepool in the 1930s.

the Hartlepool Dock & Railway Company, was built to carry coal from the Haswell area and arrived along the coast in 1835 at a point adjacent to Victoria Dock. The coal business was to grow to over 3 million tons a year and the railway docks to cover a water area of 180 acres. The latter also handled ½ million tons of iron imported for the South Durham Steel & Iron Company, and a similar amount of timber and wood pulp. Fish landings, and the subsequent railway forwardings, were also significant. The docks had the usual cranage, storage, timber pond and dry dock facilities, plus belt conveyors and gravity discharge spouts for shipment coal.

Hartlepool's second railway was the Stockton & Hartlepool which opened along the north bank of the estuary on 12 November 1840 (10 February 1841 for passengers). The terminus was in the Middleton area and there was a connection round to the HD&R line. This route was truncated by the opening of the Jackson and Swainson docks in the 1850s which forced the railway route inland. A new station was opened at West Hartlepool in 1853 when the West Hartlepool Harbour & Railway Company was formed from the Stockton & Hartlepool, Clarence Railway and Hartlepool West Harbour & Dock companies. A further period of dock and railway alteration produced the present station in 1880, with the adjacent earlier site being turned

over to goods traffic.

The old Hartlepool station slowly lost status, especially after the completion of the coast route northwards in 1905, but the various rail services—Middlesbrough, Ferryhill, Sunderland etc—continued to serve both; there was also a 15 minute interval shuttle between Hartlepool and West Hartlepool which gave the former connections with the trains on the direct Newcastle-Middlesbrough route, Hartlepool closed on 16 June 1947 and today's station carries that name rather than West Hartlepool. Its modern Newcastle-Middlesbrough trains plus those to and from Darlington give it excellent local coverage plus connections with the Inter-City network.

The approach to Hartlepool begins at Cliff House Down side signal box (70 m 6 ch) where the now disused Cliff House branch (see separate entry) still joins. On the opposite side of the main line the site of Newburn Yard is still obvious, but the two adjacent engine sheds are now but a memory. Stranton level crossing and signal box (71 m 22 ch) recalls another early station but the route ahead to the docks, though clear, is now inactive and the running lines curve into the passenger station instead. The main buildings here are on the Down side and in an indented formation surrounding the stairs to the footbridge although, in fact, the Up platform is not normally used. The Up side has a retaining wall for the lattice girders supporting the overall roof.

Beyond the station the BR route curves on past Clarence Road signal box (71 m 70 ch) on the Down side and the surviving docks area line on the Up. It then continues to Cemetery North box (73 m 49 ch) where formerly West, South and North Junctions bounded the triangular link with the original approach to Hartlepool. The course of this is still visible as an extension of the connection to the private sidings of the Steetley chemical works.

Beyond Cemetery North the present line veers away from the trackbed of the 1835 line to Castle Eden (for Ferryhill and Sunderland) at the site of the former Hart station. This lay 5¾ m from Hartlepool via West Hartlepool and had been followed by Hesleden (8½ m), Castle Eden (9¾ m), Wingate (11 m), Trimdon (12¾ m), Coxhoe Bridge (17 m), West Cornforth (18½ m) and then Ferryhill (19 m). After Castle Eden, the Sunderland trains had run via Wellfield (8½ m), Thornley (9¼ m), Shotton Bridge (10½ m), Haswell (12¼ m), South Hetton (13¼ m), Murton (14¾ m), Seaton (16½ m), Ryhope (18½ m) and then into Sunderland (21½ m). These services ended on 9 June 1952.

H.9   Haverton South—see Billingham-Seal Sands Storage Line

H.10   Haydon Bridge—see Newcastle-Carlisle Line

H.11   Headfield Branch—see Dewsbury

H.12   Headingley—see Leeds-York Line

H.13   Healey Mills
Eastwood-Normanton line, between Thornhill LNW Junction and Horbury Junction. 42 m 64 ch from Manchester Victoria

The vast marshalling yards either side of the main line are now just a memory and Healey Mills signal box just controls its section of the former L&Y main line and the various through and local freight activities. Responsibility for the latter begins at Thornhill Junction (40 m 50 ch) where the single line freight route from Liversedge joins on the Down side after the separation of the Leeds and Wakefield routes. Then the Dewsbury Railway Street link, the Headfield Branch, joins at Dewsbury East Junction (41 m 43 ch) and a Down Slow line is added between the Up and Down Fast lines at Healey Mills 'A' Junction (42 m). An Up Slow brings the main running lines up to four from 'B' Junction (43 m 31 ch).

In addition to these local freight connections and extra running lines, the Healey Mills box coverage extends west to Bradley Wood where the 1847 Huddersfield line joins the 1840–41 Manchester & Leeds Railway route. In the opposite direction, the box controls Horbury Station Junction (44 m 13 ch) where the 1902 single freight line turns off south toward Crigglestone Junction and Barnsley.

Thornhill station, the first to serve Dewsbury, stood just east of Thornhill Junction but lost much of its initial status when the LD&M line through Dewsbury to Leeds opened in 1848. The L&Y's 1867 attempt to serve Dewsbury by a branch from the main line fared little better and passenger services lasted only until 1 December 1930.

The Midland Railway route from Royston Junction to Dewsbury crossed the L&Y line near Thornhill Junction, and further east the trackbed of the connection between the two is still visible. This line opened to goods in 1905 and to passengers from 1 July 1909, but it had a chequered history with a First World War closure period and the end of normal services in 1946.

A 1987 view of Hartlepool station, looking towards Stockton and with a Darlington train in the Down side bay.

Despite its modern train service, Hebden Bridge retains the air of an earlier age, from the period signs and hydraulic lift on the station to the neat, austere signal box.

Designed to improve the MR access to Bradford and Halifax it did come to carry some important through services but made little use of the intermediate stations at Crigglestone and Middlestown.

H.14 Heaton—see Newcastle

H.15 Heaton Lodge Junctions—see Mirfield and Manchester-Leeds Line

H.16 Hebden Bridge
Manchester-Normanton/Bradford line, between Regional Boundary and Milner Royd Junction. 23 m 50 ch from Manchester Victoria

Proud of its Calder Civic Trust and Best Kept Station awards, Hebden Bridge is also a station where it is easy to capture the atmosphere of the past railway scene. It retains its period signs, damp subway, hydraulic lift machinery and even a 'Lamp Room', but enjoys an efficient modern service of hourly Sprinters between Manchester Victoria and Leeds. Apart from the early turnround workings which give Hebden Bridge originating services, most trains continue on from Leeds to York or Scarborough.

The Hebden Bridge platforms are partially staggered and there are substantial buildings on both sides. The main ones, including the booking office, are in typical L&Y style and are on the Down side. Here, too, are the visible remains of the coal yard with a surviving dock and wagon turntable area. The attractive wooden signal box is on the Up side at the eastern end and with a refuge siding beyond.

The LMR/ER boundary is at Eastwood (29 m 3 ch) where there is an Up Goods Loop controlled by the Preston panel. The Pennine hillsides crowd in as the line crosses Dover Bridge and nears the end of its 5 mile descent at 1 in 182 from Summit Tunnel. After passing through the 109 yd Weasel Hall Tunnel (23 m 12 ch to 23 m 17 ch), the stretch to Hebden Bridge affords a view of Stoodley Pike, the Battle of Waterloo monument on Lanfield Moor.

This section of the line dates from 1840–41 when the Manchester & Leeds Railway followed the old coaching route and that of the Rochdale Canal, and used the tumbling valley of the River Calder as part of its Pennine crossing. Trains had reached Hebden Bridge from Normanton (Goose Hill Junction) on 5 October 1840, but a coach link had then been needed until the completion of Summit Tunnel early in the following year.

H.17 Heighington—see Bishop Auckland Branch

H.18 Hendon Branch—see Ryhope Grange

H.19 Hensall—see Wakefield-Goole Line

H.20 Hessle
Doncaster/Leeds-Hull lines, between Brough and Hull. 4 m 64 ch from Hull

A significant number of Hull-York, Doncaster and Sheffield trains serve this dormitory area of Kingston-upon-Hull throughout the day. The route originated in 1840 when the Hull & Selby line was opened on 2 July, and the station now comprises long platforms reached by ramp from the Down side brick entrance building.

East of Hessle the railway passes beneath the approaches to the Humber bridge.

H.21 Heworth—see Newcastle

A view of Hexham station from the Carlisle end overbridge. The bay once used by Allendale and Reedsmouth trains is just discernible.

H.22   Hexham

Newcastle-Carlisle line. 20 m 68 ch from Newcastle

Hexham can trace its history back to Saxon times. The abbey site dates back that far although the original Saxon cathedral was destroyed in Danish raids in the ninth century. Today the river that carried the Danish invaders does a more peaceful job by permitting easy access for the Newcastle-Carlisle railway route and its service of Newcastle-Hexham and through trains.

The Newcastle & Carlisle Railway reached Hexham from Blaydon on 9 March 1835 and extended west to Haydon Bridge on 28 June 1836, through services over the whole route commencing two years later. Subsequently two branches were to be linked to the N&C route just west of Hexham. The first of these was the Border Counties Railway line north to Reedsmouth which opened under North British Railway con-

trol in 1862, and the second was a branch south west to Allendale which was opened in 1868/9.

Passenger trains on the Allendale branch only lasted until 22 September 1930, although the line remained open for freight for another 20 years. In North Eastern days the number of travellers warranted only three trains each way daily, with one extra on market days. On the 33-minute journey from Hexham they called at Elrington (6¼ m), Langley (8¾ m), Staward (10¾ m) and then Allendale (13½ m). The North British also provided three trains each way daily on its route through Reedsmouth to Riccarton Junction. They called at Wall (3¼ m), Humshaugh (5 m), Collerton (6¼ m), Barrasford (7¾ m), Wark (11¼ m), Reedsmouth (15¼ m), Bellingham (17 m), Tarset (20½ m), Thorneyburn (21¾ m), Falstone (25 m), Plashetts (30½ m), Kielder (33¼ m), Deadwater (36¼ m), and Saughtree (39¼ m) on the 42 mile, 1¾-hour journey—

A dmu waits in the rain at Hexham in 1988 having just completed a journey from Sunderland and soon to start the return one.

although Thorneyburn only got one call by one train, and that only on Tuesdays! The Reedsmouth line passenger services ended on 15 October 1956, and freight two years later.

Happily Hexham and its N&C station survives, although without its overall roof. The main buildings are on the south side and house the local civil engineering management as well as the ticket office. The Down side goods yard east of the station is still active, as is one of the two signal boxes and the Up side ballast yard. Hexham has, admittedly, lost its loco depot, the branch lines, and their bays, but it has through trains to Carlisle and South West Scotland plus a good service of all-stations trains to Newcastle and Sunderland.

H.23   Hickleton—see   Swinton-Milford Line

H.24   High   Level   Bridge—see   New-castle

H.25   Hipperholme Tunnel—see Halifax

H.26   Holbeck Junctions—see Leeds

H.27   Honley—see   Barnsley-Huddersfield Line

H.28   Hopetown Junction—see Bishop Auckland Branch

H.29   Horbury Junction
Eastwood-Normanton line, between Thornhill LNW Junction and Wakefield Kirkgate. 45 m 38 ch from Manchester Victoria

Horbury Junction signal box controls a portion of the four-track line between Healey Mills and Wakefield Kirkgate boxes, as well as the westbound connection from the Sheffield/Barnsley line. The location is also notable as the home of the Procor (former Charles Roberts) private wagon works.

This section of the east-west route opened on 5 October 1840 as part of the Manchester & Leeds Railway's main line, but the line south to Barnsley was not operational until 1 January 1850, by which time it had been leased to the M&L and thus became part of the Lancashire & Yorkshire Railway empire. The single line west-south freight spur runs from Horbury Station Junction (44 m 13 ch) round to

Crigglestone Junction (45 m 56 ch) and is controlled by Healey Mills box. This was a 1902 afterthought, the original line being that from south to east which joins the main line after a deep cutting and under the eye of the wooden Down side signal box. The access to the Procor works lies in the vee between these two routes.

The trackwork in this area is complicated and there is a substantial number of train movements. These include the Huddersfield-Wakefield services which have gained the M&L route at Bradley Junction and then reverse from Wakefield Kirkgate round to Westgate, also the Sheffield-Barnsley-Leeds trains which cross all the tracks to get to the Down side at the junction.

There are still some remains of Horbury & Ossett station, notably the Up side goods shed.

H.30   Horden—see Easington

H.31   Horsforth—see Leeds-York Line

H.32   Howden—see Leeds-Hull Line

H.33   Huddersfield
Manchester (Victoria) to Leeds (Holbeck East Junction) line, junction with Barnsley line. 25 m 60 ch from Manchester Victoria

There were all sorts of early schemes to bring railways to Huddersfield, and a fair amount of in-fighting between them. The first really positive development came when local interests set up the Huddersfield & Manchester Railway company early in 1844, this then merging with the canal opposition to form the Huddersfield & Manchester Railway & Canal Company. The intention was to reduce the costs of construction by following the route and using the experience of the Huddersfield Canal.

The H&M's main rivals were the Manchester & Leeds and Leeds, Dewsbury & Manchester companies. Failing to thwart the H&M, the Manchester & Leeds concern became involved with the Huddersfield & Sheffield Junction Railway's plan for a line to Penistone and secured an enabling Act for this on 1 July 1845. Just 20 days later, Parliament also approved the Huddersfield & Manchester Bill to link Mirfield and Manchester via Huddersfield, and both concerns got down to the fairly daunting construction tasks facing them.

The town of Huddersfield lies on a hilly site created by its three deep valleys. Their waters were invaluable to the woollen industry which brought the town into prominence in the seventeenth century, but the landscape they had carved forced the railway engineers to cling to hillsides and level out gradients by the provision of expensive tunnels and viaducts. The approach from the north required a viaduct 663 yd long, but a single line was laid on this to link Heaton Lodge Junction to Huddersfield's partly-built station from 3 August 1847. A second track was soon added but the tunnel immediately south of the station proved another major obstacle and, coupled with the further tunnels and viaducts beyond, delayed opening of the line through to Stalybridge until 1 August 1849. Nor was the H&SJ approach to Huddersfield any easier, and it was 1 July of the following year before the Sheffield line was opened from Penistone. The only other line then to come was the Midland Railway's goods line to Newton depot which dates from 1 November 1910.

By the time the two main routes to Huddersfield were opened the old rivals had largely solved their differences. The H&M and the LD&M merged with the London & North Western Railway from 1847 and the Manchester & Leeds eventually became part of the L&Y. In the meantime it was able to get to its Penistone line by running powers from Cooper Bridge and a jointly-owned section from Huddersfield station to Springwood Junction.

The original Huddersfield station, which survives as a Grade I listed building, is perhaps one of the most impressive of British railway stations. Begun in 1846 and completed in 1850, it is the work of York-based architect J.P. Pritchett (Jnr). The rising approach to the station enhances the stature of the 416 ft long frontage whose centrepiece is a huge portico with eight tall Corinthian columns. Beyond is the ticketing area leading to the main platform and the subway access to the Down island.

In addition to the imposing central portion of the station the two end sections are also quite dramatic. These originally housed the LNW and L&Y partners, the former having its booking, waiting and administrative rooms at the north end and the L&Y at the south. The frontage as a whole was taken under the wing of Huddersfield Council in 1968, with more recent restoration and re-roofing by Kirklees Council. The station's overall roof dates from the 1880s when there was also a major widening of the Huddersfield Viaduct.

The main Up side platform at Hud-

dersfield is served by No 1 platform line and the Down side island by No 4 and No 8 platform lines. Between lie the Up and Down Main lines and, beyond, the Down Slow which passes in front of the incredible functional bulk of the old L&Y warehouse. Now quiet and gloomy but once filled with the rattle of barrow on bench plate and the creaking of the hoists which linked its floors, the warehouse typifies an era when goods activity earned the railways more revenue than the carriage of passengers. It was built as part of the 1870s/'80s expansion and had a wagon hoist to the second floor where positioning was by electric traverser and capstans. Now the warehouse is a listed building, as are the station and several approach structures.

The main line approach to Huddersfield from the Manchester direction begins with the 20-arch Longwood Viaduct which leads to the separate bores of the 243 yd Gledholt North and South Tunnels (25 m 20 ch to 25 m 51 ch), the Down tunnel being the original. Then comes the station with Huddersfield signal box, which controls the area over Huddersfield Viaduct and on to Hillhouse Junction (26 m 26 ch) and Deighton (27 m 60 ch), located on the station's Down island platform.

Huddersfield derives an excellent cross-country service from the Scarborough-Liverpool and Hull-Chester line hourly workings. These are supplemented by the Leeds-Manchester locals and by the services to Penistone and Sheffield and to Wakefield, the latter using the north end bays. Liverpool-Newcastle trains also call.

H.34   Hull

Terminus for routes from Leeds, Doncaster and Scarborough. 31 m 12 ch from Selby

To maintain its commercial traditions and further its ambitions as a port, Hull needed to share in the railway age, so when an early Leeds & Hull Railroad scheme got no further than Selby local interests promoted the Hull & Selby Railway as part of a grand plan for a link with the inland manufacturing districts. The company got its Act on 21 June 1836, opened on 1 July 1840 and was leased to Hudson's York & North Midland Railway from 1 July 1845, after disagreements with its early Manchester & Leeds Railway associates.

The lease of the Hull & Selby brought the Y&NM the former's newly-authorized Hull-Bridlington route, designed to connect with its own Scarborough-Bridlington ven-

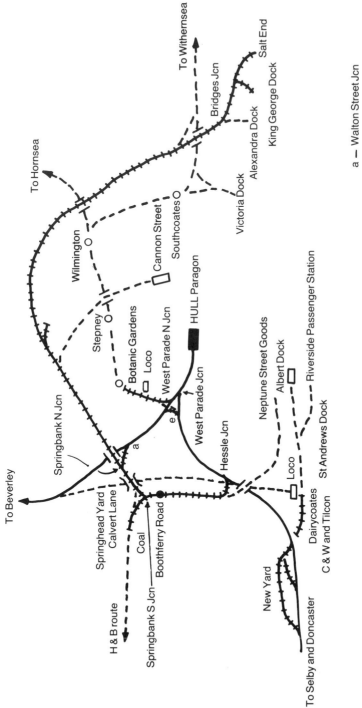

To Withernsea
Salt End
Bridges Jcn
King George Dock
Alexandra Dock
Victoria Dock
To Hornsea
Wilmington
Southcoates
Cannon Street
Stepney
HULL Paragon
Botanic Gardens
Loco
West Parade N Jcn
Springbank N Jcn
Neptune Street Goods
Riverside Passenger Station
Albert Dock
West Parade Jcn
e
Hessle Jcn
To Beverley
a
St Andrews Dock
Loco
Springhead Yard
Calvert Lane
Coal
Dairycoates
Springbank S Jcn
Boothferry Road
C & W and Tilcon
H & B route
New Yard
To Selby and Doncaster

a – Walton Street Jcn
e – Anlaby Road Jcn

Top *Electric coal conveyors at King George Dock, Hull sometime in the mid-1930s.*

Above *Discharging fruit from ship to wagon at Hull Docks some 50 years ago.*

Below *Swing bridge over the River Hull. Dated 1944, this scene has a ghostly quality helped by the old wreck rotting on the low-tide mud.*

If the length of this fish train is anything to go by the Hull trawlers and drifters had enjoyed a good catch, which was then despatched to Billingsgate Market.

ture. Authorized on 30 June 1845, the line north from Hull was opened on 6 October 1846, a route round Hull to the new Victoria Dock following in 1853. The area's other two coastal lines, both connected with the Y&NM route round the city, were much more modest: the Hull & Holderness Railway opened to Withernsea on 28 June 1854 and the Hull & Hornsea Railway to the latter point from 28 March 1864.

By the 1860s all these concerns had become part of the North Eastern Railway and the passenger services had been concentrated on the Paragon terminus. In addition, freight traffic to and from the docks was considerable and, altogether, the monopoly company was doing quite nicely—at least in its own eyes. But, as more docks opened and traffic increased still further, the NER became hard pushed to cope and dissatisfaction with its shortcomings led to the emergence of a rival in the shape of the Hull & Barnsley Railway.

In 1880 the Hull & Barnsley was authorized to construct a railway between Hull and Cudworth and this was duly opened five years later, on 20 July for goods and 27 July for passengers. However, the H&B's approach to Hull across the Wolds, the costly embankment route round the city to the docks and the rather modest traffic levels meant that the new company was never to be affluent. It was helped by the opening of two branches—to Denaby in 1894 and to Wath in 1902—which produced considerable quantities of coal traffic, but suffered a reverse when the North Eastern acquired the Hull Docks Company. A passenger service operated between Hull and Sheffield from 1905 to 1917, but despite a plan to serve Doncaster

in partnership with the Great Central the H&B route became increasingly a coal railway.

The original H&B route ran via Beverley Road (1 m), Willerby & Kirk Ella (6 m), Little Weighton (9 m), South Cave (14 m), North Cave (15 m), Newport (18 m), Sandholme (19 m), Eastrington (21 m), Howden (24 m), Barmby (28 m), Drax (30 m), Carlton (31 m), Kirk Smeaton (41 m), Upton & North Elmsall (45 m) and Hemsworth & South Kirkby (49 m) to Cudworth (53 m), and the few through trains took nearly two hours on the journey. The present century brought more cooperation between the two railways serving Hull, of which a 1914 product was the new King George V dock. Eventually, the Hull & Barnsley merged with the NER from 1 April 1922. Cannon Street station closed in favour of Paragon two years later. H&B route passenger services west of Howden ceased on 1 January 1932 and those to the east on 1 August 1955.

Hull was an important centre under the LNER administration with a District Office and the full panoply of railway activities. In addition to the passenger services of the Withernsea, Hornsea, Scarborough, York and South Howden routes, there were express workings to and from King's Cross via Doncaster and cross-Pennine trains on the original line via Selby. The ferry from Corporation Pier across the Humber to New Holland provided a link to the railways radiating through Lincolnshire and Special Boat Trains operated regularly to the Riverside Quay station in connection with the Rotterdam and Hamburg steamers. At one time four locomotive sheds were needed for all the goods and passenger services and there were many ancillary activities ranging from the docks pumping station to Springhead Locomotive Works.

The LNER's docks at Hull developed from a port tradition that provided Edward III with 16 ships and 461 seamen to fight the French Wars. Along a river frontage of over 7 miles the Salt End oil jetties were followed, east to west, by King George V Dock, Alexandra Dock, Victoria Dock, the three older docks (Prince's, Railway and Humber), Albert Dock and St Andrew's Dock. The total water area was 200 acres and at its peak the activity was served by 300 miles of railway track, 31 coal conveyors, hoists and cranes, 6 grain elevators with a capacity of 120 tons an hour, and no less than 257 hydraulic, steam and electric cranes up to 40 ton capacity. Timber, grain, coal and wool were all major traffics and a 275,500 sq ft area was devoted to handling the catches of the trawlers and drifters working in the North Sea. The railway system used to handle most of the inland movement of the fish landings, with Class 'C'

The furthest of the arched spans at Hull Paragon now only protects a car parking area. The station remains very busy, despite this empty look on a rainy day.

express freight trains thundering southwards during the night hours to serve the London markets.

After the end of the Hull-York service via Market Weighton in 1959, workings on the Hornsea and Withernsea branches were simplified to reduce costs. The Hornsea route served Botanic Gardens (1 m), Stepney (1¾ m), Wilmington (2½ m), Sutton-on-Hull (4½ m), Swine (7 m), Skirlaugh (8¼ m), Ellerby (9¾ m), Whitedale (10¾ m), Sigglesthorne (12¼ m), Hornsea Bridge (15 m) and then Hornsea (15½ m). That to Withernsea followed the same course as far as Wilmington and then served Southcoates (3¼ m), Marfleet (5 m), Hedon (8¼ m), Rye Hill & Burstwick (10¾ m), Keyingham (12¼ m), Ottringham (13¾ m), Patrington (17 m) and Withernsea (20¾ m). Both closed to passengers on 19 October 1964.

The approach to Hull from the Hessle direction passes Priory Sidings and the former Freightliner terminal on the Down side. From Hessle East Junction (3 m 20 ch) a stub of the old route to St Andrew's Dock drops down to serve a stone terminal and the Carriage & Wagon sidings, leaving the main line to turn away from the estuary. The latter then passes beneath the former link to Neptune Street and past those to the older docks and Riverside, to come to Hessle Road signal box (1 m 74 ch) and overbridge. This was once a busy, even notorious, level crossing, just one of several on the NER routes and a factor that eventually contributed to the concentration of the surviving docks traffic on the raised embankment route of the H&B which leaves the main line here.

Beyond Hessle Junction come CCTV crossings at Chalk Lane (1 m 49 ch) and St George's Road (1 m 24 ch) and then Anlaby Road Junction (73 ch), with its 24 chain spur to the Scarborough line. The connection from Botanic Gardens motive power depot joins at West Parade Junction which is followed by Hull Paragon signal box (18 ch) and the station.

Hull Paragon station took over from the 1840 Hull & Selby station in 1848 and is the work of G.T. Andrews, although a 1904/5 reconstruction added to the shorter platforms on the north side and produced the impressive umbrella of five glazed roof spans. The older Up side area, once used to handle the flow of emigrants to the New World via Liverpool, retains No 1 bay platform which has a canopy, plus locomotive sidings beyond. Some of the Down side has, however, been turned over to car parking. Paragon is a station of contrasts, a highly styled, modernistic travel centre in the passenger circulating area differing dramatically from the high, period ticket hall with its tiled surrounds. The frontage contrast between the pleasant hotel and the over-functional look of Paragon House is equally striking.

Trains departing from Hull on the Scarborough line run past Hull Paragon box (25 ch) and then carry on to West Parade North Junction (72 ch) where the spurs to the Selby line and to Botanic Gardens MPD depart. It was on this section that a signalling error produced a head-on collision on 14 February 1927, a Scarborough train departing on the wrong line and running into an arriving Withernsea service, with 12 deaths resulting from the ensuing impact.

The next section of the Scarborough line, past the old carriage sidings to Walton Street Junction barrier crossing (1 m 25 ch) is bi-directional on the Up line and is controlled by Hessle Road box. There is a 25 chain spur to the old H&B route above before the Scarborough line sets off in earnest on its journey northwards.

The ex-Hull & Barnsley route round Hull is controlled from Hessle Road box (0 m), using Track Circuit Block on the double track section as far as Bridges Junction. After 78 chains comes Springbank South Junction, just beyond the Boothferry Road halt which was built for the football ground traffic. At the junction the mileage changes to 4 m 59 ch, and a 45 chain One Train single line round to Springhead Yard serves Calvert Lane coal depot and marks the course of the former H&D main line to Cudworth. At Springbank North Junction (4 m 20 ch) there is a 25 chain connection to the Scarborough-Hull line, the high level H&B route then continuing round the city via the former connection to Cannon Street, Sculcoates coal depot and the swing bridge across the River Hull. This brings it to Bridges Junction (14 ch/0 ch) and the final section to King George Dock where the acetic acid tank trains from the BP Chemicals Salt End installation are handed over.

Hull was badly bombed in the war and has suffered much from railway rationalization since. Its branches have been pruned back but there are compensations, eg, the HST services that reach King's Cross in less than three hours, excellent links across the Pennines and their connections with Liverpool and Blackpool services, the more local links to Doncaster, Sheffield and York and the generous service north to Bridlington and Scarborough.

H.35 Hull-Scarborough Line
Hull to Seamer West. 50 m 43 ch

A line north from Hull formed part of the expansion plans of the pioneer Hull & Selby Railway and, indeed, that company obtained an authorizing Act for a line north to Bridlington just one day before becoming part of the growing York & North Midland Railway empire. The latter company was about to open its line from York to Scarborough and was already planning the connection south to join the Hull line at Bridlington. In the event, the two end sections were opened first—Filey-Seamer on 5 October 1846 and Hull-Bridlington one day later—with the more difficult middle section coming into use a year later, on 20 October 1847.

After leaving Hull, the new route headed almost due north to Beverley and Great Driffield before turning towards Bridlington and the coast. A climb of nearly 5 miles at 1 in 92 behind the cliffs of Flamborough and Bempton then preceded a descent back to the coast at Filey and then the final, curving section to join the York-Scarborough line 2½ miles inland, at Seamer, rather than tackle the heights of Deep Dale on the southern outskirts of Scarborough.

The line has always enjoyed a good Hull-Scarborough service, with the semi-fasts of the steam era covering the 54 miles in an hour and a half. The through, Saturday and excursion workings to Bridlington and Filey joined the line via Market Weighton until that route closed. Now there is a substantial service out from Hull to Beverley, better than one train an hour to Bridlington with about a dozen of these going on to Scarborough. A Sunday service runs in the summer period.

The Scarborough line leaves Hull between Walton Street, site of the notable October Fair, and Spring Bank Cemetery where the victims of Hull's 1849 outbreak of cholera are buried. It takes a straight course via Thwaite Gates remotely controlled barrier crossing (3 m 63 ch) to Cottingham station (3 m 72 ch) just beyond. Crossing and station set the tone of the line straight away, demonstrating the style of the architect G.T. Andrews who made much use of local brick in the buildings along the route. The crossing houses are single-storey in the main and owe their pleasing appearance to bays, which break up an otherwise severe outline, and to a few decorative touches such as the arched chimney stacks. The station buildings vary a little with the location, but generally com-

A signalling showpiece, the Hull Paragon signal box in 1938.

prise substantial house and office on one side and just waiting rooms on the other. Their austere appearance is generally relieved by some stone dressing and by quite a lot of decorative ironwork and pleasing footbridges.

Beyond Cottingham's Down side buildings and bowed footbridge comes Cottingham North barrier crossing and signal box (4 m 17 ch), the route then heading via two more crossings—Beverley Parks AOCR (6 m 51 ch) and Flemingate (8 m 2 ch)—to Beverley (8 m 20 ch). A separate entry deals more fully with this location which is notable for its Andrews station, not far from the impressive thirteenth-century Minister.

Beyond Beverley the trackbed of the former Market Weighton line heads off north west, leaving today's route to skirt east of

Leconfield Airfield, still used by RAF rescue helicopters and shared with the Army. Next comes the modest station at Arram with its gated crossing and brick buildings (11 m 16 ch), and then a long section across Holderness Plain. This includes five crossings, the RG-X one at Scarborough (12 m 24 ch) and AOCR-X installations at Lockington (12 m 74 ch), Beswick (13 m 53 ch), Kilnwick (14 m 1 ch) and Watton (14 m 44 ch). Crossing keepers' accommodation still exists at most such locations on the line, and at Kilnwick goods buildings survive from the role it exercised as a goods station until 1960.

Hutton Cranswick (16 m 21 ch) comprises platforms with Down side buildings, signal box and level crossing. There is another crossing and cottage combination

*The station yard at Driffield with liveried coachmen and a motor bus with its side curtains drawn (*Lens of Sutton*).*

Class 144 set arriving at Scarborough on a wintry day.

at Hutton Lane (16 m 73 ch) with the line then moving on to Driffield (19 m 38 ch), where it is joined by the former Selby route after crossing a tributary of the River Hull. Beyond Driffield, which has its own entry, the next station is Nafferton (21 m 44 ch). In addition to its gated crossing, Down side buildings and typical LNER signal box, there is considerable evidence of former goods activity in the shape of a traditional loading dock and goods shed, left over from the days when Nafferton's mills and maltings were part of the extensive rail freight business.

The Hull-Scarborough line is now heading for Bridlington and the coast, passing through the crossings at Nether Lane (25 m 45 ch), Lowthorpe (23 m 64 ch), Burton Agnes (25 m 45 ch) and Carnaby (28 m 54 ch) on the way. The last three had stations until 5 January 1970 and both Burton Agnes and Carnaby retain their signal boxes. Not far from the former, on the inland side of the line, can be seen the fine Elizabethan mansion of Burton Agnes Hall.

Like Beverley and Driffield, Bridlington (30 m 72 ch) has its own entry, the line beyond running parallel with North Sands before cutting across the Flamborough Head peninsular via the substantial former station marked by Flamborough's gated crossing (33 m 31 ch) to Bempton. This section, from Bridlington to Hunmanby, is single track and worked on the Electric Token system. Thus only one platform is used at Bempton (34 m 43 ch) which,

again, has substantial station buildings as well as its gated level crossing.

The flat, open landscape of the southern section of the route has now become more undulating. High embankments and deep cuttings have become necessary to achieve the 5 mile rise at 1 in 92 from just outside Bridlington, through Flamborough, Bempton and an AOCR crossing at Buckton Lane (35 m 16 ch) to a summit just before the next level crossing at the site of the former Speeton station (37 m 34 ch). This is grassy chalkland with Speeton Moor, Hills, Cliffs and Sands to the right and the Wolds beyond the plain to the left, the latter bisected by Argam Dykes and dotted with other early sites and earthworks.

Descending at gradients varying from 1 in 112 to 1 in 672, the single line comes to Hunmanby (41 m 51 ch) where it reverts to double track as far as Filey. Hunmanby station house is on the Up side, just after the gated crossing, and on the Down side are the signal box, a wooden waiting room and the former brick goods shed. The station still has its clock by Barnet & Rust of Hull.

The section on to Filey commences with the AOCL-X crossing at Hunmanby Depot (41 m 72 ch) where the former Up side goods yard and weighbridge are still evident. The line then descends at 1 in 106/228, past the embankments of the former triangle to Filey Holiday Camp station, and through the AHB-X crossing at Royal Oak (43 m 4 ch) to Filey itself. The curving single line section on to Seamer then has crossings at Muston (45 m 41 ch), Gristhorpe (46 m 38 ch), Lebberston Road (46 m 72 ch) and Cayton (48 m 19 ch), with the former station sites at Gristhorpe and Cayton still marked by their old platforms and buildings. Having moved inland behind the coastal rise, our route finally turns east again to effect its junction with the York-Scarborough route at Seamer Junction (50 m 2 ch).

The Hull-Scarborough line, known as the Wolds Coast Line for promotional purposes, has received considerable support from the local authorities of the area, including a contribution of £692,500 over five years towards the cost of modernizing 22 level crossings. Over the years BR and local interests have worked hard to attract additional business, including campaigns with Ken Dodd—who rechristened Beverley as 'Treacle Well' and Driffield as 'Diddy Town'—with the Army Museum of Transport at Beverley, and with various tourist bodies. The introduction of Pacers has also helped to increase passenger business and the numbers who 'Coast the Wolds'.

H.36   Hunslet—see Leeds

H.37   Hunmanby—see Hull-Scarborough line

H.38   Hutton Cranswick—see Hull-Scarborough Line

I.1   ICI Wilton Branch—see Middlesbrough-Saltburn Line

I.2   Ilkley Branch
Leeds-Skipton line, branch from Apperley Junction. 9 m 20 ch

From the industrialized Aire Valley, single lines from both the Bradford and Leeds directions unite south of Guiseley to head into Wharfedale, running adjacent to the river as far as the terminus at Ilkley. Agriculture and medium-sized housing communities have always been more important than the modest industrial activity of the area, and so the undulating landscape along the route remains unscarred and the journey quite a scenic one.

In addition to the surviving lines, there was formerly a triangular junction south of Burley with the line through Otley to Arthington on the Leeds-Harrogate route. The present route was also extended beyond Ilkley to rejoin the Midland line at Skipton, and there was a short branch from Guiseley to Yeadon. The section through Burley to Ilkley was a joint venture of the North Eastern and Midland railways, as a result of a rare piece of inter-company co-operation in the original rail penetration of Wharfedale.

The NER and MR companies obtained their Acts on the same day, 11 July 1861,

Baildon station being tidied up in 1972.

These Class 144 Metrotrain units have helped to popularize rail travel on lines like the Ilkley branch, now busy throughout the day as well as at the peaks.

but the former had its section from Arthington to Otley opened by 1 February 1865 whereas the Midland's longer section up from Apperley Junction to Ilkley was not ready until 1 August. The section from Shipley to Guiseley then waited until 4 December 1876 and the extension from Ilkley to Skipton until 1 October 1888. Both the latter and the Arthington-Otley line closed to passengers on 22 March 1965, ending any further prospect of Bradford-Otley-Harrogate services or of the once popular excursions to Bolton Abbey further up the Wharfe.

The Ilkley branch leaves the Leeds-Skipton line by courtesy of the wooden signal box at Apperley Junction (202 m 3 ch), parallels the main line for a short way and then curves north into a cutting and the 75 yd Apperley Lane Tunnel (202 m 61 ch to 202 m 26 ch). It continues its wooded course via hillside and embankment to a second tunnel, the 77 yd Springs Tunnel (204 m 7 ch to 204 m 11 ch) and then a third, the 134 yd Greenbottom Tunnel (204 m 61 ch to 204 m 67 ch). Between the last two the other single line from the Bradford direction has arrived.

The Bradford-Shipley-Guiseley leg of the route leaves the Skipton line at Guiseley Junction (3 m 41 ch) and takes a very scenic course through a succession of tun-

nels and viaducts. The station at Baildon (2 m 29 ch) was closed for 20 years between 1953 and 1973 and follows a crossing of the Aire river and its adjacent canal. North of Baildon comes the first of two tunnels bearing that name, the 156 yd Baildon No 1 (2 m 14 ch to 2 m 7 ch), which is then followed by the 274 yd No 2 (2 m 3 ch to 1 m 71 ch). Two viaducts follow, with the site of the former Esholt station between and the 548 yd Esholt Tunnel (52 ch to 27 ch) then preceding the former junction between the two lines.

Only the site of Esholt Junction signal box remains, the two single lines running parallel but not joining until they reach Guiseley. On this section there was also a junction with the Yeadon branch which closed in 1964. Despite early ambitions to continue on to Leeds, this had lasted only 70 years as a modest goods line contributing to the grading of the station master at Guiseley. Guiseley itself (205 m 22 ch) now consists just of platforms, shelters and footbridge, with the signal box (205 m 7 ch) and a former goods shed on the Down side.

The scenery becomes more open as the now double track heads for Menston (206 m 53 ch) which still has ornate stone station buildings on the Down side. Before Burley-in-Wharfedale (208 m 2 ch) the trackbed of the Otley line joins, and then Burley station itself which consists of just platforms, shelters and footbridge, although a former bay and signal box are still apparent and the station house is set back on the Up side. From the ensuing embankment there are good views, first of Burley town and then of the riverside meadows. Ben Rhydding (210 m 21 ch) also has a surviving station house, but few traces of its former spa status. The platforms show evidence of having been raised, as at Guiseley.

There is a wooden signal box at Ilkley Junction (211 m 7 ch), so named because the through lines separate here from the terminating ones. The platforms for the former were being demolished in 1988 when it was still possible to visualize Ilkley as it used to be. Lying opposite the Town Hall, the station's simple but classic exterior led to a high ticket hall and then out on to the Down platform of the terminus section, now used for most trains. Under a glazed area with canopy extensions the lighting was still by replicas of MR three-mantle gas lamps with a long rocker arm for turning the gas on or off.

Beyond Ilkley station (211 m 23 ch) the route used to continue through Addingham (19¼ m), Bolton Abbey (21¾ m), Embsay (25¼ m) and on to Skipton (27¾ m).

Apart from the industries at Guiseley, this is a line of people, farms and sheep with some notable riverside and dales scenery. The alternate hourly trains combine to give a half-hourly service to either Leeds or Bradford and this is well used by shoppers as well as by peak period commuters.

I.3   Isabella   Colliery—see   Benton-Morpeth Line

J.1   Jarrow—see Simonside Branch

J.2   Joan Croft Junction—see Shaftholme Junction

K.1   Keighley
Leeds-Skipton line, between Shipley and Skipton. 212 m 6 ch from St Pancras

A line from Shipley to Keighley was one of the commitments made by the Leeds & Bradford Railway in the Parliamentary proceedings on its original line, and this was duly honoured in the Leeds & Bradford (Shipley-Colne Extension) Act of 30 June 1845. When the line opened on 16 March 1847 only a temporary wooden halt was available for Keighley passengers, but an imposing new station, with ornate gables and chimneys and much decorative stonework, was provided with the extension to Skipton on 7 September 1847. Keighley then became part of a through route to Burnley and Liverpool in 1849, and later part of the Midland Railway's new main line to Carlisle.

Of the two other lines from Keighley one still survives by courtesy of the railway preservation movement. This is the MR branch up the Worth Valley to Ingrow (1¼ m), Damems (2¼ m), Oakworth (2¾ m), Haworth (3½ m) and Oxenhope (4¾ m) which was originally opened on 15 April 1867, closed to passengers on 30 December 1961 (and to freight on 23 June 1962) and then reopened by the preservation society on 29 June 1968. The other was the Great Northern branch to Queensbury (for Halifax and Leeds) via Ingrow (1 m), Cullingworth (3¾ m), Wilsden (5 m), Denholm (6 m) and Thornton (7½ m) which opened in stages between 1882 and 1884. Both routes involved a climb south of Keighley and the GN route, which closed on 23 May 1955, had two tunnels—Lees Moor and Well Heads—and two viaducts—Hewenden and Thornton.

Access to Keighley station today is from the road overbridge which leads to a domed booking hall and then, by ramp, to the platforms. A separate ramp with period posters

Keighley enjoys an excellent local service to Leeds and Bradford, and both the Morecambe and Carlisle trains call.

and a Midland colour scheme leads down to the platforms of the Keighley & Worth Valley Railway. The signal box, Keighley Station Junction (212 m 18 ch), lies on the Skipton side of the station and is followed by level crossing and box combinations at Steeton (215 m 3ch), Kildwick (216 m 52 ch) and Cononley (218 m 22 ch) and then the end of ER territory at Skipton Station South (221 m 13 ch).

Keighley enjoys an excellent service from the Leeds-Carlisle, Leeds-Morecambe and Leeds-Skipton trains, plus the hourly workings to and from Bradford.

K.2   Kelloe Bank Foot Branch
East Coast Main Line, branch from Ferryhill. 3 m 3 ch

This short single line branch leaves the East Coast Main Line just north of Ferryhill and runs east along the course of the former route to Hartlepool as far as the foot of Kelloe Bank. It serves Raisby Hill Quarry at the east end and has another quarry link at the main line end which gives access to the rapid loading bunkers of Thrislington Quarry.

The distances on the branch reflect its origins as a scheme of the Great North of England, Clarence & Hartlepool Junction Railway to provide an alternative coal route to the coast. It opened west from Wingate to the bottom of Kelloe Bank for goods on 18 March 1839, with passenger trains commencing on 13 October 1846 when connections were established with the main line (northwards) and the Byers Green line westwards. An east-south curve into Ferryhill was brought into use on 19 October 1873 and permitted a passenger service from Hartlepool which called at Trimdon, Coxhoe Bridge and West Cornforth on the section east of Wingate.

The branch leaves the main line at Kelloe Bank Foot Branch Junction (14 m 9 ch from Hartlepool) where the Thrislington connection is located. Track Circuit Block applies on the section which rises up from the main line and turns east to Kelloe Bank Foot Staff Instrument (14 m 3 ch), with One Train working then coming into force for the section on through West Cornforth TMO LC (13 m 16 ch) and past the former incline connection to Kelloe Bank Foot North End (11 m 6 ch) where the running line ends.

K.3   Kildale—see Middlesbrough-Whitby Line

K.4   King Edward Bridge—see Newcastle

K.5   King George Dock—see Hull

K.6   Knaresborough
Leeds-York line. 16 m 45 ch from York

Knaresborough's station occupies a difficult site and one can have some sympathy with the original engineers who, having had a relatively easy approach for the rest of their line from York, decided to use a temporary station on the eastern outskirts of the town for the initial services. The promoting company was the East & West Yorkshire Junction Railway which obtained its Act on 16 July 1846 for a rail link from York to join the line being built by the Leeds & Thirsk Railway. The York-Knaresborough scheme had L&T backing, but following a disagreement between the two concerns, the services which began on 30 October 1848 were operated by the York, Newcastle & Berwick Railway. Later they were to be put in the hands of a contractor, E.B. Wilson & Company.

The present station site at Knaresborough dates from 1 October 1851 (the buildings are much later) when the link between the L&T at Starbeck and the line from

Knaresborough station looking towards York and with the Knaresborough Tunnel portal just visible.

York was brought into use. This entailed a dramatic viaduct across the Nidd, a structure which had delayed the opening of the new link by collapsing while under construction in 1848. The approach from the eastern side used a combination of cutting with retaining walls and the 178 yd Knaresborough Tunnel (16 m 48 ch to 16 m 40 ch). Between the tunnel and the viaduct lies the station with its signal box and level crossing. Its traditional-style Up side buildings have now been put to private commercial use and house a tea room-cum-restaurant called 'Off the Rails'.

The town of Knaresborough itself holds much of interest including the castle, ruined in the Civil War, Mother Shipton's Cave, and the Dropping Well. On the north-east side of the river is Fort Montague, a dwelling carved out of the living rock.

Knaresborough also had a branch line north east to Boroughbridge and Pilmoor. This had opened between those two points on 17 June 1847 and between Boroughbridge and Knaresborough on 1 April 1875. Boroughbridge got a new through station on that occasion, the old station being relegated to goods use. Passenger services on this route ended on 25 September 1950 and the line was cut at the Pilmoor end three years later. Goods trains continued to Brafferton and Boroughbridge until 1957 and 1964 respectively.

In the 1930s Knaresborough enjoyed a service of over 50 trains a day to and from Harrogate where passengers could pick up the Leeds, Stockton and Pateley Bridge trains. It had all-stations and semi-fast trains to York, plus the two weekday and four Saturday trains to Copgrove (7½ m from Harrogate), Boroughbridge (11 m), Brafferton (14½ m) and Pilmoor (17 m). Less varied, the train service nevertheless remains good with hourly Leeds-York and Leeds-Knaresborough services which combine to give a half-hourly service to Harrogate and Leeds, plus the InterCity links at each end of the Leeds-York route.

K.7   Knottingley
Wakefield/Leeds-Goole line, junction with freight line to Doncaster. 58 m 37 ch from Manchester Victoria

A notable glassware town, Knottingley appeared on the railway map when the Wakefield, Pontefract & Goole Railway opened on 1 April 1848. Before the year was out it had additionally been linked to

Askern and Doncaster (6 June) and two years later became part of the route from London to York with the opening of the link north to Burton Salmon. Passenger services over the latter route ended on 11 July 1947 and to Doncaster on 27 September 1948, but Knottingley retains a service of a dozen trains a day to and from Leeds, half of which continue to or originate from Goole. It also has an important role in connection with the provision of traction and stock for the extensive local movements to and from power stations.

From the Pontefract direction, Knottingley station is approached via Knottingley West Junction (58 m 20 ch) where the double track freight spur from Ferrybridge joins. There are coal sidings on the Up side in advance of the station which has wooden platforms superimposed on the original brick base. Then come the wagon maintenance shops and Knottingley East Junction (58 m 70 ch) where the UGL link to the Askern line at South Junction departs. On the Down side England Lane barrier crossing (59 m 5 ch) is followed by Knottingley signal box (59 m 26 ch).

Knottingley station was a joint L&Y and Great Northern station from 1 February 1854 reflecting the latter's use of this route for its London-York trains and the close connection between these two companies.

L.1   Leeds
Meeting point of lines from Hull, Goole, Doncaster, Sheffield, Manchester, Bradford, Skipton, Ilkley, Harrogate and York. 20 m 47 ch from Hull

Leeds has a very significant place in the annals of railway history because it was the home of the first railway to be authorized by Act of Parliament. This was the 4 ft 1 in gauge Middleton Railway, authorized on 9 June 1758 and opened shortly afterwards, with conversion to steam haulage as early as 12 August 1812 when the agent John Blenkinsop and engineer Matthew Murray put two rack locomotives to work. The later years of the system were undistinguished, but after closure in 1958 the Middleton Railway again entered the record books as the first standard gauge line of the railway preservation movement.

The woollen merchants of Leeds needed the best of transport to maintain their flourishing businesses and were talking of posssible rail routes as early as the 1820s. However, the first practical development took the form of the Leeds & Selby project whose trains began conveying passengers

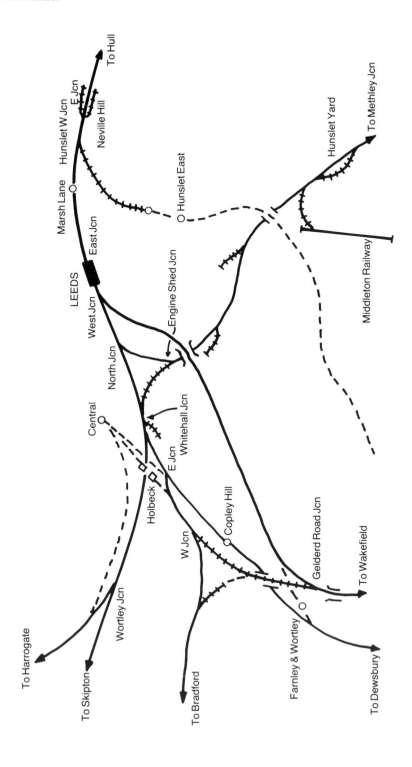

Leeds City station in the 1930s.

to Selby and the waiting Hull steamer from 22 September 1834. The rail extension to Hull was not completed until six years later (2 July 1840), by which time Leeds had one day earlier been linked to Rotherham and Derby—and thence to London—by the North Midland Railway. The Leeds & Selby used a station at Marsh Lane and the North Midland one at Hunslet Lane.

The North Midland line gave Leeds a link to Manchester via Normanton where it connected with the Manchester & Leeds, and the York & North Midland company gave it access to York via the connection with the Leeds & Selby. Thus by 1840 Leeds had rail connections radiating outwards in each direction, although its two terminal stations were less than conveniently sited in relation to the centre of the town.

The Leeds & Bradford Railway did not make the same mistake. Its line north from Bradford to Shipley and then east along the Aire valley was opened on 1 July 1846 and used a Leeds terminus by the river and much nearer the Leeds activity centre. This was in Wellington Street, the location taking in the York & North Midland services re-routed via Methley and then rapidly growing in importance during the years of Midland control.

The late 1840s brought a second wave of railways to Leeds and with them the new Central station, although the plans for and development of the latter were the subject of much alteration and altercation before it was eventually brought into use in 1849. The three new railways authorized in 1845–6 were the Leeds, Dewsbury & Manchester, the Leeds & Thirsk, and the

ill-fated West Riding Union. After two official openings the LD&M's shorter line to Manchester started to carry passengers to and from a temporary station on the Central site in 1847, the Leeds & Thirsk contributing its trains to the expanded facility from 10 July 1849, with the LNWR cross-Pennine and GNR via Wakefield services being added about the same time.

At this stage common sense would have suggested the completion of Central, but by 1850 its users were again at loggerheads and most moved out to overtax the station in Wellington Street, eventually leaving the L&Y in solitary splendour. The Great Northern later used Central when it improved its access to Leeds from 1854 by courtesy of the Leeds, Barnsley & Halifax Junction Railway, and the station was finally completed in 1857.

Leeds got a further station 12 years later when the North Eastern extended from Marsh Lane by means of a viaduct section to a 'New' station just south of the Midland's Wellington Street. The LNWR constructed a similar link to Leeds New to create an east-west through route and lay the foundations of today's coast-to-coast services. One other major nineteenth-century extension of the Leeds railway system gave Hunslet two new goods lines in 1899, one NER link from Neville Hill on the old L&S line to Hunslet East, and the long GN branch from south of Beeston to Hunslet West.

At the 1923 grouping, Leeds had settled down to a three-station status, Wellington terminus contributed by the Midland Railway becoming LMS, and the joint LNW and NER New station becoming joint

Above *The final combined station at Leeds with London and local trains about to depart from the west end.*

Right *The ticket office at Leeds with the main concourse beyond.*

LNER and LMS, with the same position applying to the Central terminus which had been used by the GN, NE, LNW, L&Y and GC railways. This situation lasted until 1938 when Wellington and New stations were combined into a single Leeds City station. Finally, all trains to and from Leeds began using a single station from 17 May 1967, when track alterations on the approach lines allowed the remaining Central services to be diverted into the remodelled City station, with Central closing on 30 April 1967.

The planning and construction process for the new, single station complex had begun back in 1959, with major modifications to the plan in 1963. The final result was a 12-platform station, spanning the River Aire and with an additional parcels area, new concourse and adjacent office block. The parcels area lies on the former Wellington terminus site behind the Queen's Hotel, which was part of the 1938 alterations. Next is a bay area and then the main

No 5 platform with two islands beyond. In total there are five through platforms, two Selby end bays and five Bradford end bays.

In addition to the car parking facilities in the former Wellington station area, Leeds' surviving station has a good approach road alongside Bishopsgate Street. This leads to the South Concourse with ticketing and information facilities adjacent and with refreshment and shopping facilities around. There are subway, barrow-way and footbridge links to the outer platforms, and the main station area is covered by an inverted vee span roof of welded steel portal construction with a low level section over the ticket barrier. The basement area of the station accommodates the electrical supply, relay rooms, workshops and ventilation plant.

The approach to Leeds station from Wakefield is via the 297 yd Ardsley Tunnel (180 m 61 ch to 180 m 75 ch) and the 1967 Gelderd Road Curve put in to link the ex-

The impressive Leeds station frontage.

GN line with the LNWR route from Manchester. From Gelderd Road Junction (184 m 22 ch) the route runs on arches to Leeds West Junction (185 m 44 ch) and on into the station. On the LNW line from Manchester the approach is past the old loco shed site, near the former junction with the Gomersal line, through Farnley Branch Junction (40 m 65 ch) to join the Bradford line at Holbeck East Junction (42 m 5 ch). This involves using the 1967 Whitehall Curve instead of continuing to Central station as before.

The Farnley branch consists of a 71 chain single line from Farnley Branch Junction to the premises of Dunlop and Ranken. It is worked on the One Train basis under the control of the Leeds panel and has a 25 mph upper speed limit.

Armley Gaol is visible west of Leeds on both the Bradford routes. The direct ex-GN line leaves Leeds station via Whitehall Junction (42 m 23 ch), Holbeck East Junction (42 m 5 ch/185 m 4 ch) and Holbeck West Junction (185 m 1 ch/2 ch) and then climbs past the gaol to the 80 yd Armley Tunnel (1 m 2 ch to 1 m 6 ch). On the Skipton route the bi-directional station lines end at Leeds West Junction (20 m 70 ch/0 ch) with the Up and Down Shipley and Up and Down Main then continuing through Leeds North Junction (5 ch) and Whitehall Junction (25 ch/195 m 54 ch).

Holbeck High Level station was located above Holbeck Low Level where the ex-MR main line passed below the routes into Central. The approaches to the latter are still visible north of the line and the access

to Whitehall yard lies to the south. The ex-Midland line on to the Ilkley branch junction at Apperley also had stations at Armley, Kirkstall, Newlay & Horsforth and Calverley & Rodley. There is an Up side signal box at Kirkstall Junction (197 m 78 ch) after Wortley Junction (196 m 19 ch) and the departure of the Harrogate line, and then views of both Kirkstall Abbey and the Leeds & Liverpool Canal.

East of Leeds station the Through line between platforms 8 and 9 becomes the Up Main and No 6 Platform Line the Down Main at East Junction (20 m 26 ch). The Up and Down Goods lines, which have passed around the outside of the station, also join in, although a separate Up Goods line continues with the main line through the 118 yd Richmond Hill Tunnel (19 m 44 ch to 19 m 39 ch) and on past Neville Hill West Junction (18 m 74 ch) to the East Junction (18 m 25 ch). This is initially a high-level route and once had an extra tunnel. The remains of the Marsh Lane site, now largely occupied by a cement depot, are visible before the route passes into a brick-lined cutting and the 1 m 21 ch double line from the engineers' and oil sidings at Hunslet East joins at West Junction. Neville Hill carriage sidings and traction maintenance depot then parallel the main line to East Junction.

South east from Leeds, the Sheffield and Goole trains depart via West Junction (20 m 70 ch/0 ch), Leeds North Junction (195 m 53 ch) and Engine Shed Junction (195 m 20 ch). On the Up side the former LMS loco shed area survives in modernized form as a washing, fuelling and signing-on point. Then, on the Down side, comes the former link to the Hunslet Engine Company, a reminder of the prominence Leeds firms achieved in the building of industrial locomotives.

Hunslet Station Junction (194 m 10 ch) is a reminder of the former station and of the ex-GN line which crossed over the present route, and that of the Aire river, to Hunslet goods depot. Extra running lines on the stretch through Hunslet South Junction (193 m 40 ch) on to Stourton signal box (193 m 17 ch) and junction (192 m 42 ch) serve the Up side freight activity of Hunslet Yard and the following British Steel and Freightliner terminals. The Middleton Railway lies beyond.

There was formerly a loco shed at Stourton, plus a carriage and wagon works, marshalling yard and a link with the East & West Yorkshire Union Railway. The latter had been conceived as a line to link the

Rothwell area collieries with the Hull & Barnsley, but the eventual 1891–8 openings produced only a complex of local and colliery lines between Stourton (Mid) and Lofthouse (GN). A passenger service ran for nine months in 1904 and there was a 1963 plan to make a trunk route of the line, but this came to nothing and closure followed on 3 October 1966.

Leeds today is one of the great railway centres and interchange points. The train service pattern of the past has been considerably simplified, but Leeds has gained much and lost little in the process. The hourly service of HSTs gets travellers to London in under two and a half hours, with even better to come under electrification; HSTs also provide links to the North East and Scotland and via Birmingham to the South West and Wales. Across country the trains from Hull and Scarborough link Leeds to Manchester, Liverpool, Chester and North Wales and the city also has longer distance services north to Newcastle and Scotland, to Preston, Morecambe and Carlisle, and towards Nottingham and Scunthorpe.

As a result of the BR/PTE partnership there is considerable local traffic on the Sprinter and Pacer trains, on both routes to York, on the Summit and Calder Valley lines, east to Selby and Goole, and south towards Sheffield and Doncaster.

Leeds has, admittedly, lost its 'Midland main line' status, but even the old 10 am from St Pancras was not at City station until 1.48 pm. The other LMS loss is the

former route out via Farnley & Wortley (2 m), Birstall Town (6¾ m), Gomersal (8 m), Cleckheaton (9½ m), Liversedge (10½ m), Heckmondwike (11¼ m), Northorpe (13 m), Battyeford (14¼ m) and Bradley (16 m) to Huddersfield (18¾ m). An interesting past activity on this side of Leeds was the 'circular' service which called at Holbeck (½ m), Beeston (2½ m), Ardsley (5½ m), Lofthouse & Outwood (7½ m), Alverthorpe (9¾ m), Flushdyke (11¼ m), Ossett (12 m), Earlsheaton (13¾ m), Dewsbury (14¾ m), Batley Carr (15 m), Batley (16 m), Woodkirk (17¾ m), Tingley (19 m) and then back into Leeds Central via Beeston and Holbeck.

The LNER direct route between Leeds and Bradford via Bramley took 33 minutes for the 10½ miles but a 60–70 minute, 17¾-mile alternative was available via Holbeck (½ m), Beeston (2½ m), Ardsley (5½ m), Thingley (7 m), Morley (8 m), Gildersome (9¾ m), Drighlington & Adwalton (11 m), Birkenshaw & Tong (12 m), Laister Dyke (15¾ m) and St Dunstan's (17¼ m). Another circuitous route unable to stand the acid test of railway costing awareness was the great loop up to Wetherby and down again to Church Fenton, and a further loss was the local service from Leeds to Castleford via Kippax.

In the heyday of railway freight traffic, Leeds had a welter of goods station depots and private sidings, running to over two pages in the *RCH Handbook of Stations*. The main locations for general goods traffic

Oil traffic in block train loads of high capacity tank wagons is an important element of the ER freight business. These wagons are discharging at a Leeds terminal.

In the pre-Metrotrain period a three-car dmu set heads from Bradford to Leeds.

were the individual Hunslet depots where 40 ton lifting capacity was available and Whitehall Road which had a 20 ton crane. No less than 27 cattle docks are recorded in the area.

Apart from the bulk oil and steel traffics and the Freightliner activity, most of the freight business has gone, but Leeds has gained much from the changes in the railway industry and its single, central station is busy nearly all day and every day. It stands to gain even more with the advent of electrification for the London services.

L.2   Leeds-Bradford Line

Local link and part of Manchester-Leeds cross-Pennine route. 9 m 36 ch

Although the 1846 Leeds & Bradford Railway had an easily-graded route between these two great West Riding cities, its use of the valley of the River Aire added something like 3 miles to the direct distance and a competing line was virtually inevitable. This duly appeared in 1852 when the Leeds, Bradford & Halifax Junction Railway obtained its Act for a line through Pudsey and Stanningley. When it opened to passengers on 1 August 1854 this cut the railway distance between Leeds and Bradford quite significantly and the route not only became the major link between the two cities but also a vital part of the Great Northern Railway's penetration of West Yorkshire.

The route leaves Leeds via Whitehall

Junction (42 m 23 ch), Holbeck East Junction (42 m 5 ch/185 m 4 ch) and Holbeck West Junction (185 m 1 ch/42 m 2 ch). There is a view of Armley Gaol to the north as the track rises through cuttings and at a gradient of 1 in 50 to the 80 yds of Armley Tunnel (1 m 2 ch to 1 m 6 ch) and the former station nearby. The climb continues, albeit at 1 in 128 and then 1 in 146, to Bramley station (3 m 15 ch) which was opened by West Yorkshire County Council in 1984 and has staggered wooden platforms with shelters.

From Bramley there is a 3½ mile climb at 1 in 100 through New Pudsey (4 m 77 ch) to the 455 yd Stanningley Tunnel (5 m 22 ch to 5 m 43 ch) and on to the summit at Laisterdyke. New Pudsey station was opened on 1 May 1967 and is of modern design with shelters, footbridge and ramp access.

Stanningley station formerly lay on this section, but to get nearer to the heart of Pudsey the GN opened a branch round to a terminus at Pudsey (Greenside) on 1 April 1878. From 1 November 1883 this was remodelled and extended to provide a 'loop' line from the Bramley direction, through a tunnel beyond Greenside and on to Dudley Hill and Low Moor. The new loop came to carry an alternative Leeds-Bradford service through Greenside and back to the original line via Dudley Hill, the Shipley branch and Laisterdyke, and taking five minutes longer than trains on the 1854 line.

After leaving Stanningley Tunnel, today's

An early view of Selby, complete with bookstall and a schoolboy waiting with his trunk for a Down train.

route reveals some evidence of its former four-track status as it passes beneath the route of the old Shipley line and along the site of the Laisterdyke connection. The GN's trains to Halifax ran this way and there was also a connection with the important access route from Ardsley. However, today's services just head on through Hammerton Street (191 m 18 ch) and the 132 yd Wakefield Road Tunnel (191 m 36 ch to 191 m 42 ch) to join the Manchester line at Mill Lane Junction (191 m 78 ch) and on for the final 24 chains into Bradford Interchange station.

L.3   Leeds-Hull Line

Leeds-Selby-Hull. 20 m 47 ch Selby South Junction to Leeds and 31 m 12 ch Hull to Selby South Junction

The official distances for the two sections of the line reflect its origins as two separate railway promotions, although the idea of linking the West Riding to the Humber, at Hull, had been the intention of a scheme mooted as early as 1824. As it turned out those early ideas were replaced by the Leeds & Selby Railway project which received the Royal Assent for its Act on 29 May 1830.

The pioneer line from Marsh Lane, Leeds to a station on the west bank of the Ouse at Selby was opened for public traffic on 22 September 1834. The trains ran in conjunction with a paddle steamer service down the Ouse and along the Humber estuary to Hull but this was not really good

enough for the commercial men of that city who secured an Act for the Hull & Selby Railway on 21 June 1836 and opened it from Manor House Street at Hull to a new, through station at Selby on 2 July 1840. This involved crossing the Ouse by means of a bascule-bridge which lasted until replaced by the present swing-bridge after 51 years' service.

The York & North Midland Railway's line was linked to the Leeds & Selby from 1839–40 to permit through services between York and Hull, but when George Hudson secured a lease of the L&S for his growing Y&NM ambitions he brought about the closure of the former west of Gascoigne Wood in favour of his own company's York-Leeds route via Methley. This piece of blatant self-interest lasted for some years, but the Leeds-Hull route was soon gaining in importance again with the Selby-Market Weighton line added in 1848, the Church Fenton-Micklefield line in 1869 and intersection by the East Coast Main Line from 1871. Other important connections came to be the Cross Gates-Wetherby, Garforth-Castleford and Selby-Goole lines, while character was added by its links with a short rural light railway, the Cawood, Wistow & Selby.

The Leeds-Hull route leaves Leeds station (20 m 47 ch) via Leeds East Junction (20 m 26 ch) and takes a high level course out towards the original Marsh Lane terminus, the site of which is visible on the Down side. There are also traces of the suburban station at Marsh Lane which closed

in 1958, but the tunnel which early passengers had to be persuaded to brave by
whitewashed walls and light reflectors is
now just a cutting and today's trains just
accelerate smoothly on from Marsh Lane
Junction (19 m 48 ch) where there is a
Down Goods Loop. An Up Goods Line is
added to the passenger pair as the route
continues through the 118 yd Richmond
Hill Tunnel (19 m 44 ch to 19 m 39 ch),
past Neville Hill West Junction (18 m 74
ch) and its branch to Hunslet East, and
alongside the maintenance depot and carriage sidings to Neville East Junction (18 m
25 ch). As the route begins to leave Leeds
behind, the Up side of the track reveals fine
and continuing examples of the North Eastern Railway's square milepost signs with
the one, two or three-starred roundels for
the quarter miles in between.

Cross Gates (16 m 11 ch), where the
trackbed of the former Wetherby line can
still be seen, has its own separate entry, as
has Garforth (13 m 23 ch) which follows
the R/G crossing at Manston (14 m 77 ch)
and formerly had its own branch, south to
Castleford. Between Garforth and the
crossover and Down side signal box at
Peckfield (11 m 17 ch) a new halt has been
opened at East Garforth (12 m 56 ch),
comprising modern wooden platforms with
shelter and a high, ramp-access footbridge.
Micklefield (10 m 69 ch) and the junction
(10 m 63 ch) for the Church Fenton line are
controlled by Peckfield signal box and also
have their own entry.

South Milford (7 m 57 ch), now simplified to a shelter and platform combination, was one of the 1834 stations which
Hudson closed for 10 years. There is a R/G
level crossing before the route starts its rise
to cross over that of the old Y&NM. Then
comes Gascoigne Wood (6 m 27 ch),
which also has a separate entry and is
where the north and south spurs from the
Y&NM lines join our west-east line. There
is a Down Goods Loop and a signal box
which controls access to the Up side loading point for coal from the Selby coalfield.

Some period gradient boards appear by
the lineside as the L&S route continues east
through more R/G level crossings at Hagg
Lane (5 m 36 ch) and Philip Lane (4 m 48
ch) and then passes over the East Coast
Main Line. The new junctions and old station at Hambleton are covered in the entry
for that point, West Junction lying at 4 m
43 ch and East Junction at 3 m 34 ch, the
latter carrying the trains of the York-Hull
service reverting to a tradition lost while the
route via Market Weighton was extant.

Having originally risen west of Garforth
and then dropped again to Gascoigne
Wood the L&S line has become completely
level for the section through Hambleton to
Selby. Its pleasant agricultural course is
broken only by crossings at Harrymore
Lane (2 m 78 ch), Thorpe Hall (2 m 41 ch),
Thorpe Gates (2 m 27 ch) and Sandhill
Lane (1 m 42 ch). The Cawood, Wistow &
Selby line joined from the north along this
portion and the old dock of the former
Thorpe Gates goods siding is a reminder of
the cut-off line that used to run from here to
Brayton East Junction on the Selby-Goole
line. The final, curving section into Selby is
heralded by Selby signal box and its barrier
crossing (40 ch), followed by Selby West
Junction (36 ch) where the original CW&S
platform was located and where a single
line spur now connects with the Doncaster
line, and then Selby South Junction where
the ex-ECML tracks join the Leeds-Hull
line.

Selby, which has its own separate entry,
lay on the East Coast Main Line until the
Selby Diversion was opened in 1983. At
South Junction the L&S 'zero' mileage
changes to the 31 m 12 ch of the H&S, with
the line then continuing through the station
(30 m 79 ch) and over the swing bridge (30
m 70 ch). Until 1983 the main line turned
away north at East Junction and the
Market Weighton line continued straight
ahead from Barlby LC (30 m 34 ch), but
now only the Hull line remains. It does,
however, retain Up and Down Passenger
Loops and there is a connection into the
Melmerby Estates private sidings network,
which has its own diesel shunter.

West of Selby the Hull line is very level
and nearly straight. It is signalled by
traditional signal boxes using mainly semaphore signals, the first box being located on
the Up side at Hemingbrough LC (28 m 2
ch). Hemingbrough lost its passenger trains
on 6 November 1967, but traces of the station remain and the 28 milepost still stands
on the former Up platform. Next come
crossings at Hagg Lane (26 m 77 ch) and
Wood Lane (25 m 77 ch), followed by a
crossing of the River Derwent and views of
Wressle Castle and church. Wressle station (25 m 3 ch) has a signal box, modest
period buildings and an open crossing.

Further crossings at Cross Common (24
m 52 ch) and Rowland Hall (24 m 6 ch)
precede Howden crossing, signal box and
station (22 m 27 ch), which once had a
branch to the R100 airship sheds. Howden
has much in common with the preceding
Wressle and the following Eastrington (19

m 23 ch), all three representing a class of rural station that have survived from the earliest days of railway activity. The route of the old Hull & Barnsley crossed the Leeds-Hull line between Howden and Eastrington, the latter then joining the Doncaster line at Gilberdyke Junction (17 m 7 ch) and its remaining locations being covered by individual entries, viz Gilberdyke (16 m 76 ch), Broomfleet (14 m 33 ch), Brough (10 m 38 ch), Ferriby (7 m 42 ch), Hessle (4 m 64 ch) and Hull.

The Leeds-Hull line carries a cross-country service with a broad pattern of hourly trains originating at Chester or at Bangor or beyond. Worked by Sprinters with a refreshment trolley service, the units call only at Selby and Brough after Leeds and take under an hour for the 51¾ miles between Leeds and Hull. The intermediate stations east of Selby are served by the York-Hull trains and those west thereof by the York-Leeds workings.

L.4   Leeds-York Line

From Wortley Junction, Leeds to Harrogate (17 m 10 ch) and thence to a junction with the East Coast Main Line at Skelton, York (18 m 68 ch)

Although the first half of the line, from Leeds to Harrogate, was once part of a through trunk route on to Northallerton and Stockton, the line today is more concerned with carrying its substantial local traffic plus such important flows as the conference

business to and from Harrogate and those who come to explore the beauties of the dales and the attractions of places like Knaresborough. The main route between Leeds and York is that via Micklefield, but the service on the Harrogate line includes trains which run through between those two cities.

From Leeds, its initial northbound course forces the route to tackle the high east-west ridges, starting with a dramatic climb to a summit near Horsforth. This is followed by a steep descent through Bramhope Tunnel into Wharfedale and then a further, wooded climb back to the level of the two pleasant elevated towns of Harrogate and Knaresborough. Turning east towards York, the line then drops gently through the valley of the River Nidd amid the pleasant woods and pastures of this part of Yorkshire.

Today's lines east and south from the Harrogate/Knaresborough area are the survivors of six former routes which served these towns. Of the first one—the York & North Midland Railway's line from Church Fenton, opened to Harrogate on 20 July 1848—only a small portion survives as today's access to the spa town from the Leeds direction. The section from Leeds to Pannal originated as part of a Leeds & Thirsk Railway project which extended its ambitions to Stockton and changed its name to the Leeds Northern Railway to match them. Opened throughout on 9 July 1849, the section from Weeton to Wormald Green which had been brought into

A two-car dmu photographed in 1955 between Arthington and Bramhope Tunnel.

Knaresborough, looking towards Harrogate (Lens of Sutton).

use the previous August, actually bypassed Harrogate and passed beneath the Crimple Valley viaduct of the Y&NM line. Now trains leave the Leeds Northern route at Pannal Junction, climb steeply to the Y&NM route and use its viaduct to cross the original trunk line as part of their approach to Harrogate.

The Leeds-Knaresborough portion of the line is double track throughout and is worked on the Absolute Block system with a maximum line speed of 60 mph. The southern end is controlled by the Leeds panel, but over most of the route traditional semaphore signalling applies. The journey from Leeds turns away from the Skipton route at Wortley Junction (14 ch) and uses the long Aire Viaduct to cross both the Leeds & Liverpool Canal and the River Aire. Then through a deep cutting the gradient steepens to 1 in 98 to lift the route to the 70 yd Headingley Tunnel (1 m 72 ch to 1 m 75 ch) and reach the staggered platforms of Headingley station (2 m 11 ch). The traditional stone buildings of the old station on the Down side seem to dwarf their modern shelter replacements.

After a glimpse of Kirkstall Abbey, the route starts to shake itself free of the Leeds suburbs and, climbing steadily at 1 in 100 through an area of woods, mills and streams, comes to Horsforth (4 m 61 ch), a simplified station with two platforms, shelters, overbridge and signal box. The stone goods shed survives, albeit in private hands. Then, at the end of the 3½ mile

climb at 1 in 100, a short level section precedes the 3 mile descent, mostly at 1 in 94, into Wharfedale. The 2 mile 241 yd Bramhope Tunnel (5 m 65 ch to 7 m 76 ch), which has its own entry, dominates this stretch.

Before the level section across the bottom of the valley, the discerning eye can just spot the evidence of a former triangle at Arthington. The first station here was closed on 1 February 1865 when the opening of the route up the valley to Ilkley produced a new station south of the junction. There were branch platforms on the curve, from which the trains then continued on via Pool-in-Wharfedale (10 m from Leeds), Otley (12¾ m), Burley-in-Wharfedale (15½ m) and Ben Rhydding (17¾ m) to Ilkley (18¾ m). The Leeds-Ilkley trains, which took a few minutes longer than their Midland route rivals, lasted until 22 March 1965, and at one time the line carried a Bradford-Harrogate service.

Crossing the Wharfe valley floor by means of a substantial 21-arch viaduct, the curves in the Harrogate line then attract 20 and 30 mph speed restrictions either side of the 100 yd Wescoehill Tunnel (10 m 14 ch to 10 m 18 ch). This is followed by a cutting and then Weeton station (10 m 62 ch) with its simple shelters on each platform. More cuttings, interspersed with views of rolling countryside, follow on the 1 in 195 climb via Rigton crossing and box (12 m 15 ch) to Pannal (14 m 3 ch). This station, too, has been simplified, but its former buildings still exist and have been joined by Pullman Car No 332 to function as a restaurant.

North of a cutting and skew bridge at Pannal, the old Leeds & Thirsk route took an easy course beneath Crimple Viaduct and on to Starbeck, but this closed in 1951. Today's trains leave the L&T course at what used to be Pannal Junction and make a screeching curved climb up to join the former Church Fenton-Harrogate route at Crimple Junction, between Crimple Tunnel and the viaduct. They then cross the latter (see the separate entry) and, via a long stretch of cuttings and overbridges, come to Harrogate where the mileage changes from 17 m 24 ch from Leeds to 20 m 38 ch from York, and the direction from Down to Up. The link between the two early routes and the new, central station at Harrogate (see separate entry) represent part of the dividends from the formation of the North Eastern Railway and date from 1 August 1862.

Beyond Harrogate station the surviving double-track route continues past former sidings and an oil terminal. This section was part of the 1862 improvements, as was a spur from Dragon Road Junction to Bilton Road Junction which rejoins the L&T route on its way from Starbeck to Ripon. It is still possible to spot the overgrown junction before coming to Starbeck (18 m 27 ch) itself, where the simple combination of platforms, shelters, barrier crossing and signal box is all that survives from a former railway crossroads and all the railway hardware that would have entailed. Both Starbeck and Knaresborough also have separate entries.

The original Leeds & Thirsk route had approached Starbeck from the east and then turned north on the opposite side of the station, and this is all it did to serve Harrogate until the later NER line produced today's route. It did, however, do more to fulfil early commitments to Knaresborough which the East & West Junction Railway's line from York had reached on 30 October 1848. The link from Starbeck, via Belmont barrier crossing and former frame (17 m 69 ch), was opened on 1 October 1851. It produced the present dramatic approach to Knaresborough over the high river viaduct and into a new station for the town, including a level crossing and signal box and the 178 yd Knaresborough Tunnel (16 m 48 ch to 16 m 40 ch).

Beyond the Knaresborough eastern approach tunnel the embankment course of the old line to Boroughbridge and Pilmoor (also covered in the Knaresborough entry)

is still visible, although young trees have seized the opportunity of a clear growth field. At 16 m 24 ch the route then becomes single using a token obtained at Knaresborough. Two crossings on the single line section —at Oakwood Farm (14 m 47 ch) and Whixley (11 m 8 ch)—survive in place of the two earlier stations—Goldsborough which used to serve Princess Mary's home at Goldsborough Hall and an extant buffer depot, and Hopperton (formerly Allerton). These both closed to passengers on 15 September 1958, as did Hessay and Marston Moor.

The countryside is mellow, level and wooded as this first single line section ends at Cattal's traditional buildings, signal box and level crossing gates (10 m 20 ch). Absolute Block then applies on the double track portion via gates and cabin at Hammerton Road (9 m 17 ch) as far as Hammerton station (8 m 61 ch)— similar to Cattal, its brick station house and buildings are to a familiar railway pattern.

The second Electric Token section produced by the 1973 singling has level crossings at Wilstrop (7 m 45 ch), Marston Moor (6 m 5 ch) and Hessay (5 m 11 ch). Wilstrop used to have a 'market day only' service to Knaresborough until 1931, Marston Moor is not far from the 1644 Civil War battlefield, and Hessay has ground frame access to the Down Refuge Siding and military depot there. At the end of the single line section, Poppleton (2 m 74 ch) is a simplified version of the preceding stations. Nearby there are railway-run nursery gardens with a 60 cm gauge internal railway system. After Poppleton there just remains the Nether Poppleton LC (2 m 34 ch) before the route curves south to join the main line at Skelton (1 m 50 ch) and its trains run on to terminate at York.

The Leeds-York route was never a significant through line, this role being filled by the service via Church Fenton. The Leeds end emphasis is, in fact, recognized in the half-hourly Leeds-Knaresborough frequency, with an hourly extension to York. Apart from the HST service, successor to former Pullman and *White Rose* trains, the line's workings are normally in the hands of Class 141 Pacers. All stations except Harrogate are unstaffed.

L.5   Liversedge   Branch—see   Manchester-Leeds Line

L.6   Lockwood—see Barnsley-Huddersfield Line

L.7 Longbeck—see Middlesbrough-Saltburn Line

L.8 Low Fell Junction—see Newcastle

L.9 Low Moor

Manchester-Milner Royd Junction-Bradford line, between Halifax and Bradford. 37 m 37 ch from Manchester Victoria

Only the signal box remains active at Low Moor now, but up to the First World War it was a location of considerable importance, and traces of some of its former routes are still visible. This was Lancashire & Yorkshire Railway territory, opened up by the West Riding Union as the L&Y agent when the line from Mirfield was brought into use on 18 July 1848. Two years later, the extension to Bradford opened on 9 May and that to Halifax on 7 August. The link with the Great Northern, to Dudley Hill, dates from 1 December 1893 but then lasted only 23 years.

Low Moor lost its station on 14 June 1965 with the closure of the Mirfield route. This had formerly carried trains like the 9.5 am *Yorkshireman* which was in St Pancras by 1.21 pm, plus a Huddersfield service and the Thornhill locals. The latter called at Bowling Junction (1¼ m), Low Moor (3 m), Cleckheaton Central (5½ m), Liversedge Central (6¾ m), Heckmondwike Central (7¾ m) and Ravensthorpe (9½ m).

L.10 Lynemouth Colliery Branch

Benton-Morpeth line, branch from Bedlington. 6 m 12 ch

The trains to Newbiggin-by-the-Sea ended on 2 November 1964, but part of their route north of Bedlington survives to serve Ashington Colliery and the complex of works and collieries at Lynemouth. The output of the Ashington seams had been responsible for the first railway links to the staiths at Blyth and the colliery used to operate its own railway system which carried miners to and from work as well as handling the coal they produced. Ashington station, when it was open, used to have nine sidings under its control, mostly originating coal wagons but also serving a granary.

From Bedlington North crossing and signal box, the route separates from the Morpeth line and heads northwards to the triangular junction with the branch to North Blyth. The connections with the Bedlington-Lynemouth route are at West Sleekburn Junction (78 ch) and Marchey's House

Junction (1 m 35 ch), with the double line then continuing north past Marchey's House signal box and LC (1 m 41 ch) to the level crossing at the old North Seaton station (1 m 76 ch). This section dates back to 7 November 1859, that on to Newbiggin from 1 March 1872.

The next location is the AHB LC at Green Lane (2 m 43 ch), followed by Ashington (3 m 2 ch) where the Butterwell Colliery line and its connection to the Ashington complex departs. The Lynemouth line operates on the No Block system from this point and completes its journey along the coast through Hirst Lane LC (3 m 21 ch) to Lynemouth Colliery (6 m 12 ch).

The main traffic movements over this line are the coal from the Ellington/Lynemouth colliery sidings and from Butterwell opencast mine plus traffic to the aluminium works at Lynemouth.

M.1 Malton

York-Scarborough line. 21 m 12 ch from York

Malton, the railhead for a considerable area of agricultural Yorkshire, was formerly a junction, with lines north to Gilling and south-east to Driffield. The first trains to arrive at Malton were those of the York & North Midland Railway's York-Scarborough line and the present station is the one that Y&NM architect G.T. Andrews built in 1845 to deal with them. The other routes from Malton date from 19 May 1853, that to Gilling and Pilmoor being the work of the York, Newcastle & Berwick Railway and the single line across to the Scarborough-Hull route belonging to the Malton & Driffield Railway.

The Gilling line was of some importance and for many years carried the through services which ran, mainly on summer Saturdays, between Scarborough and Newcastle. At one stage a spur between the two routes was proposed, but nothing was done and the through trains had to continue to reverse over the curve (between Scarborough Road Junction and Malton proper) which carried the Malton-Driffield trains to the higher level through Gilling-Driffield line.

Local traffic on both the York-Scarborough and Malton-Gilling lines benefited, or suffered, according to one's point of view, from an early piece of road-rail rationalization when the intermediate stations on both routes were closed in favour of the alternative buses. This took effect from the first day of 1931 and displaced the previous four trains each way between Malton and Gilling which had been linked with the York-Pilmoor-Gilling-Pickering workings, and had called at Amotherby (4½ m), Barton-le-Street (6 m), Slingsby (7¾ m) and Hovingham Spa (9½ m) on the 13 mile, 32-minute journey to Gilling.

The Malton-Driffield passenger service ended from 5 June 1950 and the line closed completely eight years later. At that time the holiday services between Scarborough and the North were still passing via Gilling, as the awkward reversal at Malton was preferable to adding to York's peak traffic problems. However, these came to an end in 1963 when a derailment at Pilmoor destroyed the junction with the main line there.

In the days when walking was more acceptable and horse vehicles provided a common alternative, stations did not have to be built close to the centre of the community they served. In Malton's case there was no incentive to provide another crossing of the Derwent to get into Malton proper and the 1845 York & North Midland engineers thus stayed in the East Riding and built their station in Malton's Norton suburb. This survives in much the original form with pleasant stone buildings on the town side and an overall roof to the arched Up side wall. A yard area and water tower precede the station, and both sidings and a dock survive near the former loco depot site. After the former bay area at the country end of the station, Malton's brick signal box stands on the Up side with its barrier crossing (21 m 32 ch) nearby. Beyond, a surviving overbridge abutment and the trackbed of the former spur to Scarborough Road are all that remain to mark the Gilling and Driffield lines.

Malton is well served by the hourly trains between Scarborough and Liverpool/Manchester. Its station is one of considerable architectural merit, but something less than modern in its convenience for passengers. At the time of writing the future of the station buildings was under discussion between BR and the local council.

M.2   Manchester-Huddersfield-Leeds Line

From the Regional Boundary at Diggle Junction to Holbeck East Junction, Leeds. 34 m 2 ch

Now the principal route between Manchester and Leeds, this line originated with the Huddersfield & Manchester Railway and subsequently became part of the London &

North Western Railway empire. The Act of Incorporation for the H&M received the Royal Assent on 21 July 1845, four years after the pioneer Manchester & Leeds had linked the two cities mentioned in its title with a route through the Calder Valley.

The H&M's section of the developing new route started with a single line from Heaton Lodge Junction, opened to a partly built station at Huddersfield on 3 August 1847 (goods 16 November). The onward section through the Colne Valley to Stalybridge involved some difficult viaducts and tunnels, and was not ready for use until 1 August 1849.

Between Heaton Lodge Junction and Dewsbury East Junction the route is that of the Manchester & Leeds, with the section north to Leeds via Dewsbury originating with the Leeds, Dewsbury & Manchester Railway. Incorporated by an Act of 30 June 1845, this concern was amalgamated with the LNWR from 9 July 1847 and opened its line on 18 September 1848.

The line from Manchester via Stalybridge uses the Tame Valley for its approach to the Pennine barrier, gradually becoming more and more overwhelmed by the 1,500 ft moors on either side until even a 1 in 125 gradient is not enough. After Diggle Junction signal box (14 m 59 ch), the first Eastern Region location, the unequal struggle is abandoned in favour of the level 3 m 66 yd of Standedge Tunnel (15 m 11 ch to 18 m 14 ch). This leads directly to the valley of the River Colne which has just become a significant waterway, thanks to the efforts of half a dozen tributaries draining down from the heights above.

The level summit section continues as far as Marsden (18 m 54 ch), one of the original stations, now simplified, but still served by the Leeds-Manchester locals, and handling some Leeds turnround trains. The remains of the goods yard are on the Up side and there is an Up Goods Loop. Ahead, the line clings to the northern side of the narrow valley and begins a descent of 7 miles, largely at 1 in 105, with views of the mills along the river and of the locks of the Huddersfield Canal. The A62 road makes up the transport quartet exploiting the valley.

Slaithwaite station (21 m 19 ch) was closed in 1968 and then brought into use again by the West Yorkshire PTE 14 years later. It is followed by a section of cuttings and viaducts along which there were formerly stations at Linthwaite Goods, Golcar and Longwood & Milnsbridge. The route is now nearing Huddersfield and a section

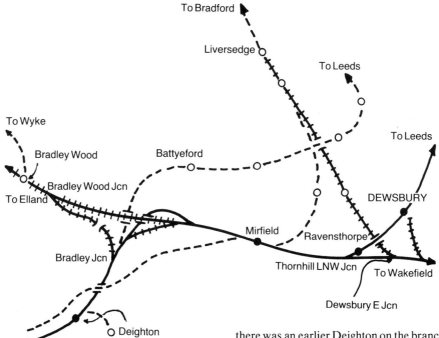

To Bradford

Liversedge

To Leeds

To Wyke

Bradley Wood

Battyeford

To Leeds

Bradley Wood Jcn

To Elland

DEWSBURY

Mirfield

Ravensthorpe

Bradley Jcn

Thornhill LNW Jcn

To Wakefield

Dewsbury E Jcn

Deighton

To Huddersfield

To Kirkburton

which caused the H&M engineer, A.S. Jee, many headaches. It starts with Longwood Viaduct and then the 243 yd Gledholt North and South Tunnels (25 m 4 ch to 25 m 15 ch). At Springwood Junction (25 m 20 ch) the line from Penistone joins the Manchester line for the final approach to Huddersfield through the 695 yd Huddersfield North and South Tunnels (25 m 20 ch to 25 m 51 ch).

Huddersfield, which has its own entry, has a dramatic station with imposing Up side buildings and a great goods warehouse on the Down side. The signal box (25 m 60 ch) is located on the station which has a total of six running lines, one of which, the Down Slow, continues over the long Huddersfield Viaduct and on as far as Hillhouse Junction (26 m 26 ch). The Midland's goods line previously ran parallel to the LNW route and the latter had its own goods station at Hillhouse.

The simplified station at Deighton (27 m 60 ch) was opened by the PTE in 1982, but there was an earlier Deighton on the branch line which ran along the valley of the Fenny Beck to Kirkburton. This was a LNWR enterprise, authorized by an Act of 28 July 1863 and opened for passengers on 7 October 1867 after some nasty problems with a viaduct; goods traffic began on 1 January 1868. The branch left the Manchester-Huddersfield-Leeds line in a facing direction at Kirkburton Branch Junction and then looped south over both canal and river to start its journey along the east side of the valley. The trains from Huddersfield called at Deighton (2 m), Kirkheaton (3½ m), Fenny Bridge & Lepton (4¾ m) and Kirkburton (6¼ m), taking 18 minutes one way and 21 the other. The branch lost its passenger trains on 28 July 1930 but kept the goods workings until 5 April 1965 when the route was cut back to Deighton. It finally closed on 1 February 1971.

Just before Bradley Junction (28 m 39 ch), where the single line freight link round to the Mirfield-Milner Royd Junction line departs, there are traces of the old Midland goods branch from Huddersfield. This took a parallel route to that of the LNW line initially and then crossed both its rival and the two adjacent waterways to complete the journey to Mirfield south of the M&L line.

Beyond Bradley Junction the line from Huddersfield divides at Heaton Lodge

South Junction (28 m 78 ch) with 76 chains of double track passing beneath the M&L line and then rising on the other side to join it at Heaton Lodge East Junction (29 m 54 ch). Meanwhile, the single line of the Up Main has curved directly to the latter.

From the underpass route the Spen Valley line used to continue a further 13¼ miles to Farnley Junction, Leeds. Authorized to the London & North Western Railway by Acts of 27 June 1892 and 6 July 1895, it had first carried a through passenger service on 1 October 1900 and then continued to do so until 2 August 1965. The service on the line ran between Huddersfield and Leeds and called at Bradley (2¾ m), Battyeford (4¼ m), Northorpe Higher (5¾ m), Heckmondwike (7½ m), Liversedge (8¼ m), Cleckheaton (9¼ m), Gomersal (10¾ m), Birstall Town (12 m), Farnley & Wortley (16¾ m) and Leeds (18¾ m), taking 45–40 minutes on the journey.

The trackwork of Heaton Lodge loco shed lies on the Down side as the main line continues to Mirfield, which has a separate entry.

The former L&Y line to Low Moor and Bradford left the main line immediately east of Mirfield station, but now our route just continues over the river and on to Thornhill LNW Junction where the 39 m 72 ch distance via Hebden Bridge reverts to the Huddersfield route mileage of 32 m 16 ch. At Thornhill LNW Junction the LD&M route to Leeds separates from the Wakefield/Normanton line, the former coming immediately to Ravensthorpe (32 m 28 ch) where the station has period wooden buildings in the vee between the two routes. A single freight line is crossed on the section to Dewsbury; this is the surviving portion of the Thornhill-Low Moor line, now serving a coal depot at Liversedge.

Dewsbury (33 m 62 ch) has a separate entry and is followed by Batley (35 m 9 ch), the area between revealing a succession of textile mills affirming the strong woollen and cloth traditions of the locality. Our surviving LNW line crossed the Great Northern's route twice between Dewsbury and Batley and a few traces of this can still be spotted. Beyond Batley, which retains its traditional stone buildings on the Down side, there used to be a link to the GN from Birstal Junction as well as the LNW branch in the opposite direction, out to Birstal itself. This short, 2 mile line, of which some traces still remain, ran via an intermediate station at Carlinghow. It was opened on 30 September 1852 but had its 'service suspended' from 1 January 1917 and then handled only freight until final closure on 18 June 1962.

The Great Northern line through Batley divided after the connection from Birstal Junction, one arm turning east towards Ardsley and the other crossing over the LNW line, continuing up the valley through Upper Batley, and eventually reaching Laisterdyke and Bradford. Our line passes beneath the GNR again after leaving Batley level crossing and signal box (35 m 57 ch) and plunging into the 1 m 1,609 yd of Morley Tunnel (36 m 25 ch to 39 m 19 ch). The gradient is 1 in 138 on the approach, with the summit in mid-tunnel and a down gradient then prevailing all the way to Leeds.

Immediately after Morley Tunnel comes

A line of ventilation shafts marks the course of Standedge Tunnel under the A670 road. The Pennine Way passes just beyond Redbrook Reservoir.

the simplified Morley station (38 m 24 ch), and then the final section into Leeds past the former Churwell station and on via Farnley Branch Junction (40 m 65 ch) to Holbeck East Junction (42 m 5 ch).

The Manchester-Huddersfield-Leeds route is of considerable importance with a high volume of local traffic as well as the North Wales/Liverpool to Hull/York/Scarborough Sprinters. It also has a link to the North East, with every second hourly 'fast' extended to Newcastle.

M.3   Manors—see Newcastle

M.4   Marchey's House Junction—see Lynemouth Colliery Branch

M.5   Marsden—see Manchester-Leeds Line

M.6   Marsh Lane—see Leeds

M.7   Marske—see Middlesbrough-Saltburn Line

M.8   Marton—see Middlesbrough-Whitby Line

M.9   Melton Halt
Doncaster/Leeds-Hull lines, between Brough and Hull. 8 m 46 ch from Hull

One morning train out from Hull and one evening train home again may be valuable to their users, but they are not sufficient to earn Melton Halt a conventional line in the timetable. Its two trains, reminders of an era when 'workmen's' services were extensive, are just dealt with by a footnote.

The halt is provided with wooden platforms and basic shelters, and stands at the beginning of a short three-track section to Ferriby. The turnout from Up Slow to Up Fast is controlled by Melton Lane LC signal box, as is the barrier crossing.

At the beginning of 1988 the Up side cement works west of Melton was being used to store bulk cement wagons. Beyond it lies Welton LC (9 m 35 ch).

Melton Halt was proposed for closure in a notice issued on 26 May 1988.

M.10   Menston—see Ilkley Branch

M.11   Methley Junction
Sheffield-Leeds line, junction with Castleford/Milford line. 187 m 37 ch from St Pancras

Today Methley Junction is no more than the point at which the Normanton and Castleford routes join on the way to Leeds. There is a wooden, Midland-style signal box on the Down side at the junction and a R/G crossing at Methley North LC (188 m 30 ch). The junction itself consists of a trailing crossover and then an Up side lead which doubles again for the 1 m 11 ch curve round to the Castleford line at Whitwood.

The line from Normanton to Methley and on to Leeds dates from the opening of the North Midland Railway between

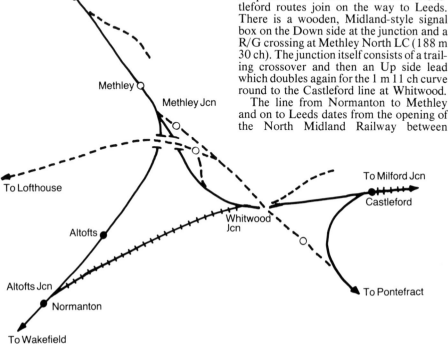

Rotherham and Leeds on 1 July 1840. The curve from the York & North Midland Railway was added on 27 July to complete a triangular junction between the two concerns. Later this curve was to carry trains from York and Hull to Leeds, diverted away from the Leeds & Selby line allegedly because of the latter's inconvenient Marsh Lane terminus at Leeds (but just possibly because it would lengthen the journey at a time when passenger fares were directly related to mileage).

The Wakefield, Pontefract & Goole Railway, which had opened the route detailed in its title on 1 April 1848, followed this first line with a branch from Pontefract to Methley which the Great Northern planned to use as its access route to Leeds. The Midland tried to insist that the use of the section on from Methley should be conditional upon the GN forsaking any right to an independent access to Leeds and blocked Methley Junction to try to enforce this. However, matters soon quietened down and the Pontefract-Methley line was officially brought into use, under L&Y auspices, on 1 December 1849.

Although the Great Northern's express trains were later diverted to today's Wakefield route, Methley came back into the limelight with the opening of the Methley Joint line east to the latter at Lofthouse. This West Yorkshire Railway/Great Northern enterprise opened to goods in 1865 and to passengers from 1 May 1869, later carrying a frequent Leeds-Castleford service and a rather sparse Wakefield-Castleford one. Both served the MJ intermediate stations at Methley and Stanley until closure on 2 November 1964. The line also had coal traffic links to the East & West Yorkshire Union Railway.

In all, Methley had three stations, all now closed. The first to go was the ex-L&Y Methley Junction which closed on 4 October 1943. Methley North, the former Midland station located on the Leeds side of today's junction, closed on 16 September 1957, but traces of this are still visible on the Up side of the line. Methley South was the Methley Joint station and this ceased work from 7 March 1960. The abutments of the bridge which used to carry the joint line's route over the surviving Y&NM/NER are, however, still visible.

M.12 Micklefield

Leeds-Hull line, junction with York line. Micklefield Junction is 10 m 63 ch and the station 10 m 69 ch from Selby South Junction

Although the Leeds & Selby Railway was opened on 22 September 1834, the early routings between York and Leeds were circuitous and it was not until 1 April 1869 that the NER opened the 5 mile connection between Micklefield and Church Fenton to create today's direct link between the two major cities. This is used by the Sprinter trains from Scarborough/York to Manchester and by the through services between Leeds and the North East. The former, together with the Hull line trains, give Micklefield an excellent interval service which is supplemented at peak times.

Micklefield station now consists simply of staggered platforms plus shelters. However, the 1834 buildings are still standing on the Down side—shed, station rooms and station master's house—and provide an interesting example of early railway facilities.

M.13 Middlesbrough

Darlington-Saltburn line, junction with Whitby branch. 15 m from Darlington

Middlesbrough owes its existence to the decision of the Stockton & Darlington Railway to extend its original line across the River Tees to an area down river which would give improved loading for the coal shipments that had brought this pioneer railway into existence. The area chosen for the new loading point was a marshy site in a bend of the Tees, and horse-worked trains started using the new extension from 27 December 1830, locomotive haulage commencing on 7 April 1834. The original Middlesbrough township grew up around this initial activity and then became increasingly industrialized with the exploitation of the ironstone deposits of the Cleveland Hills to the south.

The 1830 line into Middlesbrough headed straight towards the bank of the river instead of turning east as today's line does, the present route dating from the extension to Redcar from 4 June 1846. The line to Guisborough, which forms the beginning of the present Whitby branch, was added on 25 February 1854, and the Redcar line was extended to Saltburn on 17 August 1861.

The area of the river bend penetrated by the original S&D extension came to house important iron and steel works, along with the wharfs to serve them. Their rail access was via a freight connection with the main line, west of Middlesbrough station, at Marsh Bridge Junction. This led to Marsh and Bridge sidings where traffic for and from the Cleveland, Acklam, Ayrsome and

Loading general cargo between the wars at No 6 Quay at Middlesbrough Dock.

Britannia works was assembled and distributed. A second access route from the main line took the course of the 1830 line from Old Town Junction and served Middlesbrough goods, the coal depots and Tyne/Tees Wharf where the 1830 station had been located. From this second access line the former 'Middlesbrough Owners'' line ran parallel with the river to join the dock lines east of the station.

The LNER owned the docks system at Middlesbrough. This covered an area of 25½ acres and had nearly 7,000 ft of quays. Hoists, cranes, conveyors, storage etc were all provided, the main traffics being the iron and steel products of the local works which produced a great deal of rail 'trip' working. The main rail access was from just east of the passenger station, although there was a second connection at the dockyard, stockyard and tube works end, and a single line bridge connection over the entrance lock.

Although it has a through service to and from King's Cross, Middlesbrough is catered for mainly by the frequent Saltburn-Darlington/Bishop Auckland trains, those via Hartlepool to Newcastle and its services on the Whitby branch. The approach to the station in the Down direction is from Newport East Junction (14 m 3 ch), where the Tees Yard goods lines reduce from four to two, and past Middlesbrough panel box

Another view of Middlesbrough Dock, with the River Tees beyond and the Saltburn line in the foreground.

(14 m 71 ch). Beyond the station the Nunthorpe line veers off south at Guisborough Junction (15 m 23 ch), opposite Middlesbrough docks, with No 1 Up and Down Goods Lines then continuing as far as Whitehouse signal box and level crossing (15 m 67 ch).

The present station at Middlesbrough was brought into use on 1 December 1877. It was the work of the North Eastern Railway's architect William Peachey and seems to owe some of its Gothic features to Barlow's then newly completed St Pancras. Originally there was an outer concourse, an inner concourse and an overall roof (attributed to W.J. Cudworth), but the latter, together with a locomotive, was destroyed in a daylight German bombing raid on 3 August 1942.

The surviving outer concourse station building at Middlesbrough is on the Up side. Constructed in grey stone, it comprises a two storey block with a steep roof rising from decorative parapets and two sizeable dormers. The station also has a considerable amount of decorative ironwork, including the east end underbridge which carries the legend 'Albert Bridge NER'. A rather more recent feature is a modern travel centre complete with ticket and information facilities and the latest in customer-care technology.

Freight traffic, dealt with in association with Cobra Railfreight and Stockton Haulage, remains an important activity. Commodities range from steel to cider.

M.14   Middlesbrough-Saltburn Line

Eastern section of Bishop Auckland/ Darlington-Saltburn route. 12 m 57 ch

This surviving section of the sizeable east-west railway built up by the Stockton & Darlington Railway is a healthy part of a modern route either side of the East Coast Main Line, carrying hourly trains between Saltburn and Bishop Auckland with additional services as far as Darlington hourly in between. The portion of the route east of Middlesbrough provides an interesting journey, passing first through an industrial part of Tees-side, then through some of the housing areas that provide the labour force, and finally through the retirement and relaxation areas along the coast.

The line was opened in two sections, that from Middlesbrough to Redcar on 4 June 1846 and the extension to Saltburn on 17 August 1861. The Middlesbrough & Redcar Railway was leased to its S&D backers in the year following opening and the extension to Saltburn was a wholly S&D project, the route duly passing to the NER, LNER and finally to British Rail (Eastern). Redcar and Saltburn are described in separate entries.

Immediately east of Middlesbrough station the Whitby line departs at Guisborough Junction (15 m 23 ch), and a view of the docks is then followed by the connection to a modern tank farm and the depot of Stockton Haulage. On the Up side, White-

Class 143 Pacer unit takes on mail at Saltburn prior to starting its journey to Bishop Auckland.

At the opposite end of Saltburn station the former main platform has been absorbed in a remodelling scheme and no longer leads directly to the Zetland Hotel.

house barrier crossing and brick signal box (15 m 76 ch) is followed by a now-cleared area which once carried the connection from the Cleveland Railway's line. This had been opened on 23 November 1861 to bring ironstone to a jetty on the River Tees, but it was subsequently cut back to the mines at Normanby and Eston, although its Guisborough station survived to be used by the Middlesbrough-Brotton trains.

Cargo Fleet station (16 m 6 ch) consists of an island platform with waiting shelters and is followed by the little-used Down Goods line which ends in a connection to the British Steel coking plant. More TCB goods lines commence at South Bank Junction (17 m 31 ch) with South Bank station

then following (17 m 40 ch). A closure notice for the previous station was published at the end of 1983 to facilitate moving the location 700 yds east with access to the Normanby road. The site has wooden platforms and waiting shelters.

The next portion of the route is dominated by heavy industry, with views of modern chemical installations and the works, ancient and modern, of British Steel. At Beam Mill Junction (18 m 3 ch) the first connection departs to Slag Road (Lackenby) LC, crossing over the main line to the British Steel network where wagons of coil, billets and finished steel are assembled. The first of the two connections to Teesport and Grangetown Refinery used to come at

Grangetown, with the British Steel Lackenby plant in the background.

Grangetown Junction (18 m 76 ch), with Shell Junction (19 m 32 ch) then providing the second (and surviving) access to the Shell Refinery via a 1 mile 47 chain single line. This is also the route of the link with ICI Wilton which passes beneath the Saltburn line and then under the A1085 road. Redcar Ore Terminal Junction (20 m 5 ch) follows. There are passenger stations along this section at Grangetown (18 m 41 ch) and at British Steel Redcar (20 m 56 ch) which gives access to BS's Redcar works and the Teeside Divisional Headquarters; it also uses the steel product in its shelters and railings. The modern Down side Grangetown signal box (18 m 65 ch) controls the area.

As the Saltburn line turns towards the coast, the trackbed of a former route represents the final connection with the industrial area. Redcar, detailed in a separate entry, is served by Redcar Central (22 m 64 ch) and Redcar East (23 m), with the route then continuing south to Longbeck where the combination of wooden platforms and waiting shelters is followed by a barrier crossing and Up side signal box (25 m 29 ch). After Marske (25 m 65 ch), with its partially-staggered platforms and coal drop remains, the route heads for the terminus at Saltburn (27 m 57 ch) via Saltburn West Junction (27 m 5 ch). From the latter the former line to Whitby is still in use as far as Boulby Potash Mine.

M.15   Middlesbrough-Whitby Line

Branch from Darlington-Saltburn line, from Guisborough Junction, Middlesbrough to Battersby, 10 m 62 ch, and on to Whitby, 24 m 1 ch

One of the most interesting lines in the North East, this route starts off as a Mid-dlesbrough commuter line and then turns east through the beautiful scenery of the narrowing valley of the River Esk to carry walkers to the moors and through travellers to the historic port and resort of Whitby.

For most of its life the service over this route ran from Stockton to Picton over the old Leeds Northern line and then turned east to Battersby and on to Whitby. This provides a clue to its origins as a York & North Midland Railway scheme for a branch to Castleton which was opened at the Picton end on 3 March 1857 by the North Yorkshire & Cleveland Railway.

The lure of ironstone for the Tees furnaces had included a branch to Swainsby in the 1857 opening, and this also prompted the extension on from Stokesby to Ingleby on 1 February 1858. There the new railway met the Ingleby Mining Company, a move that under North Eastern Railway ownership was to lead to the building of the dramatic Rosedale branch. This mineral line, which climbed the slopes of the Cleveland Hills by a 1 in 5/6 incline and then ran for 11 lonely miles across the moors, lasted from 27 March 1861 to 29 September 1928.

The line from Picton towards Whitby was extended from Ingleby to Kildale on 6 April 1858 and then passed into North Eastern ownership from the first day of the following year. This seemed to slow the project down and it was 1 April 1861 before trains reached Castleton and 2 October 1865 before the gap to the 1835 Whitby & Pickering line at Grosmont was filled.

The first section of the present route, from Middlesbrough to Nunthorpe, was opened for freight on 11 November 1853 and for passengers on 25 February 1854, as part of a Middlesbrough & Guisborough Railway project supported by the Stockton

A goods train on the lonely and remote Rosedale ironstone branch in LNER days.

1986 scene with a Pacer unit leaving Egton for Whitby, with Egton Low Moor in the background.

& Darlington. Completion of the present route was then delayed by the NER's reluctance to construct the section between Nunthorpe and Battersby as this would have provided a cheaper outlet for Rosedale ore than their existing, but circuitous route via Picton. However, the link was finally built, coming into use for freight on 1 June 1864 and for passengers on 1 April 1868.

At first passenger services on the Esk Valley line were between Stockton/Picton and Whitby with the Middlesbrough-Battersby trains connecting with them, but from the late NER era the number of through Middlesbrough-Whitby workings began to rise despite the existence of the alternative coastal route. Increasing leisure brought more and more people to walk in the delightful areas surrounding the line or to take advantage of an excursion to Whitby itself.

In the Beeching era the Esk Valley line was proposed for closure but only the Picton-Battersby section succumbed, resulting in the end of passenger services and the closure of the intermediate stations at Trenholme Bar, Potto, Sexhow, Stokesley and Ingleby from 14 June 1964.

Under the control of Middlesbrough signal box, today's Whitby trains quickly leave the Saltburn route at Guisborough Junction where the route's distances commence. This section through suburban Middlesbrough heads via crossings at Cargo Fleet Road (14 ch) and North Ormesby (38 ch) to the simple platform at

Marton (2 m 56 ch), not far from the birthplace of Captain Cook. Open countryside now begins as the route continues via the short wooden platform at Gypsy Lane (3 m 60 ch) and the line's first open crossing at Marston Lane (3 m 62 ch). The suburban service portion of the route then ends at Nunthorpe (4 m 25 ch), a traditional station with signal box, barrier crossing and passing/run-round loop.

After Morton Carr AOCL crossing (4 m 68 ch), the line turns south away from the trackbed of the former Middlesbrough & Guisborough Railway. This used to carry a service via Pinchinthorpe, Hutton Gate and Guisborough and then on via Boosbeck to Brotton. The latter section was part of an 1861 Cleveland Railway route which took its own course to Guisborough, where the use of a terminus meant that all trains had to reverse. There were various iron ore mine connections along the whole of the Nunthorpe-Brotton route which lost its passenger services west of Guisborough on 2 May 1960 and between Nunthorpe and Guisborough from 2 March 1964. The once-extensive freight traffic did not last much longer.

Returning to the surviving Whitby line, Captain Cook used to go to school at Great Ayton (8 m 14 ch) where the platform and shelter combination stands on the green arable plain below the Ice Age height called Roseberry Topping. The adjoining heights of Easby Moor carry a monument to Captain Cook, dominating the lower landscape as the Whitby trains pass round

Middlesbrough-Whitby dmu at Grosmont, the junction with the now-preserved line to Pickering.

the 20 mph curve and parallel their onward route past Battersby signal box (10 m 54 ch) and on into the station, where the mileage changes from 10 m 62 ch to the 12 m 3 ch of the original line from Picton. The station itself now uses the original Down platform and bay, with the Up side platform and main buildings no longer operational. At the country end a 1907 NER water crane survives near the signal box, and its scissors crossover linking the parallel Middlesbrough and Whitby lines. Both of these use Electric Token working on the sections to Nunthorpe and Glaisdale respectively.

On from Battersby Road AOCL crossing (12 m 46 ch), the route curves through gentle farmland to the modest platform with shelter combination at Kildale (13 m 64 ch), and then through Guisborough Road AOCL crossing (14 m 56 ch) to another such combination at Commondale (17 m 71 ch). Castleton Moor (19 m 38 ch), the next station, is more substantial, as befits the small market town it serves. A loading dock survives, along with the stone-built station house that has a viewing bay overlooking the platform.

The youthful River Esk is now the railway's companion as it heads for the platform and small stone house at Danby (20 m 74 ch), home of the Moors Centre, and then continues with excellent views of the dales to Lealholm (24 m 43 ch). There the station house is the work of Thomas Prosser, and a stone goods shed also survives. Both Lealholm and the following Glaisdale have ancient bridges across the

river. Glaisdale station (26 m 50 ch) is a passing loop controlled by the small brick signal box on the Down side. It has approach viaducts in each direction, the eastern one affording a view of the ancient Beggar's Bridge which spans the Esk near the line. Glaisdale had a small iron industry in the 1860–70 period with iron ore workings, three blast furnaces and an uncompleted mineral railway.

At Glaisdale One Train working replaces the previous Electric Token operation, and the character of the route also changes as the valley narrows. Using a double-span tied girder bridge to cross the Esk, the line then needs a cutting and a hillside ledge to get it to the single platform, station house and reputedly haunted but none the less very pleasant Postgate hotel at Egton (28 m 17 ch). After a rare straight section the winding course is resumed, and our line makes a long viaduct crossing of the Murk Esk river which has been used by the trains of the preserved North Yorkshire Moors Railway on their scenic course from Pickering.

The Whitby & Pickering Railway was the area's first railway, being authorized by an Act of 6 May 1833 and opening inland from the port to Grosmont 25 months later. It then climbed south out of the narrowing valley by a 1 in 15 incline of nearly a mile, reaching Goathland on the moors plateau and heading on through the Ice Age Newtondale to Pickering. This section became operational from 26 May 1836. The route was originally horse-worked with water-

A Middlesbrough-Whitby train crosses the River Esk just outside Ruswarp station.

balance operation on the incline, but modernization came with the take-over by the York & North Midland Railway from 30 June 1845 and linking with the latter's branch from Rillington on the York-Scarborough line. Accidents on the incline were frequent and led to its replacement by a more easily graded section which was brought into use from 1 July 1865, although the section to the foot of the incline at Beckfoot carried a local passenger service from 1908 to 1914 and a skeleton freight service until 1951.

In the 1930s there were four all-stations trains each way daily on the line to Pickering and Malton calling at Ruswarp (1¾ m), Sleights (3¼ m), Grosmont (6½ m), Goathland (9¾ m), Levisham (18¼ m), Pickering (24½ m), Marishes Road (27¾ m) and then Malton (35¼ m). The through journey took just under an hour and a quarter, but the longer distance trains omitted all but Pickering, Goathland and Grosmont and cut this down by five minutes or so, and the local Whitby-Goathland trains took less than 30 minutes. The journey, still available by the trains of the NYM concern, is a dramatic one.

The BR station at Grosmont (29 m 59 ch) lies on a 15 mph curve, with the NYMR station adjoining and the two routes meeting at Grosmont Junction, where the mileage changes from the 29 m 66 ch of the Esk Valley route to the 24 m 44 ch of the earlier Whitby & Pickering line. On towards Whitby, the BR line now enters the lovely

Esk Dale stretch, winding through woodland and crossing the river no less than seven times on the way to Sleights (27 m 66 ch) where only the Up platform is now used. Another river crossing then heralds Ruswarp's AOCL crossing and station (29 m 31 ch), where the period station house has a new career as a cafe.

Railway and widening river are now on the final stages of their journey, the former cutting across a bend of the latter and then passing beneath the high 13-arch viaduct of the former coastal route from Scarborough to Middlesbrough. Finally comes the terminus at Whitby (30 m 26 ch) which has its own separate entry.

The Whitby line carries a basic winter service of seven through trains each way daily with extra local workings over the Middlesbrough-Nunthorpe section. Extensive and imaginative publicity for the route has given it a good level of patronage, but the scope for extra or special workings is limited by the One Train section at the Whitby end. At the time of writing this is the subject of a study financed by local councils and the Development Council for Rural England to establish the cost and practicability of running North Yorkshire Moors trains into Whitby.

M.16   Milford—see Swinton Junction-Milford Line and Gascoigne Wood

M.17   Mill   Lane   Junction—see Bradford

M.18 Milner Royd Junction-Mirfield Line

Freight-only link between the Manchester-Halifax-Bradford and Manchester-Huddersfield-Leeds routes. 8 m 8 ch

Although this section no longer carries a passenger service it remains open for freight, and is historically significant as the course of the first railway between Manchester and Leeds. The Manchester & Leeds Railway had obtained its enabling Act as early as 4 July 1836 and had opened sections at each end of its Manchester-Normanton route until the completion of Summit Tunnel not only joined Lancashire and Yorkshire but also permitted the first train services between the two. This began on 1 March 1841, the section under comment dating from 5 October of the previous year.

Normal passenger services over the route ended on 5 January 1970, but it continued to be used for some summer Saturday services until 1984 when their routing between Wakefield and the Greetland/ Dryclough/Milner Royd Junction(s) triangle was abandoned in favour of other alternatives. Now the line is just used for through freight and for access to the oil installation at Elland.

Control at the western end is in the hands of Milner Royd Junction signal box (29 m 21 ch) from which point the two tracks fall away from the Halifax line to stay with the River Calder and the Calder & Hebble Navigation on the valley floor. Overlooking all this, on the crest of the valley opposite the signal box, stands Wainhouse Tower, a nineteenth-century viewing point with a spiral staircase inside.

At Greetland (30 m 77 ch) the Normanton line is joined by the twin tracks that have left the Halifax line at Dryclough Junction (0 m) and run south through Salterhebble Down and Up Tunnels (91 yd between 21 ch and 25 ch) to Greetland (1 m 11 ch). Now freight only, this was the first line to reach Halifax, having been opened to the Shaw Syke terminus there on 1 July 1844. It came to carry the important Bradford-Halifax-Huddersfield service as well as the L&Y 'Motor Cars' on the Stainland branch.

The short Stainland branch from Greetland, or North Dean as it was formerly, was an L&Y undertaking opened to passengers on 1 July 1875 and to freight on 29 September of that year. Trains originated at Halifax and called at Greetland station (1¾ m) before turning south along a minor valley to West Vale (2¾ m) and then Stainland (3½ m). A halt was added at Rochdale Road in 1907 and prior to grouping the service ran as many as 15 trains each way daily. However, such lines were very vulnerable to early road competition and its passenger services ended on 23 September 1929, although the line remained open for goods for another 30 years.

Back on the 1840 line to Normanton, Greetland is followed by the 420 yd of Elland Tunnel (31 m 25 ch to 31 m 44 ch) and then by Elland signal box (31 m 61 ch). Staying with its canal and river companions, the route loops north to Brighouse where the Pickle Bridge branch used to run along the other side of the river before joining at Anchor Pit Junction. A direct Bradford-Huddersfield service used the Pickle Bridge line, calling just at Low Moor, Wyke and Clifton Road and giving a 34-minute journey time. Opened originally on 1 March 1881, the line was closed to passengers in the year of nationalization and to freight four years later.

The M&L route makes its first connection with the LNW line from Bradley Wood Junction (35 m 59 ch) where there is a spur towards Deighton, 1 m 17 ch long and using the 132 yd Bradley Tunnel between 24 and 30 chains from Bradley Junction on the Huddersfield line. The Normanton line continues on via Heaton Lodge Junction (37 m 29 ch) and Heaton Lodge East Junction (37 m 49 ch) to Mirfield (38 m 32 ch). There is an extra Up Slow line over this last section and a 76 ch spur between South and East Junctions to connect the higher level freight line with the Up direction of the passenger line below.

M.19 Mirfield

Eastwood-Normanton line, between Heaton Lodge Junctions and Healey Mills. 38 m 32 ch from Manchester Victoria

The large, grey stone buildings on the island platform at Mirfield have a sad air and convey a sense of being left over from the days when Mirfield was an important interchange point between the L&Y and LNW systems, and even dealt with such oddities as the Great Northern links with East Lancashire. Now all that has gone, but Mirfield still does quite well from the Manchester-Huddersfield-Leeds trains and from the local service between Huddersfield and Wakefield.

The two early main lines which made Mirfield a railway crossroads were the Manchester & Leeds Railway's trunk route

The classical exterior of Monkwearmouth station, now housing a museum (Sunderland Museum & Art Gallery)

to Normanton which opened along here on 5 October 1840, and the combined routes of the Huddersfield & Manchester and Leeds, Dewsbury & Manchester concerns which were opened throughout from 1 August 1849. The L&Y took over the M&L route through the Calder Valley, while the other route through Huddersfield became the LNW's Yorkshire tentacle, joining the original M&L line west of Mirfield and leaving it east thereof to continue through Dewsbury to Leeds.

The L&Y's first probe towards Bradford was opened from Mirfield to Low Moor by the West Riding Union Railway on 18 July 1848, just before the LD&M's Thornhill-Leeds line which came into use two months later. The WRU route, which lasted until 14 June 1965, ran via Northorpe (6½ m from Huddersfield), Heckmondwike Central (8 m), Liversedge Central (9 m) and Cleckheaton Central (10¼ m) and carried a normal service of some 14 trains each way daily. From Mirfield there was also a Midland Railway goods line to Huddersfield (Newtown), opened in 1910 and closed on 1968.

The approach to Mirfield is via Heaton Lodge Junction (37 m 29 ch) and Heaton Lodge East Junction (37 m 49 ch) where the Calder and Colne routes join, and it is followed by Mirfield East Junction (29 m 26 ch) where the Wakefield and Dewsbury routes separate. There is an extra Up Slow line over this section.

M.20 Monkwearmouth

Northallerton-Newcastle line, between Sunderland and Gateshead. 90 m 26 ch from Leeds

The Brandling Junction Railway opened a line from the Tyne to the Wear on 19 June 1835, using a terminus to the east of the present Monkwearmouth station. Passenger traffic began on this line and on the BJR's line to Gateshead on 5 September of that year, by which time the two routes had been linked and a goods branch had been opened to North Dock at the mouth of the Wear.

The present station site was brought into use in 1848 and became a through station in 1879 when the route was extended over the Wear to Ryhope Grange. Three years earlier a line had been opened from just north of Monkwearmouth, along the north bank of the Wear, to join the old Stanhope & Tyne route at Southwick Junction.

Latterly just a local station rather than the terminus of a proud independent railway, Monkwearmouth retains its impressive 1848 stone buildings on the Up side. The dock and platforms are screened by a high, arcaded wall so that the functional part of the station should not detract from the high portico frontage! Passenger services were withdrawn from 6 March 1967 and since then a museum has been set up in the non-operational buildings. There is even a convenient period milepost on the platform.

Monkwearmouth signal box controls the main line and the access to the 1876 goods line, the eastern end of which has been retained as a freight-only branch to Austin & Pickersgill's shipyard. The connection from the Down side (4 m 28 ch) leads to a short double-line 'sidings' section, then to the start of One Train Working (4 m 13 ch) over the single line portion on to Southwick Goods Yard (3 m 46 ch), and finally to the shipyard (2 m 71 ch). On the Up side of the main line the trackbed of the route from North Dock junction can be seen from the Sunderland-Newcastle trains. It is hard to believe now that this route once served half a dozen busy sidings, with more on the Southwick line, including Swan Hunter and Castletown shipyards, Hylton and Wearmouth collieries, and the goods depot at Southwick, where traffic warranted a 10 ton crane.

M.21   Moorthorpe—see Swinton-Milford Line

M.22   Morley Tunnel
Manchester-Huddersfield-Leeds line, between Dewsbury and Leeds. 36 m 25 ch from Manchester Victoria

The substantial heights between Batley and Morley look innocent enough now as golfers and walkers enjoy their hobby above the 1 m 1,609 yd railway tunnel (36 m 25 ch to 38 m 19 ch), but they are the gathering places for the waters of the Aire and Calder rivers and presented the original tunnelling engineers with plenty of problems. Even so, the work was completed in just over two years to enable the opening of the Leeds, Dewsbury & Manchester Railway's line on 18 September 1848. The summit of this lies in the middle of Morley tunnel, with rises of 1 in 138 and then 1 in 410 from Batley, a change to 1 in 500 down inside the tunnel and then continuing steeper descents all the way to Leeds.

M.23   Morpeth
East Coast Main Line, between Newcastle and Alnmouth. 16 m 50 ch from Newcastle

The Newcastle & Berwick Railway's trains reached Morpeth on 1 March 1847 and by 1 July of the same year were running through to Tweedmouth. Morpeth itself is a venerable town where the Cistercians founded an abbey in the twelfth century and where Northumberland County Council now has its headquarters. It got its second railway when the Blyth & Tyne opened a mineral line from Bedlington in 1857 and began to carry passengers on it from 1 April 1858, using a separate station at Morpeth.

On 8 August 1859 an Act was passed that was to bring the North British Railway to Morpeth. This related to the Wansbeck Railway which was the NBR's creature and which opened from Morpeth west to Scotsgap on 23 July 1862, on to Knowesgate in 1864, and through to Reedsmouth, on the Hexham-Riccarton Junction line, on 1 May 1865. The Wansbeck Railway was amalgamated with the NBR in 1863, but continued to be worked by the Blyth & Tyne whose station was used until a new connection in 1872 allowed the use of the main line station. The B&T trains moved into the modified ECML station about 1880, their former station then doing duty as a goods depot.

Another line linked to Morpeth was that of the Northumberland Central Railway which was conceived as a north-south link between Cornhill on the Berwick-Kelso line and Scotsgap on the Wansbeck Railway. Authorized on 28 July 1863, the NCR opened from Scotsgap to Rothbury on 1 November 1870 but got no further. It became part of the North British system on 1 February 1872.

The basic '30s service on the routes west of Morpeth was one of four trains a day, two going through to Rothbury with a connection from Scotsgap to Reedsmouth, and

A North Eastern Railway single coach push-pull train.

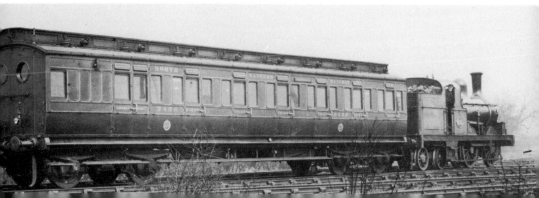

two to Reedsmouth with a connection to Rothbury. The intermediate stations to Reedsmouth (25 m from Morpeth) were at Meldon (5¼ m), Angerton (7½ m), Middleton North (9 m), Scotsgap (11 m), Knowesgate (14¾ m) and Woodburn (21¼ m); between Scotsgap and Rothbury (24 m) lay Longwitton (14¼ m), Ewseley (16¼ m), Fontburn Halt (17½ m) and Brinkburn (21¼ m). Services ended on 15 September 1952.

Benjamin Green's stations for the Newcastle & Berwick Railway are all impressive, and Morpeth is no exception. The style is Tudor, with an entrance arcade and plenty of decorative touches throughout—gables, chimneys, finials and ornamental canopy brackets. Opposite the main two-storey block on the Up side is the former Down island, provided with a waiting shelter and with a dock and sidings beyond.

North of the station stands the modern Up side signal box (16 m 63 ch) where a Slow line is added through Morpeth North CCTV crossing (16 m 78 ch) and on to signal M141. At Morpeth North Junction (17 m 26 ch) the old Blyth & Tyne, now a coal route, departs. The junction is a triangular one with one spur from the B&Y at Hepscott Junction north to Morpeth North Junction and the other one south to Morpeth Junction.

South of Morpeth. an attractive station house survives near Stannington box and crossing (13 m 74 ch), and there is a stone cottage and CCTV LC at Clifton (14 m 56 ch). The route of the old Wansbeck Railway has now been built over.

Morpeth is the turnround point for a local service from Newcastle and is also served by the Alnmouth and Berwick trains. Some longer distance trains also call.

M.24 Mytholmroyd
Manchester-Normanton/Bradford line, between Hebden Bridge and Milner Royd Junction. 24 m 68 ch from Manchester Victoria

Mytholmroyd is on a gently-graded section of the line opened by the Manchester & Leeds Railway on 5 October 1840. Even so, its platforms are raised to viaduct height and have to be reached by using the five flights of stone stairs inside the three-storey Down side building. From the latter a subway leads to the Up side which has an attractive, but smaller, building of its own.

The station at Mytholmroyd dates from 1847 and previously had a companion to

the east at Luddenden Foot. Notable as once having Branwell Brontë as its clerk in charge, the latter closed to passengers on 10 September 1962 and to freight on 3 May 1965. Further east still there were water troughs, but these, too, have now gone. The crane plinth in Mytholmroyd's former goods yard is still visible, but only its passenger station remains active, deriving a service from the Manchester/Hebden Bridge-Leeds/York/Scarborough trains.

N.1 Nafferton—see Hull-Scarborough Line

N.2 Neville Hill—see Leeds

N.3 Newburn Branch
East Coast Main Line, branch from Newcastle West Junction. 5 m 33 ch

Today this branch is just a single freight route running westwards along the north bank of the Tyne to serve the Stella North power station at Newburn and various sidings in between. At one time, however, it carried most of the passenger services from Newcastle to the west and south west and its origins go back to 21 May 1839 when the Newcastle & Carlisle Railway crossed the Tyne to Scotswood and Shot Tower (passengers from 21 October 1839). At the eastern end the route was extended to Newcastle Forth on 1 March 1847 and then Central station on 1 January 1851. The extension westwards through Newburn was a separate enterprise of the Scotswood, Newburn & Wylam Railway which had shipping traffic ambitions for Scotswood. It was opened as far as Newburn on 12 July 1875 and continued to rejoin the N&C route west of Wylam in the following year.

The route lost its passenger service on 10 March 1968, although there had been intermediate station closures before then. In LNER days the line had carried a half-hourly service, with trains calling at Elswick (1¾ m), Scotswood (3 m), Lemington (4 m), Newburn (5½ m), and then Heddon-on-the-Wall (6¾ m) on the 21-minute journey to North Wylam (8½ m).

Today's surviving freight line leaves Newcastle West Junction (11 ch) and descends to the civil engineer's sidings in the old Forth Goods Depot area and the cement terminal in the Railway Street depot. This 'siding' section (51 ch to 1 m) is followed by the commencement of One Train working at 1 m 3 ch, with the 1839 section mileage ending at 2 m 66 ch in favour of that of the 1875–6 extension. On this the 269 yd Scotswood Tunnel (22 ch to 34 ch) is followed by Newburn LC (2 m 47 ch) and then the end of the line (2 m 58 ch).

N.4 Newcastle

East Coast Main Line, junction with Carlisle and Middlesbrough/Northallerton routes. 80 m 16 ch from York

Its strategic position near the mouth of the Tyne made Newcastle important to the Romans who built a fort there, and then to the Normans who gave the location its 'new castle'. Commercial and manufacturing activity then grew over the years, linked closely with the discovery of coal deposits and then the shipping, engineering and wagonways associated with the carriage and use of that commodity.

Newcastle's first conventional railway was the pioneer Newcastle & Carlisle enterprise which formally opened the Hexham-Blaydon section on 9 March 1835 and added passenger services to the earlier goods carriage from the following day. An objection to the use of locomotives brought about the N&C's closure for a short period, but extensions of 1836 and 1837 carried the line further east to Redheugh, with a boat link across to the north bank of the Tyne. By 18 June 1838 the route was opened throughout to Carlisle, and two years later (goods 21 May and passengers 21 October) crossed the Tyne from Blaydon to Scotswood, proceeding on to Shot Tower and later to Forth (1 March 1847) and eventually Central (1 January 1851). The N&C became part of the North Eastern in 1862.

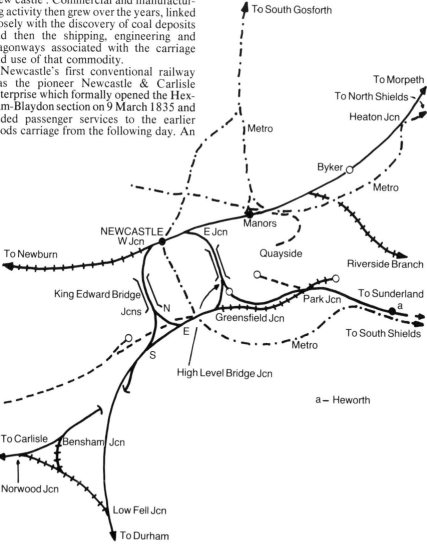

A period view of the Tyne at Newcastle, looking downstream to the High Level Bridge. Note the twin-stacked paddle steamer.

East of Newcastle the lines along either bank of the Tyne date from 1839. The Newcastle & North Shields route from Manors to North Shields was opened on 22 June, and doubled in the following year, extending into Central station on 1 September 1848. In the previous year the Newcastle & Berwick had been linked to the North Tyne route at Heaton Junction from 1 March 1847, so that the 1848 section on to Central connected it with both the Newcastle & Carlisle system and with the lines south of the river, via the newly-opened High Level Bridge.

To the south of the Tyne, the Brandling Junction Railway had opened from South Shields and Brockley Whins to a Gateshead terminus on 5 September 1839 (minerals 30 August). The Redheugh Incline from the N&C route linked the two systems for passenger traffic from 18 June 1842 and then this network was connected to the one north of the river with the opening of a temporary crossing on 1 September 1848 and a permanent one from 15 August of the following year. The new East Coast Main Line began to take shape in 1868, when the section from Durham was linked to the High Level Bridge and then took over from the route via Washington from 1 October 1871.

The other main element of the Newcastle railway system was added when the Blyth & Tyne Railway opened its line from Gosforth to New Bridge Street on 1 May 1863 (passengers 27 June 1864). This was con-

nected to the North Tyne route on 1 January 1909, after the second Tyne crossing over King Edward Bridge had come into service three years earlier, on 1 October 1906.

The various development stages of the railways of Newcastle eventually produced a 'box' layout configuration, with the two Tyne bridges forming the east and west sides, Central station the north, and Gateshead the south. From each corner of the box or circle, main routes departed—to Scotswood, to Darlington, to South Shields and Sunderland, and to North Shields and Berwick. The box/circle layout permitted a great deal of operational flexibility, although Newcastle-originating and terminating services have usually passed over the High Level Bridge in order to use the dead end platforms on the east side of the station.

The end of the 1840s must have produced some dramatic scenes at Newcastle as the York, Berwick & Newcastle Railway constructed the High Level Bridge and the station/hotel complex. The former was the work of Robert Stephenson and used bowstring girders to carry road and rail routes high above the old road bridge just downstream. The High Level Bridge has six spans which lift the present rail route 120 ft above the river, and the whole structure has recently had a £200,000 repair and renovation programme.

Central station opened the year after the High Level Bridge. Again, Robert Stephenson was the engineer and worked to the

Above *Streamlined A4 6001 at the head of the Up* Flying Scotsman *on 30 July 1952. The 600 ton train is seen crossing King Edward Bridge over the Tyne.*

Below *The era of the Tyneside electrified lines; a South Shields train at Newcastle Central station in July 1948.*

Bottom *The exterior of Newcastle station, clearly showing the Prosser portico added to the 1850 Dobson frontage.*

Newcastle station interior view.

designs of John Dobson, a noted local architect, the two of them achieving one of the finest classical buildings of its kind. The long frontage, including the Royal Station Hotel, is original, but the planned central portico was omitted as an economy measure and the present one added later under the guidance of Thomas Prosser. The great roof spans are part original and part 1893 additions. They cover the central access area of ticket hall, concourse, and the ends of the bay platforms, and then pass over the through lines and four carriage sidings beyond. Avoiding lines then pass outside the functional south side retaining wall.

A prominent feature of the concourse of Newcastle Central is a new travel centre, begun in 1984 and costing £1 million. Built on the old bookstall site, the structure has, at the request of the local planners, a futuristic appearance deriving from the deep blue armour-clad glazing which forms the outer skin of the back and side walls, the tension supports which form an overhead lattice frame, and the clear armour-plated glass of the frontage. The complex has six InterCity and three local ticket windows, plus one business and eight information counters, and the main station indicator is positioned above it.

Even more dramatic changes lie ahead for Newcastle under a £31 million scheme of remodelling linked to the electrification

The famous diamond crossings and the castle keep outside Newcastle station.

of the East Coast Main Line. This will simplify the pattern of diamond crossings between the High Level Bridge and North Tyne routes and create a new, through platform on the south side of the station for use by local through services.

Approaching Newcastle on the East Coast Main Line, Tyne Yard is followed by Low Fell Junction (73 m 37 ch), from which a double line leads past Low Fell engineers' sidings to Low Fell Sidings Junction (79 ch), and the Norwood Junction (1 m 42 ch), with the route to Hexham and Carlisle. From Low Fell Sidings Junction another double line spur runs for 25 chains to the Carlisle line, but this time to Bensham Junction and facing towards the route's Bensham Tunnel beneath the main line.

The ECML, after passing through the 53 yd Askew Road Tunnel (79 m 26 ch to 79 m 29 ch), is joined by the Carlisle lines which have passed below it and risen on the Up side to King Edward Bridge South Junction (79 m 42 ch). Through ECML services then continue to KEB North Junction (79 m 57 ch), over the bridge to Newcastle West Junction (80 m 5 ch), and then into the through platforms of the station. Those terminating continue via KEB East Junction, past the loco depot, then round from Greensfield Junction to High Level Bridge Junction and on into the station from the East end past the Castle Keep.

The route from Newcastle to Sunderland in the Up direction picks up its 'Leeds' distances at Newcastle East Junction (101 m 59 ch), with trains then crossing the High Level Bridge to High Level Bridge Junction (101 m 33 ch). There they meet the three lines from KEB East Junction and then continue east via Park Lane Junction (100 m 68 ch), St James Bridge Junction (100 m 23 ch) and Heworth station (99 m) to Pelaw Junction (98 m 16 ch), where the Ferryhill line departs. A separate pair of freight lines runs from Greensfield Junction to Park Lane Junction to serve the Up side Tyneside Central Freight depot. Just after High Level Bridge stand the remains of Gateshead East station, the route subsequently running alongside the Metro lines, through the modernized interchange station at Heworth.

On the north side of the River Tyne the mileage changes from 80 m 16 ch to zero at Newcastle signal box. From this point to East Junction (14 ch) the three through platform lines (8, 9 and 10) are bi-directional and there are two Up and two Down avoiding lines (W, X, Y and Z). The single freight line to Newburn departs beyond the west end bays, now used for parcels services, while the main line—together with the unused Up and Down Tynemouth lines—takes a viaduct course to Manors (46 ch). The Morpeth trains still call at the main line platforms here but the location is only a shadow of what it once was, and the platforms of Manors North are now derelict.

The Blyth & Tyne system opened its terminus in the New Bridge Street area in 1864. The B&T route was then linked to the North Tyne line on 1 January 1909 using new through platforms at Manors and a bay for Blyth trains. The alterations to the site also produced New Bridge Street goods

Heaton servicing and maintenance depot.

depot, which was to be badly bombed during an air raid on 28 September 1941. A spur linked the two routes at Manors and also connected with the 1,306 yd Quayside branch which took a semi-circular course from Trafalgar Yard down to the Quayside exchange yard with the Newcastle Corporation lines and Hamburg Wharf. Opened in 1870 and with a ruling gradient of 1 in 25, mostly in tunnels, the branch had the distinction of using four forms of traction. Steam was followed by NER third rail electric operation, then overhead electrification, and finally diesel power, the first alteration being influenced by the fact that smoke rarely cleared from one sharply-curved tunnel, whatever the wind direction. The line carried a large volume of traffic at one time and latterly was taken over by the Port of Tyne Authority. It closed on 14 June 1969.

After Manors, the ECML passes through the 98 yd Red Barns Tunnel (65 ch to 70 ch) and continues to Riverside Junction (1 m 25 ch) where the declining Riverside branch departs. Then comes Heaton South Junction (1 m 74 ch), Heaton signal box (2 m 16 ch) and Heaton North Junction (2 m 48 ch), all serving the main Newcastle rolling stock and traction depot situated on the Up side of the line. Down side accommodation is used by BR and Balfour Beatty engineers as a construction depot, and there is also a cement terminal. Beyond Heaton, the old Tynemouth route continues ahead in the hands of the Tyne & Wear Metro, while the ECML turns north for Benton and a pleasant coastal course through Northumberland.

Much has changed at Newcastle over the years. Losses include such things as the closure of Gateshead locomotive works and the passing of the special Bergen Line facilities, but 50 years ago the best trains from London reached Newcastle in just under five hours, and now the timing is down to three or less. The city still has excellent cross-country links with Carlisle and South West Scotland, Manchester/Liverpool, and to the West Riding, West Midlands and Wales/South West, plus a good service to Edinburgh and beyond. The Durham service via Blackhill and the one to Blackhill via Pelton have gone, but there is still a useful service to Durham on the main line and another north to Morpeth and Berwick. Local services also continue on the Middlesbrough and Hexham routes, including some trains running between the two and serving the incredible new Gateshead shopping and leisure complex.

Part of the former railway role in connection with suburban services has been perpetuated by the Tyne & Wear Metro system, which is described separately. The North Eastern Railway, losing over half its suburban business to tramway competition, responded positively and had electrified its North Tyne services by 1904, five years before London learned the same lesson. Now the main line's Metro successor perpetuates the railway tradition on former routes to South Shields and over the circular line to Tynemouth and Whitley Bay.

Three of Newcastle's former passenger services have not survived, those to Newbiggin, to North Wylam, and on the Riverside branch. But the NER spirit which pioneered electrification, electro-pneumatic signalling and experiments with locally-built railcars can still be seen in the facets of transport interchange which come together at Newcastle station and in the modern rail services and facilities available there.

N.5   Newcastle-Carlisle Line
Gateshead, High Level Bridge Junction to Carlisle. 58 m 48 ch

This double-track, east-west line has great scenic attraction in addition to its value as an important link between the East and West Coast Main Lines. Its companions on the cross-country journey are the River Tyne and, a little further away, that great fortification of Roman Britain, Hadrian's Wall. The Newcastle-Carlisle line also has a standing as one of the pioneers of the railway age and for a short period it had the distinction of being Britain's longest railway.

There had been talk of a canal route across the relatively narrow 'neck' of northern Britain from the late eighteenth century. Nothing came of this until its conversion to a railway alternative about the time of the Stockton & Darlington Railway. The new scheme, entitled the Newcastle-upon-Tyne & Carlisle Railroad Company, secured its enabling Act as the Newcastle & Carlisle Railway on 22 May 1829, and construction was started at the two ends of the line in the following year.

With valleys to be spanned, rivers to be crossed and hills to be surmounted the N&CR's construction task was not easy, but Francis Giles, the company's engineer, managed to avoid having more than one short tunnel. However, some of the viaducts and other works border on the spectacular, and it was four years before the first section

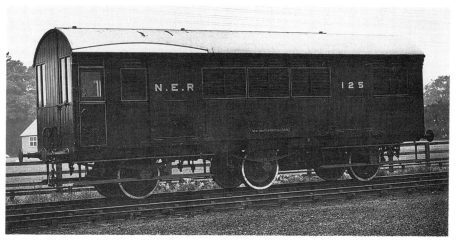

A product of York Works, this NER six-wheeled milk van with slatted sides was used on the Newcastle & Carlisle section.

of the line was ready for opening. This was the 16 mile eastern portion between Blaydon and Hexham which was subjected to the usual boisterous opening festivities on 9 March 1835, after having carried goods traffic since the previous November. An objection by a local landowner to the use of the locomotives then closed it again for a period until new Parliamentary powers were obtained.

In 1836 the N&C opened a further 8 miles from Hexham to Haydon Bridge and nearly 20 miles at the western end, out from Carlisle to the colliery at Blenkinsop, the former on 28 June and the latter on 19 July. Two short extensions from Blaydon in 1836/7 brought access to Redheugh, Gateshead and thence by ferry across the Tyne to Newcastle itself. A more effective entry to Newcastle via Scotswood and the north bank of the Tyne was achieved on 21 October 1839, by which time the missing centre section between Haydon Bridge and Blenkinsop had been at work since 18 June of the year before. The final extensions were from Shot Tower to Forth on 1 March 1847 and into Central station on 1 January 1851.

Today the Newcastle & Carlisle line carries a local service as far as Hexham, plus through workings by locomotive and coaches over the whole route, pending the full introduction of Sprinters and Pacers. The local services originating at Sunderland are routed out of Newcastle via King Edward Bridge, but trains starting from the bay platforms there travel via High Level Bridge Junction (0), Greensfield Junction (16 ch)

and the Up and Down Gateshead West tracks to KEB East (38 ch) and West (48 ch) junctions. The Up and Down Carlisle lines then pass through the 53 yd Askew Road Tunnel (62 ch to 64 ch) and use the 125 yd Bensham Tunnel (1m 1 ch to 1 m 6 ch) to pass below the main line and rise on its west side to Bensham Junction (1 m 30 ch). This and the following Norwood Junction (1 m 71 ch) provide the connections to Low Fell Sidings Junction and back to the ECML north of Tyne Yard.

This section of the route is made up of three short lines opened between 1893 and 1909 and running slightly south of the original 1837 N&C route to Redheugh. The area of the latter has now been landscaped, but after Norwood Junction, where the 1893 line crossed the Tanfield Railway, a trackbed towards the Tyne marks the former connections to Dunston Staiths and an S loop to the Dunston Junctions, back to Whickham Junction and then to West Dunton Staiths. A rusting siding from the latter area now joins at Swalwell Junction (3 m 78 ch) which follows the island platform of Dunston station (2 m 17 ch) and the new Gateshead Metro Centre station (3 m 41 ch) which was opened on 3 August 1987. The latter has two platforms, with stairs, ramps and waiting areas beneath, all painted bright red and leading to a covered walkway to one of Europe's biggest leisure and shopping complexes.

At Swalwell, which has its own entry, the joining of the Dunston branch is followed by the departure of the link to Swalwell Colliery, a crossing of the River Derwent, a

*An engineers' train on the Up line at Hexham which is a ballast depot for the Newcastle &
Carlisle route.*

coal depot, Down side sidings, and then
Blaydon signal box and its barrier crossing
(5 m 52 ch). Six chains further on the
mileage changes to the 3 m 78 ch of the
original route, as the old course of the line
from Scotswood and the north bank of the
Tyne joins the surviving route for the entry
into Blaydon station (4 m 3 ch). The line
from Blackhill used to cross the N&C here
from its opening on 18 June 1867 (passengers 2 December) and had joined the
cross-river line just south of the bridge. At
one time there were three other connections
between the two routes, plus the access line
to Blaydon goods.

Blaydon station itself, consisting just of
platforms and a connecting footbridge, is
followed by a stretch of line very close to
the river and then the former sidings serving
Ryton power station. Stella Crossover (4 m
44 ch), Addison AHB LC (5 m 3 ch) and
Clara Vale AOCR-X LC (7 m 40 ch) lie on
the section between Blaydon and Wylam (8
m 35 ch) where the original N&C station
survives with staggered platforms, single-
storey station buildings, footbridge, level
crossing and high signal box. George
Stephenson was born at Wylam and his
birthplace is maintained by the National
Trust. The Wylam Railway Museum displays relics of local pioneers and there are
walks along the old wagonways and over
Hagg Bridge, which used to carry the
Scotswood, Newburn & Wylam Railway
route over the Tyne to join the N&C line at
West Wylam Junction.

NER milepost signs are still visible along
the lineside as the route continues past the
old mineral sidings at West Wylam, and
there is a view of Prudhoe Castle and the
simplified station at Prudhoe (10 m 48 ch).
In addition to the basic platforms, shelters
and footbridge, this location has refuge sidings, a crossover and barrier crossing, all
controlled by the high signal box at the Carlisle end. There is a gentle climb through
Mickley R/G LC (11 m 40 ch) to the platform, footbridge and shelter combination at
Stocksfield (13 m 11 ch), but the route does
not do any serious climbing until beyond
Hexham. Riding Mill (15 m 35 ch) and
Corbridge (17 m 59 ch) stations and
Dilston AHB LC (18 m 19 ch) lie on the
way there, Corbridge with severe, ungabled
Up side buildings, restored but quite unlike
most of its surviving N&C contemporaries.

The local service from Sunderland and
Newcastle ends at Hexham (20 m 68 ch),
which has its own separate entry, and is
followed by the former Border Counties
Junction where the Allendales and Reedsmouth routes departed. Just before Warden
AHB-X LC (23 m 54 ch) the railway
crosses the South Tyne river whose valley
it will follow as far as Haltwhistle. The
climbing starts here and will continue for 18
miles before the steep descent into the Eden
Valley begins. Meanwhile, the next station
is Haydon Bridge (28 m 35 ch), where the
main brick buildings are on the Down side
with a signal box to control the conventional gated crossing on the Up. The old
yard and dock areas are still there, as is a
NER warning notice.

The South Tyne river is crossed twice on the 1 in 265/204 section on to Bardon Mill R/G LC (32 m 23 ch) and the following station and signal box (32 m 29 ch and 32 m 41 ch). The interesting station house survives, but the railway heads on to the 202 yd Winchester Tunnel (35 m 70 ch to 35 m 79 ch) and then Haltwhistle (37 m 13 ch). This former junction station has staggered platforms linked by a footbridge in the distinctive three-section style. The gabled main building and adjacent smaller block are typical of the semi-Tudor design used on the line and there is an interesting cast-iron water tank signed 'Peter Taite, Engineer, Wylie & Co, Newcastle 1861'. The approach route of the former Alston branch is visible at the east end of the station and its former yard at the west.

In search of lead traffic the N&C opened a branch south from Haltwhistle to Alston which was brought into full use on 17 November 1852 after the completion of Lambley Viaduct. This nine-arch, 110 ft high crossing of the South Tyne had a companion in the skew-arch Burnstones Viaduct, and the route also involved some significant earthworks and gradients in its climb to the Alston terminus, nearly 1,000 ft above sea level. In LNER days the five trains each way daily served Featherstone Park (3 m), Coanwood (4 m), Lambley (4¾ m), Slaggyford (8½ m) and then Alston (13 m), but the losses started at £6,000 in 1962 and a subsidy of £73,000 was being paid 10 years later. The route, which had a short mineral branch from Lambley, closed on 3 May 1976 but is now the home of the South Tynedale Railway Preservation Society which operates a 2 ft gauge line at the southern end of the former branch.

The next section of the N&C route completes the climb from Hexham and starts the descent to Carlisle after a high, level stretch through the remains of former stations at Greenhead, Gilsland, Low Row and Naworth. Active locations here now consist of Blenkinsop box and crossing (40 m 19 ch), marking the completion point of the original enterprise, Long Byre R/G LC (41 m 5 ch), Denton School AOCR-X LC (43 m 23 ch), Denton Village LC (43 m 65 ch), Upper Denton AHB LC (44 m 1 ch), Lane Head LC (45 m 38 ch), Low Row LC (46 m 24 ch), Naworth AHB LC (47 m 67 ch), Milton Village LC (48 m 60 ch) and then Brampton (49 m 21 ch).

Brampton today has just Up and Down platforms plus shelters, but it used to have a short branch north west to Brampton Town and to rejoice in the name Brampton Junc-

tion as a consequence. Brampton Town closed on 29 October 1923 after the local service had previously been suspended from 1917 to 1920. It had earlier been part of the Brampton Railway route up to Lambley Fell and a link with the branch from the Alston line, a scheme which had its origins back in an eighteenth-century wagonway. Stephenson's much-rebuilt *Rocket* ended its working life on the Brampton Railway.

From Brampton the N&C route descends at 1 in 128, and later at 1 in 107 via the signal box at Brampton Fell LC (50 m 10 ch), another at the old station of How Mill (52 m 66 ch), and AOCR LC at Broadwath (54 m 62 ch), and another box and crossing at Corby Gates (55 m 54 ch). There are three viaducts and a deep cutting on this steep, curving section which leads to another original N&C station at Wetherall (55 m 76 ch)—closed 2 January 1967 and reopened 5 October 1981—and then the Regional Boundary (58 m 60 ch). From east to west the three skew arches of Gelt Bridge are followed by the seven of Corby Viaduct and then the five 80 ft spans of Wetherall Viaduct which carries the line across the River Eden into Wetherall station.

Shortly beyond the boundary between the two Regions the N&C route curves north and into Carlisle.

N.6 Newport—see Tees and Middlesbrough

N.7 New Pudsey—see Leeds-Bradford Line

N.8 Newsham—see Benton-Morpeth Line

N.9 Newton Aycliffe—see Bishop Auckland Branch

N.10 Northallerton

East Coast Main Line, junction for lines to Eaglescliffe and Redmire. 29 m 76 ch from York

Northallerton is the administrative centre of North Yorkshire and the County Hall can be seen from the railway. For many years the town lay on two main railway lines, the East Coast Main Line being crossed by the old Leeds Northern's route up through Harrogate, Ripon and Melmerby, and on to Eaglescliffe and Stockton. Northallerton also had a single line east-west route through Wensleydale to the Midland Railway at Hawes, but this only

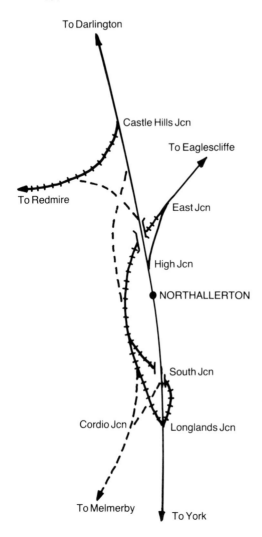

To Darlington

Castle Hills Jcn

To Egglescliffe

To Redmire

East Jcn

High Jcn

NORTHALLERTON

South Jcn

Cordio Jcn

Longlands Jcn

To Melmerby

To York

survives as a freight line as far as Redmire. The trunk route from Melmerby is closed and the direct route to the Tees has lost its intermediate stations.

However, as with the whole pattern of railway rationalization there have been many benefits in other directions, and Northallerton is well served by trains on the ECML, with calls by the Newcastle-Liverpool and NE/SW services as well as having a local service and good connections for King's Cross via York. The station has been simplified and modernized, but the location has lost its wartime avoiding loop which recognized the importance of the connection between the two main lines by building a supplementary north-south link,

in case one was put out of action by bombing. The old North Eastern had also planned to build a marshalling yard at Northallerton, but this never materialized.

The section of the main line through Northallerton dates back to 1841 and was opened by the Great North of England Railway for mineral traffic on 4 January and then for passengers on 30 March. The Leeds-Stockton services of the Leeds Northern Railway then began running through Northallerton from 2 June 1852, calling at a separate Northallerton Town station. From 1856 to 1901 the LN line services were rerouted via Thirsk, leaving the Melmerby-Northallerton section to function as a branch line, but the position was then reversed again, the direct route to Northallerton upgraded, and the layout there modified to allow Leeds-Stockton route trains to use the main station. The former LN station became a goods depot, but the redundant Melmerby branch platforms were brought back into use as part of the Second World War avoiding line.

The other line radiating from Northallerton was the single track Wensleydale route which rose to the lonely dales and a meeting with the Midland Railway at Hawes. The NER had taken over the earlier independent Northallerton-Bedale (1848) and Bedale-Leyburn (1855/6) sections from 1 January 1858 and, 20 years later, added the 16 miles on to Hawes. Although closed to passengers on 26 April 1954, the line is still open to Redmire for Tarmac traffic. The wartime avoiding line was only slightly different in level from the Wensleydale branch and the problem of crossing the latter was solved by providing a movable bridge which could be rolled aside if the avoiding line was needed.

Following the closure of the Wensleydale branch to passengers, the Leeds Northern route also began to decline. The section on to Stockton lost its intermediate stations at differing times up to 1965, and the section to the south lost its passenger trains on 6 March 1967 to leave Northallerton very much as it is today.

The four tracks of the East Coast Main Line approach Northallerton via R/G level crossings No 88 (27 m 16 ch) and No 89 (27 m 58 ch). The former station at Otterington lay about a mile ahead of No 88 and was closed to passengers on 15 September 1958. The Melmerby line trains were still running then but are now only remembered by the approach of their trackbed on the Down side. The 1901 link from Cordio Junction on the Leeds line to South

Junction on the ECML has also gone, but at Longlands Junction (28 m 71 ch) a 1 m 1 ch single line drops down to the old LN route at Boroughbridge Road CCTV LC (29 m 72 ch) and a single Up line of 69 ch runs from the latter point through the 55 yd Longlands Tunnel, beneath the main line to the Up side at Longlands Junction.

Northallerton has staggered platforms with the main station facilities on the Up side. Beyond the wide Down platform, which formerly had an outer face and a country end bay, the lower level ex-Leeds Northern route can be seen parallel and below. It passes beneath the main line and then heads north-east towards Eaglescliffe, the 1856 36 ch Up side link with the main line running between East Junction and High Junction. Northallerton box (30 m 8 ch) precedes High Junction (30 m 9 ch) on the East Coast Main Line and it is followed by Castle Hills Junction where the Redmire branch leaves. The wartime link from the Leeds Northern joined the main line here and its course can still be spotted. The wartime LN route platforms are also still in existence.

N.11 Northallerton-Eaglescliffe Line

From the ECML at Northallerton to the Middlesbrough-Saltburn line at Eaglescliffe. 14 m 54 ch

Running to the west of the Cleveland Hills, this line is part of an alternative coastal route to and from the Tyne and is used by through freight from the Tees and beyond. It originated with enabling Acts obtained by the Leeds & Thirsk Railway, later the Leeds Northern, in 1845 and 1846, and carried its first through services between Leeds and Stockton on 2 June 1852. These developed over the years until the line was carrying some interesting combinations which extended the basic Leeds-Stockton coverage west to Bradford and Liverpool and north to Sunderland, Newcastle and Berwick.

Along the Northallerton to Eaglescliffe section trains called at Brompton (27¾ m from Harrogate), Welbury (31 m), Picton (35¼ m) and Yarm (38¾ m). Until the last intermediate station closed in 1965 to end the local service activity these had, over the years, averaged about six trains each way daily. South of Northallerton the former Leeds Northern route lost its passenger trains on 16 March 1967 and was closed completely in 1969, but the northern sec-

tion retained a value as a cut-off, diversionary and freight route, and still carries the *Cleveland Executive* service between Sunderland and King's Cross.

The southern end of the line begins at Boroughbridge Junction CCTV LC (42 m 21 ch from Leeds), meeting point of the Up and Down links with the ECML at Longlands Junction. It continues via Romanby Road CCTV LC (42 m 38 ch) and Springwell Lane AOCR LC (42 m 65 ch) to Northallerton East Junction (42 m 79 ch), having passed under the East Coast Main Line in the process. The Up side double line connection from the ECML at High Junction joins the Leeds Northern route at East Junction after which it begins a modest climb, past Low Gates level crossing and box (43 m 24 ch), through Brompton AHB LC (44 m 57 ch) and through Long Lane crossing and its signal box (46 m 34 ch) to a summit near Welbury AHB LC (48 m 21 ch).

A succession of cuttings and embankments produces a gentle descent to Rounton Gates AHB LC (50 m 12 ch), with a level section then leading to the crossing and signal box at Picton (52 m 31 ch), former junction for the line to Battersby and the Esk Valley. More cuttings and embankments then mark the 1 in 170 descent to Yarm (see separate entry) where the 75 yd Yarm Tunnel (55 m 76 ch to 55 m 79 ch) and a viaduct crossing of the Tees precede Eaglescliffe South Junction (56 m 75 ch) with the Darlington line.

N.12 Normanton

Wincobank Junction, Sheffield-Leeds line, junction with Cudworth line. 185 m 11 ch from St Pancras

At the beginning of 1988 demolition contractors were at work at Normanton, clearing the buildings from the vast island platform and leaving it just a forlorn paved surface with a filled-in bay. At that time the location seemed torn between its past importance as an interchange point and the modern needs for local journeys. The sheer size of the platform area was a reminder of the fact that this was the first real junction station of the pioneer railway network in Yorkshire. It came to handle hundreds of trains a day, some halting for a refreshment stop, and the location also had freight yards, a locomotive shed and all the other paraphernalia of railway importance.

The trains of the North Midland Railway reached Normanton on 1 July 1840, capitalizing on the Stephenson philosophy of easy gradients and following the River Dearne and one of its tributaries for part of its northwards extension from Rotherham to Leeds. On the same day, the York & North Midland Railway completed its line from York, and Normanton became part of the first railway link between that city and London. Its junction status was then created by the arrival of the near-exhausted Manchester & Leeds Railway which opened from Hebden Bridge on 5 October 1840, although through trains from Manchester had to wait until the completion of Summit Tunnel and 1 March 1841.

In LMS and LNER days Normanton had an extensive and varied train service pattern. On the ex-M&L line this included many additional summer Saturday trains, eg, Bradford to Bridlington, Manchester to Scarborough, Liverpool to Newcastle etc; while on the Midland main line the *Isle of Man Boat Express* called, as did various Scottish trains. Add the local services and the justification for the sizeable station becomes even more apparent.

Normanton passengers now derive their service from the Sheffield-Barnsley-Wakefield-Leeds trains, and the longer-distance trains on its two main lines are now just a feature of the past. Today's services use the M&L route from Horbury Junction and join the North Midland route at Goose Hill Junction (50 m 31 ch from Manchester Victoria). An Up side signal box presides over the union of the two routes and their subsequent separation into Fast and Slow pairs for the progression through the station and its Footpath R/G level crossing (185 m 11 ch) and on to Altofts Junction (185 m 73 ch). There the Slow lines have a double connection with the fast pair, before the Leeds and York routes separate near the wooden Altofts Junction signal box (186 m).

The North Midland line used to leave Sheffield via Aldwarke North Junction (166 m 59 ch) and Dearne Valley North Junction (172 m 68 ch), where the 2 m 64 ch link from Grimesthorpe Colliery joined. The forward route was then through Cudworth (175 m 3 ch), Royston Junction (178 m 28 ch), Oakenshaw South Junction (181 m 77 ch)—with its links to Wakefield and Pontefract—Oakenshaw (182 m 35 ch) and then Goose Hill (184 m 56 ch). After an initial short-lived passenger closure on 7 October 1968, the mainstay of the route became the coal from Houghton Main, Grimesthorpe and Royston, but recent years have brought a second passenger closure and a general decline in activity.

The local passenger service used to call at Wath-on-Dearne (170¾ m), Darfield (173 m), Cudworth (176¾ m), Royston & Notton (179¼ m) and Sandal & Walton (183 m).

N.13   North Blyth Branch

Benton-Morpeth line, branch from Bedlington-Lynemouth line. 3 m 22 ch

The Blyth & Tyne system originally came into existence to overcome the shortcomings of Blyth harbour by transferring coal shipment traffic to the deeper waters of the Tyne, but harbour improvements by the NER revived the Blyth activity and some staith to vessel transfer still takes place there. Other shipping traffic also passes over this surviving freight line which originally came into being in 1867 and 1896 to handle coal from Ashington Colliery.

This line is double initially, with the two spurs from the Lynemouth branch—from West Sleekburn Junction and Marchey's House—joining near Winning signal box and LC (36 ch). The route continues to the box and crossing at Freemans (1 m 30 ch) where it becomes single to finish up as a One Train route through Cambois TMO LC (2 m 10 ch) and on to the end of the line at North Blyth (3 m 22 ch).

The railway activity around Blyth harbour used to consist of the passenger station and two yards to the south of the estuary, north and south staiths, and the loco sheds and dock connections on the north bank. The latter area survives to give connections to the power station, the staiths and the Alcan terminal, plus the Cambois loco depot. The latter provides local power and crews for coal trains to the south, plus the administrative control of the area.

N.14   North Shore—see Stockton

N.15   Norton-on-Tees

Northallerton-Newcastle line, junction with Ferryhill line. Norton-on-Tees South is 61 m 71 ch and East 62 m 19 ch from Leeds

Although there was a passenger station here at one time, the location now consists just of the triangular junction between the lines mentioned in the heading. At Norton-on-Tees South box the modestly-used double track freight route to Ferryhill departs via Norton-on-Tees West (33 ch) and the course of the 1833 Clarence Railway, leaving the Newcastle line to curve round to that same route eastwards at East Junction. The 29 ch section between the West and East boxes completes the triangle.

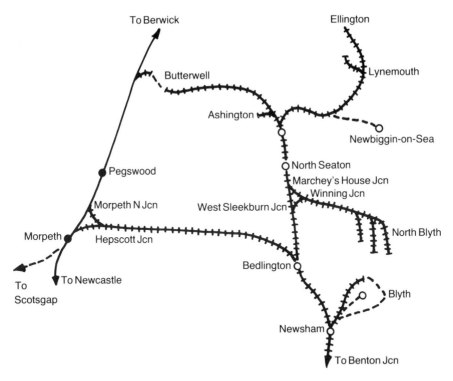

1930s scene at North Blyth staiths with a collier being loaded by chute.

South box remains operational but East box, a high brick and wood structure, is now closed and boarded up. There is another high signal box at Norton-on-Tees LC (62 m 63 ch), near the site of the former passenger halt.

N.16 Norwood Junction—see Newcastle-Carlisle Line

N.17 Nunthorpe—see Middlesbrough-Whitby Line

O.1 Oakenshaw—see Wakefield-Pontefract Line

O.2 Outwood—see Wakefield

P.1 Paddock Viaduct—see Huddersfield

P.2 Pannal—see Leeds-York Line

P.3 Pegswood
East Coast Main Line, between Morpeth and Alnmouth. 18 m 44 ch from Newcastle

The section of the East Coast Main Line through Pegswood was originally opened on 1 March 1847 and the location still has a station served by the Newcastle-Alnmouth/Berwick trains. It consists just of platforms and an overbridge.

Neighbouring Longhirst station was not so fortunate, losing its passenger services on 29 October 1951 and now comprising just a CCTV crossing (20 m 17 ch) and a

Down Refuge Siding amid remnants of the former station.

P.4 Pelaw
Northallerton-Newcastle line, junction with Ferryhill and Simonside lines. 98 m 7/16 ch from Leeds

Just south of the River Tyne, midway between Newcastle and the mouth of the river, Pelaw lies on the line opened by the Brandling Junction Railway in 1839 and now used by the half-hourly Newcastle-Sunderland/Middlesbrough trains. Pelaw itself no longer has a BR station but what is, in fact, the fourth station there is served by the trains of the Tyne & Wear Metro.

Following the opening of the BJR route on 30 August 1839, Pelaw's next railway was the route east along the bank of the Tyne to South Shields. Opened on 1 March 1872, this South Tyne route was to be electrified by the LNER and carry a 20-minute interval service calling at Hebburn (5½ m from Newcastle), Jarrow (6¾ m), Tyne Dock (9¼ m), High Shields (10¼ m) and South Shields (11 m) to the east of Pelaw. This mantle has now been taken over by the Metro system, but a single BR freight line survives on the north side of the PTE metals as far as Simonside.

Leaving Pelaw Junction (98 m 7/9 ch) the Simonside branch runs via Hebburn (1 m 50 ch), where a yard and shed survive, Jarrow (3 m), where the coal drops are still visible, and then on to Simonside (4 m 19 ch). The route is now used primarily to

An Up electric train at Hebburn in mid-1945. Note the range of connections and couplings on the buffer beam.

serve the Shell installation at Jarrow, although a rusting section does continue through to the empty and desolate wagon works buildings at Simonside.

The BR line to Sunderland and the double line freight route to Ferryhill pass beneath the Metro route at Pelaw, east of the latter's carriage sidings. The Ferryhill line dates from 1 September 1848 and from 1 October 1850 served for 20 years as part of the East Coast Main Line. It carried a passenger service to Durham and Ferryhill until 9 September 1963.

The Old Main Line from Ferryhill joins the Sunderland line at the second Pelaw Junction (98 m 16 ch). An early wagonway from Heworth Colliery to Pelaw Main Staiths ran a north easterly course nearby, while just along the Ferryhill route the Bowes Railway's Springwell-Jarrow line made its BR connection at Wardley.

P.5 Penistone

Barnsley-Huddersfield line. 13 m 36 ch from Huddersfield

Although still enjoying a useful, local, PTE-supported service between Sheffield and Huddersfield, Penistone is hardly the railway crossroads of former times. Then you could get a Bradford-Bournemouth service there, join the restaurant car express from Manchester (London Road) to Marylebone or take one of the more local services to Sheffield, Barnsley, Huddersfield, Doncaster, or even Hull. Summer Saturdays added trains to the Yorkshire and Lincolnshire coasts to the permutations.

The great Sheffield, Ashton-under-Lyne & Manchester Railway route across the Pennines via Woodhead and Penistone had been completed on 14 July 1845. It was then joined by the Huddersfield & Sheffield Junction company's line on 1 July 1850, with a branch from Barnsley Junction, Penistone to Barnsley proper coming into full use on 1 December 1859. Although L&Y-backed, the Huddersfield link was worked by the MS&L, successors to the SA&M and predecessors to the Great Central Railway, whose London extension was to lift the status of the Pennine route even further.

The original station at Penistone was about half a mile west of Huddersfield Junction, but it was replaced by a new station at the latter point on 1 February 1874. Ten years later, Penistone achieved unwelcome prominence when the derailment of an Up express resulted in the death of 24 passengers.

There was drama of another kind at Penistone on 20 September 1954 when the 1936 LNER 1,500 volt overhead electrification between Manchester and Sheffield was finally completed. The scheme, which had involved a new tunnel at Thurgoland as well as the six-year £3½ million works which produced a replacement for the Woodhead Tunnel, bore fruit for only 25 years. Declining cross-Pennine coal traffic resulted in the closure of the Woodhead route on 20 July 1981. Two years later, on 16 May 1983, the GC line between Sheffield and Penistone lost its service but, in compensation, the link between Penistone and Barnsley was restored after 13 years of closure.

Today Penistone has good links with the main rail network via Huddersfield—a 30-minute journey—and via Barnsley/Sheffield, with a 38-minute journey time to the latter. The ex-GCR mileage applies on the approach section between the former Barnsley Junction (29 m 13 ch) and Huddersfield Junction signal box (28 m 37 ch), but changes at the latter to 13 m 42 ch from Huddersfield. Between the viaduct and the station, rusting sidings and de-wired masts were still there in 1988 to act as a reminder of former times and the station, embracing the two arms of its junction, was clearly much too big for present needs. The sizeable main buildings in the vee of the junction are constructed in light brick, and although there are also outer platforms to each route and a passenger loop on the Huddersfield line, only the Huddersfield Down platform is normally used.

P.6 Pilmoor

East Coast Main Line, between York and Thirsk. 16 m from York

On the flat Plain of York, north towards Thirsk, today's East Coast Main Line runs flat and straight with few intermediate features. This has always been a high-speed stretch and the line that was opened by the Great North of England Railway in 1841 (goods traffic from 4 January and passengers from 30 March) is now a fast, four-track section carrying 125 mph services in a tradition of high-speed running.

North of York the tracks are paired with the Slow lines west of the Fast ones, but at Skelton Bridge (3 m 11 ch) this arrangement changes to the normal LNER pattern of Slow lines outside the Fast pair. There is an R/G level crossing at Beningbrough Footpath (7 m 1 ch) and crossovers near the modern looking Tollerton box (9 m 40 ch), but otherwise the only features of this section are a Pullman car lineside restaurant, some modest river crossings, and the lineside signs erected by the LNER to mark the halfway point between London and Edinburgh and those recording 200 miles still to be travelled.

Between York and Thirsk there were formerly intermediate stations at Beningbrough (5½ m from York), Tollerton (9¾ m), Alne (11¾ m), Raskelf (13¼ m), Pilmoor (16 m) and Sessay (18 m). Despite progressive quadrupling of the main line there was little scope for slow trains, and the least important stations had only two trains each way daily by the 1930s, with two more calling at the more important points. Alne, Raskelf and Pilmoor closed to passengers on 5 May 1958, Beningbrough (formerly Shipton) and Sessay on 15 September 1958, and Tollerton on 1 November 1965. A variety of docks, signal boxes and former station buildings still mark their sites.

Along this stretch of the main line, Pilmoor used to be important for the branches diverging east to Gilling, Pickering and Malton, and west to Boroughbridge and Knaresborough. The Pilmoor-Boroughbridge line was an early venture originated by the GNE and opened under its York & Newcastle successor on 17 June 1847. The original intention to serve Harrogate then lay in abeyance until the extension to Knaresborough on 1 April 1875.

On the east side of the main line the branch from Pilmoor to Malton opened on 19 May 1853. This was to develop into a through route from the North to Scarborough which only ended when the derailment of a parcels train at Pilmoor severed the junction in 1963. A Ryedale Railway Company was formed to build a line beyond Gilling, along the River Rye, to Helmsley and then east to Kirby Moorside. After a period of squabbling between local interests and the NER, harmony eventually emerged and trains replaced the NER

horse bus between Gilling and Helmsley from 9 October 1871. It then took another three years before the line reached Kirby Moorside, with opening throughout to Pickering being achieved on 1 April 1875.

Pilmoor's branches left the main line south of the station, first the one to Knaresborough, then the curve towards Gilling and finally, from 9 October 1871 when the Ryedale line reached Helmsley, the southern curve from the York direction. A proposed link between the east and west branches did not materialize although earthworks, a bridge and some signals were provided, the latter coming to be used for testing drivers' eyesight.

The York-Pickering train service gave the main line stations from York to Raskelf an extra two stopping trains each way, while two more Pickering services called only at Alne on the main line section. After using the southern curve at Pilmoor all the trains then continued via Husthwaite Gate (18¾ m), Coxwold (20¼ m) and Ampleforth (22¾ m) to Gilling (25¼ m), followed by a section parallel with the Malton branch and then on to Nunnington (28¼ m), Helmsley (31¾ m), Nawton (34½ m), Kirby Moorside (37 m), Sinnington (40 m) and Pickering (44 m)—1 hour 40 minutes in all. The Ryedale line passenger service ceased from 2 February 1953, with goods closure on the surviving section to Kirby Moorside on 10 August 1964.

The other line needing a mention here is the 2½ mile Easingwold Railway, which opened its branch from Alne on 27 July 1891 and continued to serve the small market town until 29 November 1948 (freight closure 27 December 1957). By that time the number of trains using the branch bay at Alne had dropped from the original 11 each way down to seven and eventually to two. A simple railway with one locomotive, a single line with two crossings, and a modest terminus, the Easingwold Railway served its agricultural community well for 66 years.

The East Coast Main Line at Pilmoor in 1943 with the line to Boroughbridge and Knaresborough on the right.

P.7   Pontefract

Pontefract Monkhill is on the Wakefield/
Leeds-Goole line 56 m 48 ch from Man-
chester Victoria, and Pontefract Baghill
on the Sheffield-York line 4 m 31 ch from
Milford Junction.

Pontefract's first station was opened on 1
April 1848 on the Wakefield, Pontefract &
Goole line which was to become the Lancashire & Yorkshire Railway's trunk east-
west route. In addition to serving the
historic, castled town of Pontefract, it carried great quantities of coal to Goole for
shipment and L&Y expresses to and from
Liverpool. Pontefract station, later named
Monkhill, continues to serve the Pontefract
community, although in more recent years
the Wakefield-Goole/Doncaster services
have been replaced by Leeds-Goole trains.
As a consequence of this change Pontefract
Tanshelf, about a mile west of Monkhill,
was closed on 2 January 1967.

The other Pontefract station, known as
Baghill from 1936, received its first
passenger trains on 1 July 1879 with the
opening of the Swinton & Knottingley route
to link the Midland and North Eastern
companies. This, too, remains open and
carries a Sheffield-York service.

The original WP&G route from Wakefield remains open for freight and is joined
by the Castleford line, used by the Leeds-
Goole trains, at Pontefract West Junction
(56 m 36 ch). Tanshelf lay on the Wakefield
side of this junction which is followed by
the surviving Monkhill station (56 m 48

ch), now reduced to bare platforms and a
footbridge. There is an additional goods
line and traces of a former bay and of the
curve round to the S&K station, with the
route then continuing on to Pontefract
Monkhill Goods Junction (57 m 43 ch)
where the connection to Ferrybridge power
station departs.

On the S&K line, Baghill station retains
its original brick buildings in the standard
pattern for the route. These are on the
Down side and there is a long brick shelter
opposite. The former York end bay and the
brick goods shed can also be seen.

On the L&Y route signalling control is by
Prince of Wales box as far as Goods Junction, and then Knottingley box takes over.
On the S&K the Pontefract section is controlled by Moorthorpe and Ferrybridge
signal boxes.

P.8   Pontop Crossing—see Boldon

P.9   Poppleton—see Leeds-York Line

P.10   Port Clarence—see Billingham-
Seal Sands Storage Line

P.11   Potters Grange Junction—see
Goole

P.12   Prudhoe—see Newcastle-Carlisle
Line

R.1   Ravensthorpe—see Manchester-
Leeds Line

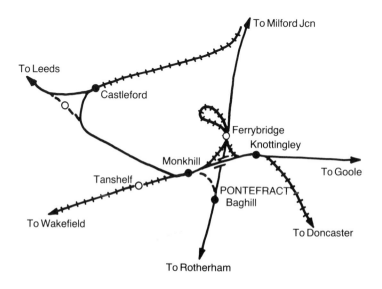

R.2   Redcar

Darlington-Saltburn line, between Middlesbrough and Saltburn. Redcar Central is 22 m 64 ch and Redcar East 23 m 60 ch from Darlington

The Middlesbrough & Redcar Railway opened its line to a terminus in the centre of Redcar on 4 June 1846. Although nominally independent, its backers were actually the Stockton & Darlington and Great North of England concerns and it could have been no surprise when the M&R was leased to the former in 1847.

On 17 August 1861 the Stockton & Darlington further extended its east-west route mileage by opening an extension from Redcar to Saltburn West Junction, starting from a point ahead of the original Redcar terminus which was displaced by the present Redcar Central location. The 1846 station was closed from 19 August 1861, but part of the access route remained in use as a coal depot.

Redcar today fulfils a residential and relaxation role aided by its trains to Darlington and Bishop Auckland which combine to provide a half-hourly service. The railway route approaches the town across Coatham Marsh, past the trackbed of a former freight route, and into Redcar Central station. This is an interesting, period location with a train shed and support wall reminiscent of G.T. Andrews but almost certainly by William Peachey. The tall, LNER era signal box near the barrier crossing (22 m 71 ch) looks quite modern by comparison.

After Church Lane CCTV LC (23 m 20 ch), the raised wooden platforms and shelters of Redcar East (23 m 60 ch) serve the 'retirement' end bungalows of this part of the town; the sea can be seen from the trains as they head on for Marske and Saltburn.

R.3   Redmire Branch

East Coast Main Line, branch from Castle Hills Junction, Northallerton. 22 m 14 ch

Just over 22 miles of the former Wensleydale branch line survive as a single freight line to Redmire, used for conveying trainloads of limestone from the Tarmac operation at that point. The route is worked on the One Train basis and is controlled by Northallerton signal box. The maximum overall line speed is 40 mph and there are 11 crossings to be negotiated.

Access to the branch is via Castle Hills Junction at Northallerton over the original connection from the Darlington direction, the mileage then jumping from 28 to 48 chains to recognize its previous calculation from the Northallerton direction via the 1882 Inner Curve. A variety of AOCL, TMO and traditional crossings then follow, at Yafforth (1 m 49 ch), Ainderby Gates (2 m 44 ch), Ainderby (2 m 71 ch), Scuton (4 m 26 ch), Ham Hall (4 m 61 ch), Leeming Bar (5 m 64 ch), Aiskew (6 m 34 ch), Bedale (7 m 42 ch), Crakehall (9 m 55 ch), Finghall Lane (13 m 17 ch) and Wensley (19 m 65 ch), with the line ending at Redmire limestone plant (22 m 34 ch). A Travelling Chargeman who rides in the rear locomotive cab draws keys for himself and the guard from Low Gates signal box and these are used for the TMO crossings, the chargeman unlocking the padlock and the guard relocking it after the train has drawn forward.

The route originated with a local line out from Northallerton to the Great North Road at Leeming Bar opened on 6 March 1848, extended to Bedale on 1 February 1855, and continued west to Leyburn on 24 November 1855 for goods and 18 May 1856 for passengers. After passing into North Eastern Railway hands in 1858, the route was extended some 20 years later to provide a link with the Midland Railway's new Settle & Carlisle enterprise. The section west from Leyburn to Askrigg was brought into use on 1 February 1877 and the link to the Midland's short line from Hawes Junction to Hawes was opened in the following year (goods 1 June, passengers 1 October).

Five trains a day in each direction was the standard late-1930s pattern for the branch, taking just under two hours for the 39¾ mile run from Northallerton through to Garsdale. On the way the trains served Ainderby (3 m), Scruton (4½ m), Leeming Bar (5¾ m), Bedale (7½ m), Crakehall (9¾ m), Jervaulx (11¼ m), Finghall Lane (13¼ m), Constable Burton (14½ m), Spennithorne (16¼ m), Leyburn (17½ m), Wensley (20 m), Redmire (22 m), Aysgarth (25 m), Askrigg (29½ m) and then the joint station at Hawes. Passenger traffic was always modest, but the route did well with stone, milk and horsebox movements and with summer excursion business.

The Wensleydale branch closed to passengers on 26 April 1954 and its goods facilities were withdrawn piecemeal in the 1960s. Complete closure of the section west of Redmire dates from 27 April 1964, leaving just the limestone operation to sustain the route, together with the occasional excursion special to climb the dales gradients and maintain a tradition of bringing visitors to their beautiful uplands.

A bridge at the Redmire end of the branch was attacked by Hurricane Charlie in 1986 and this was followed by some revision of the working there. At about the same time Class 47 traction was replaced by using two Class 20 locomotives, and train lengths were increased from 24 to 33 hoppers.

R.4 Riding Mill—see Newcastle-Carlisle Line

R.5 Riverside Branch

East Coast Main Line, branch from Riverside Junction, Newcastle. 4 m 29 ch

By 1988 this line along the north bank of the Tyne east of Newcastle was virtually out of use, with only the junction just beyond Manors and some rusting rails along its course to help recall the busy passenger service it once carried and the variety of freight sidings it served.

By the 1930s the route, which had originally opened on 1 May 1879, was carrying an intensive interval passenger service which called at Manors East (½ m) on the main line and then, on the branch, Byker (1½ m), St Peters (2½ m), St Anthonys (3¼ m), Walker (4¼ m), Carville (5¾ m), Point Pleasant (6½ m), Willington Quay (7 m), Percy Main (8 m), North Shields (9¼ m) and Tynemouth (10¼ m). Those trains covering the whole route took 28-30 minutes for their journey, but the passenger service ended on 23 July 1973 and the route was not included in the Metro scheme, partly because of the industrial and freight activity of the area it served.

In the pre-decline years the Riverside branch served the Swan Hunter yards at Walker and Carville, running from paired arrival and departure sidings at Riverside Junction through the 150 yd Byker Tunnel (13 to 20 ch) to the ground frame at St Peters, and then on as a One Train single line through the 182 yd Walker Tunnel (2 m 48 ch to 2 m 56 ch) to Carville level crossing (4 m 29 ch).

R.6 Royal Border Bridge—see Berwick

R.7 Ruswarp—see Middlesbrough-Whitby Line

R.8 Ryhope Grange

Northallerton-Newcastle line, junction with Hendon and Hawthorn branches. 87 m 63 ch from Leeds

The two surviving freight branches from Ryhope Grange mark the course of the area's first railway, that of the Durham & Sunderland which opened on 5 July 1836 for mineral traffic. Eighteen years later the present main line from the south was born with the opening of the Marquis of Londonderry's line from Seaham. This also had a terminus in the South Dock area of Sunderland, although the two routes ran separately between there and Ryhope Grange. The section of the main line north from Ryhope Grange was opened on 4 August 1879.

The signal box at Ryhope Grange controls the Newcastle-Middlesbrough passenger service on the main line plus the coal traffic over both branches. It stands on the Down side near a NER sign board displaying the junction name. Holding sidings then parallel the start of the One Train single line branch inland which betrays its origins in the

The Tyne at Wallsend in the shipbuilding days and with the Riverside line and its sidings just visible.

distance of 21 m 31 ch applying at the junction. From there the route runs via AOCL
level crossings at Seaton (18 m 34 ch),
Seaton Bank Head (17 m 74 ch) and Murton Lane (16 m 27 ch) to the boundary (15
m 44 ch) with National Coal's Hawthorn
Combined Mine and Coke Plant. Seaton
Bank is a reminder that the route is heavily
graded and was originally worked by winding engines, while Murton was a station
until the passenger service finally ceased on
5 January 1953.

The branch from Ryhope Grange towards
South Dock is single at first, passing
Grangetown open crossing (30 ch) and
becoming double in advance of Londonderry signal box (1 m 28 ch). In addition to
remembering the nobleman whose coal
promoted the original line, the frame here
controls access to the jetty lines, while that
at Hendon (1 m 53 ch) recalls the site of the
early D&S terminus and gives access to
South Bottom and the South Dock Petro-
fina depot. Track Circuit Block applies at
the start of the branch and No Block regulations at the end, where local movements
are in the hands of the train crew plus shunter
and bankrider as required.

S.1   Saltaire
Leeds-Skipton line, between Shipley and
Keighley. 206 m 51 ch from St Pancras

The line between Shipley and Keighley was
opened on 16 March 1847 but Saltaire did
not get a station until a decade later. It then
lasted until 22 March 1965 when passenger
services were withdrawn until the present
station was opened on 10 April 1984.

At one period Up expresses slipped a
Bradford portion at Saltaire, but the location is better known for the huge mill
which processed alpaca and mohair, and
was the central feature of Sir Titus Salt's

model development combining employment
and housing for over 2,000 work people.
The impressive stone complex of Salts
(Saltaire) Ltd lies on the north side of the
station. To the south, beyond ornate iron
fencing, lie the streets of enlightened period
housing, with equally period names like
Fanny Street and Herbert Street.

Today's station at Saltaire has modest
stone shelters harmonizing with its environ-
ment, and an excellent service of Bradford/
Leeds-Skipton/Keighley trains. Traces of its
former quadruple-track status are still visible.

S.2   Saltburn
Terminus of Darlington-Saltburn line.
27 m 57 ch from Darlington

At one time Saltburn had a reputation as a
haunt of smugglers, but had lived this down
by the time the Stockton & Darlington
Railway's extension from Redcar was
opened on 18 August 1861. Over the next
four years the rail network west of Guisborough was gradually extended out to
Brotton and Skinningrove in search of
additional ironstone traffic, and this network to the south of Saltburn was connected
with the Tees-side line from 1 June 1872 by
a link from Saltburn West Junction to the
Guisborough line near Brotton. This was
eventually to become part of one of the
routes to Whitby and it remains open
today, albeit for freight only, to serve the
Boulby Potash Mine.

From Saltburn West Junction only a
single line is operational for the final stretch
into Saltburn station. Only one platform is
now in use there, although an additional
platform line and a couple of sidings remain
in situ. Beyond the buffer stops, the pleasant 1862-4 stone terminal building has
been converted into a small specialist shopping and information centre.

Saltburn's former station buildings now house shopping and information facilities.

*Trains to and from Saltburn now use the for-
mer excursion platform, but rationalization
has spared the NER trespass notice.*

Saltburn station lies along one side of a
square, in the centre of this pleasant, period
town which retains a lot of nineteenth-
century charm, including glazed canopies
supported by decorative ironwork and
covering the pavements outside some of the
older shops. The town owes its original
development to the (S&D) Saltburn
Improvement Company, which also built
the large Zetland Hotel beyond the station.
Although empty and up for sale at the
beginning of 1988, the hotel remained a
symbol of past style and affluence. The
covered pathway from the hotel to the station
survives, although the latter's main platform has now been absorbed in the shopping

complex, leaving the Darlington trains—
half-hourly, with every second service
extended to Bishop Auckland—to use what
used to be an excursion platform.

S.3   Saltmarshe

*Doncaster-Hull line, between Goole and
Gilberdyke Junction. 3 m 49 ch from
Gilberdyke Junction*

Saltmarshe was the subject of a closure pro-
posal at the beginning of 1984. This arose
from the problem of funding costly repairs
to Goole swing bridge. If the matter had
gone unresolved it would have led to the
closure of the section between Goole and
Gilberdyke Junction. As it is, Saltmarshe
survives and is served by the Hull-
Doncaster local trains.

The station lies on the section of line
opened by the NER in 1869 and consists
simply of platforms with shelters, a barrier
crossing and a signal box at the Doncaster
end. On the stretch to Gilberdyke Junction
there is a level crossing at Green Oak Goit
(1 m 42 ch) and other farm crossings.

S.4   Scarborough

*Terminus of routes from York and Hull.
42 m 6 ch from York*

The tumuli on the heights around Scarborough testify to its early origins back in
the Neolithic era, and both Romans and
Vikings had some form of settlement there.
The castle built in the twelfth century was
sited on the headland which separates the
north and south bays and gives shelter to
the double harbour. Later the town developed as a spa, and then the railway age
gave it the opportunity to capitalize on the
seaside holiday habit and grow into one of
the major east coast resorts. Its attractions
are as diverse as a natural amphitheatre and

A view of Scarborough station showing the original extension on the right.

A well-loaded NER charabanc at Scarborough with a load of passengers for Filey.

four cliff railways. Also of special interest is the North Bay Railway, a miniature line opened over 50 years ago and using petrol locomotives with a Gresley 'Pacific' outline.

The various early schemes to provide Scarborough with a rail service crystallized into the York & North Midland Railway's line from York which opened on 7 July 1845, and its route south from Seamer, opened to Filey on 5 October 1846 and through to Bridlington and Hull on 20 October of the following year. About that time there was also talk of a third railway for the town, another coastal line, but this time north to Whitby. However, it was not until the 1870s that anything concrete was done and then completion was not until 16 July 1885. After 14 years of rather shaky existence, the Scarborough & Whitby Railway was purchased by the NER to become part of a coastal route all the way to the Tees.

Three years before the completion of the Whitby line a single line had been opened from Seamer to Pickering on 1 May 1882.

Railway traffic to and from Scarborough expanded rapidly over the years, becoming very heavy indeed on summer Saturdays when a host of long-distance through workings arrived and departed via the York line. The day, half-day and evening excursion business was also considerable, and the railway presence in Scarborough expanded to match its growing traffic levels.

The original and main station, Scarborough Central, took over the area allocated to the first goods shed to create additional platforms, and was then provided with some longer platforms and excursion facilities on the inland side to increase its capacity still further. A separate excursion station, named Londesborough Road, was brought into use on 8 June 1908, and extra stabling and loco servicing facilities were also provided beyond the single line tunnel of the Whitby line.

All the major seaside termini called for special railway operating skills at peak periods: releasing engines for coal and water, stabling, cleaning and recalling coaching stock, juggling with variations from booked engine, crew and stock diagrams, and controlling large numbers of arriving or long queues of departing passengers. Ticketing, luggage, seat reservations and a dozen other activities all added their complications, and Scarborough was harder to work than many places because its platforms varied greatly in the size of train they could accommodate, and movements to and from the Whitby line all involved a reversal. Scarborough was also notable as having the longest station seat in Britain, with room for up to 200 weary trippers to rest while waiting for their trains home.

In later years the service north from Scarborough ran through to Middlesbrough, and its exit from Scarborough was simplified by using an extra platform created at the south end of Platform 1. The

Whitby trains then reversed at Londes-borough Road to pass through Gallows Close Tunnel and then head out through Scarborough's suburbs to the viaduct over Sea Cut and on to the following Scalby station (2½ m). After Cloughton (5 m) the route stuck to the cliff tops, curving through Hayburn Wyke (7 m), dipping over Thorny Beck to Stainton Dale (8 m) and then head-ing for Ravenscar (10¼ m) where some hard engine work was demanded. The tun-nel at Ravenscar was followed by a steeply-graded moorland section curving through Fyling Hall (13½ m) to Robin Hood's Bay (15¼ m), with another sweeping curve to Hawsker (18½ m) and then high over the Esk by a long viaduct to reach Whitby West Cliff (21½ m). A shuttle service catered for those detraining for the main station down in the town, leaving the high level trains to add another two hours to the 70 minutes already consumed on the overall 58 mile journey to Middlesbrough. After a long fight, the route was closed on 6 March 1965.

The Scarborough-Pickering service was the first railway loss to the town, its closure dating from 5 June 1950. Beyond Seamer this modest line turned north east to a cross-ing of the Derwent near Forge Valley (6½ m) and then went on south of the rising moors through Sawdon (9¾ m), Snainton (11½ m), Ebberston (14 m) and Thornton Dale (16¾ m) to Pickering (19¾ m from Scarborough). The '30s service offered 6 or 7 trains each way on weekdays, with one running through to Gilling. A section at the Pickering end remained open for stone from Thornton Dale until 10 August 1964.

The approach to Scarborough today still reveals the extent of the siding accom-modation it used to need. There is an oil siding on the Down side, and an engine turntable funded by Scarborough Council to facilitate the summer steam specials operated in recent years; but the coal drops are empty now, as is the once-busy Up side accommodation. Londesborough Road, closed on 25 August 1963, still stands on the Down side, complete with its long bay and through platform. Falsgrave signal box (41 m 63 ch) is then followed by the tunnel of the former Whitby lines.

The interesting Scarborough terminus, currently undergoing major refurbishment, is largely the G.T. Andrews original. The long roadside block is of ashlar construc-tion, relieved by the end and centre pavilions and with the 1884 clock tower dominant. Beyond lies the roofed train shed, with the goods shed and excursion extensions very apparent, and with some delightful minor details like the lettering above the gents' toilet. Platforms 3, 4 and 5 are used for the Hull and York/Leeds services, some of the latter being extended to Manchester and Liverpool.

S.5 Seabanks Branch—see Dawdon

S.6 Seaburn

Northallerton-Newcastle line, between Sunderland and Gateshead. 91 m 33 ch from Leeds

Seaburn, which lies on the 1836 Brandling Junction Railway route, serves the Carley Hill and Fulwell communities of the north

Scarborough station decorated for Coronation year.

side of the River Wear, and the coastal area backing Whitburn Bay. It is served by the local Sunderland-Newcastle trains, with calls by some of the Middlesbrough services in the peak, and consists of platforms and shelters with access from the Up side ticket office buildings above. These date from the 1937 opening of the station and were provided with a Passimeter which housed the booking office staff in a glazed office between entrance and exit barriers.

S.7   Seaham

Eaglescliffe-Newcastle line, between Hartlepool and Sunderland. 84 m 44 ch from York

Not long after it had hosted the marriage of Lord Byron, Seaham was to see the Marquis of Londonderry commission a new harbour to serve as a point of shipment for coal mined at his collieries inland. This was brought into use in 1831, but before long the volume of coal brought in by the South Hetton Wagonway was overtaxing the harbour facilities and a railway link to Sunderland was needed to cope with the extra shipment business. The Marquis built this as well, opening his Seaham & Sunderland Railway at the beginning of 1854 and running between its own station at Seaham and the NER at Sunderland. The railway carried passengers as well as coal, and went on to have a useful independent existence for nearly half a century.

The Londonderry line was eventually acquired by the North Eastern for £387,000, although the South Hetton line remained separate and the former S&S equipment passed into the hands of the Seaham Harbour Dock Company which continued its shipment coal activity. The North Eastern began working the former Londonderry railway on 6 October 1900 and five years later, from 1 April 1905, brought the coastal route from West Hartlepool into use by completing the gap immediately south of Seaham. Seaham gained a new through station from this process and the old S&S station, later called Seaham Harbour, was eventually confined to handling the local Seaham-Sunderland service. This was still operating at a level of some 14 trains each way daily prior to closure on 11 September 1939.

The approach to Seaham is via Dawdon Junction (84 m 11 ch) where the connection from the aptly-named Seabanks Colliery joins. This comprises a 15 mph double No Block line from Seabanks (73 ch), through Bone Mill open crossing (1 m 20 ch) to the junction (1 m 65 ch), which is followed by the controlling Dawdon signal box (84 m 22 ch). There is a view of the sea on this section preceding Seaham and the fact that it is coal country is apparent even from the beaches.

There is a separate No Block line on the section between Dawdon and Seaham. This used to be busy with coal destined for the harbour connection, with additional traffic coming off the NCB South Hetton line, the last section of which passes beneath the BR route on the approach to Seaham station (84 m 44 ch).

The platforms and brick and wood shelters of Seaham station are served by the Middlesbrough-Newcastle trains, with the signal box there also controlling some originating and terminating peak services. Beyond Seaham the line continues to Hall Dene crossing and signal box (85 m 24 ch) where the connection from Vane Tempest Colliery joins on the Up side. The Marquis of Londonderry's private station was at Hall Dene and the decorative building near the barrier crossing bears witness to the private origins of this piece of modern railway.

S.8   Seamer

York-Scarborough line, junction with Hull line. 39 m 17 ch from York

Seamer is a junction rather than an interchange point, passengers usually changing between the York and Hull lines at Scarborough where a full range of station facilities is available. Even so, Seamer is significant as the point at which the two routes meet, and as such enjoys the services of the trains on both lines.

The York-Scarborough line opened on 7 July 1845 and by 5 October of the following year the Hull line was open as far as Filey. Seamer's third railway, the single line NER branch to Pickering, was not opened until 1 May 1882 and it was to last only until the beginning of the railway network shrinkage, closing to passengers on 5 June 1950.

The 'junior' routes joined the line from York on the inland side of the station at Seamer, the surviving junction there being controlled by Seamer West signal box (38 m 63 ch). Some sidings and a dock survive near the station itself, which consists of an island platform with the old brick station buildings and an LNER-era signal box at the country end. The latter is Seamer East (39 m 17 ch) whose barrier crossing is now largely redundant because of a new road overbridge. Worth noting near its replacement is the old, and probably original, signal box.

S.9   Seaton Carew
Northallerton-Newcastle line, between Stockton and Hartlepool. 69 m 36 ch from Leeds

Seaton Carew's simple platforms and shelters on the 1840 Stockton & Hartlepool line are served by some of the Middlesbrough-Newcastle and Darlington-Hartlepool trains. The remains of a former dock are visible on the Up side and the Up Goods Loop from Cliff House ends just before the country end underbridge.

S.10   Seaton-on-Tees Branch
Northallerton-Newcastle line, branch from Seaton Snook Junction. 1 m 51 ch

The North Eastern Railway opened this short goods branch to the north bank of the Tees on 1 June 1907 and it came to serve a more recent purpose as the rail connection to Hartlepool Nuclear Power Station. It

survives as a lightly-used single line operated under the One Train regulations and controlled by Cliff House signal box. The connection with the Stockton-Hartlepool line leaves at Seaton Snook Junction (68 m 60 ch from Leeds) and runs, with a maximum permissible line speed of 25 mph, via an AOCL LC at Graythorpe (25 ch) and the open West level crossing (1 m 35 ch) to the end of the BR line at Seaton-on-Tees (1 m 51 ch).

S.12   Seaton   Snook   Junction—see Seaton-on-Tees Branch

S.12 Selby
Leeds-Hull line, junction with former East Coast Main Line from Temple Hirst. Station 30 m 79 ch from Hull, South Junction 174 m 11 ch from King's Cross

The Normans were the first to develop the wet plain on which Selby stood, and the present abbey was built between 1097 and 1123. The town later became a woollen centre and prospered with the drainage of the marshes and the growth of shipping and

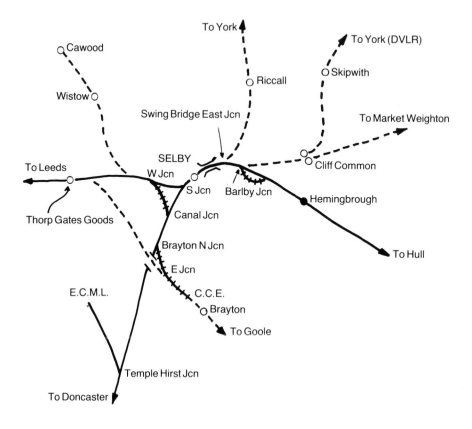

Shunting at Selby, with a two-arm upper quadrant siding signal.

shipbuilding along the River Ouse. The latter attracted the town's first railway, the Leeds & Selby, which opened to a station on the west bank of the river on 22 September 1834, passengers travelling on to Hull by paddle steamer down the Ouse and out along the Humber estuary.

The original intention had been to link Leeds and Hull by rail, and this came nearer achievement with the incorporation of the Hull & Selby Railway which eventually opened its line on 2 July 1840, crossing the Ouse on a bascule-bridge to join the L&S in a new, through station; the displaced terminus became a goods depot. At this time through trains also began running to and from York via the Milford connection with the York & North Midland line, and from 1 August 1848 that company—which by now had leased both the L&S and

the H&S—opened a line from Selby to Market Weighton (where it met the 1847 Y&NM line from York). Under NER ownership the York-Market Weighton line was completed to Beverley on 1 May 1865, and from 1 May 1890 that company worked the Scarborough, Bridlington & West Riding Junction Railway's new Driffield-Market Weighton line.

On 2 January 1871, new lines between the Great Northern Railway's system at Shaftholme Junction and Selby and then north to Chaloners Whin Junction, south of York, had put Selby on the East Coast Main Line. It had lost the York-Hull traffic when the 1865 route via Market Weighton was completed, but became part of the main route from the south to Bridlington and Filey, and on to Scarborough in 1890.

Two light railways were built in the Selby area. The first to be opened was the Cawood, Wistow & Selby Light Railway, a single line opened on 16 February 1898 and running for 5½ miles north-west to the small agricultural township of Cawood. Initially the trains on the light railway ran parallel to the ex-L&S route and into a separate platform near Selby West, but the North Eastern bought the smaller concern in 1900 and ran the light railway trains into the main Selby station from 1904. Initially tank engines were used, but from 1908 various types of railcar handled the traffic until passenger services ceased from 1 January 1930. Goods traffic, particularly potatoes, coal and sugar-beet, continued on the line until its final closure on 2 May 1960.

The other light railway in the Selby area was the Derwent Valley Light Railway, an unusual enterprise in that its prime movers were the Riccall and Escrick Rural District Councils. Although the project obtained approval from the Light Railway Commissioners in 1899, opening from York (Layerthorpe) to Cliff Common (for Selby) was not achieved until 21 July 1913. The DVLR then only operated regular passenger services until 1926, but excursions from the line continued for some years and there was a brief revival of steam services for enthusiasts a few years ago.

In the period immediately prior to the 1926 closure the passenger trains were made up of Ford petrol railbuses which called at Osbaldwick, Murton Lane (2½ miles from Layerthorpe), Dunnington Halt, Dunnington (4¼ m), Elvington (6½ m), Wheldrake (9 m), Cottingwith (10½ m), Thorganby (11½ m) and Skipwith (13 m) on the 16 mile journey. The link to Selby from Cliff Common was then by NER train, although at one period DVLR vehicles were worked through.

After 1926 the light railway continued to work its freight traffic, and survived nationalization as well as the 1923 grouping. The section south of Wheldrake was closed at the beginning of 1965 and the system subsequently cut back towards York, as the company dropped the 'Light' from its title and concentrated on developing its land for the handling and storage of coal, oil, grain, fertilizers and other rail-associated commodities. Rail traffic has now ceased.

The line east from Selby to Market Weighton carried a significant number of through trains to and from Scarborough, especially on summer Saturdays. These called only at Market Weighton on leaving Selby, not stopping again until Driffield or Bridlington. The local trains were considerably fewer, around three each way daily. They called at Cliff Common (3¼ m), Menthorpe Gate (5 m), Bubwith (6¼ m), High Field (7¼ m), Foggathorpe (9 m), Holme Moor (12 m), Everingham (13¾ m), Market Weighton (17¼ m), Enthorpe (12 m), Middleton-on-the-Wolds (24 m), Bainton (25½ m), Southburn (28¼ m), Driffield (31 m) and then on to Bridlington (42½ m), Filey (56 m) and Scarborough (65 m). The local service ended on 20 September 1954 and through trains on 14 June 1965.

Selby's other line was the 1910 route south east to Goole. Part of the NER's

expansion in the first decade of this century, the line cost the company £¼ million but helped to relieve the Hull line of some of its heavy load of South Yorkshire coal. Passenger stations were provided at Barlow (3½ m), Drax Hales (6 m) and Airmyn & Rawcliffe (8½ m), and the 12 mile journey took 26 minutes. After passenger closure on 15 June 1964 the Selby end was originally kept open as far as Drax, but was then cut back further until only a short line remained to serve a CCE tip near Brayton.

On the Leeds-Hull line the approach to Selby is via the signal box and level crossing (40 ch) and then West Junction (36 ch) from which there is a 32 ch single line spur round to Canal Junction on the former main line. The original CW&S station lay near here and was known as Brayton Gates, but today's line simply curves round to meet the Doncaster route in a welter of tracks at South Junction (0/31 m 12 ch). The former loco depot lay nearby.

The 1834 station at Selby cost £10,300, but did little more than give passengers and goods some cover while loading and unloading. It was displaced by a through station when the Hull line was opened, but there were more changes in 1871 when Selby achieved main line status. The present station dates from a round of improvements in 1891 when the swing bridge was also installed. The main brick station buildings on the Down side are fairly plain and functional, but the broad canopies rest on ornate and interesting supports.

The former four tracks through Selby

A typical G.T. Andrews station, at Market Weighton on the route from Selby to Scarborough.

station (30 m 79 ch) have now been
reduced to three, and then two over the
swing bridge (30 m 70 ch). The former
main line to Chaloners Whin used to veer
off immediately at East Junction and then
continue through the stations at Riccall
(178½ m), Escrick (181¼ m) and Naburn
(184 m), although the latter two closed in
1953 and 1958. On the surviving Hull line,
Barlby LC (30 m 74 ch) marks the junction
with the old Market Weighton line and is
followed by an active private siding location with its own diesel motive power.

The Hull-Chester/Bangor trains serve
Selby hourly, and it also has Hull-York slow
services and trains south over the old main
line to Temple Hirst and on to Doncaster.

S.13   Shaftholme
*East Coast Main Line, junction with
Knottingley line. 160 m 16 ch from
King's Cross*

The original East Coast route to York ran
from Doncaster to Knottingley over a
stretch of Lancashire & Yorkshire Railway
metals, and then made connection at Burton Salmon with the York & North Midland
system. From 2 January 1871 the route
was shortened by the opening of a line from
Chaloners Whin Junction, south of York,
through Selby, to Askern Junction, now
Shaftholme Junction.

The line from Shaftholme Junction to
Knottingley survives as a freight route, but
the main flows over the junction are now the
speeding HST services (and soon the elec-
trics) of the East Coast Main Line. Just 32
ch north of Shaftholme they encounter a
second junction where the 49 ch double line
spur from the Stainforth-Adwick route
joins the main line at Joan Croft Junction
LC (160 m 48 ch).

It is hard now to imagine a stopping service on the main line north of Doncaster but
there was one until the 1950s, although the
intermediate stations at Arksey (158 m),
Moss (163 m), Balne (166 m), Heck (168¼
m) and Temple Hirst (169¾ m) had to
make do with three trains a day each way
even in the '30s. Today the only intermediate locations between Joan Croft and
Temple Hirst junctions are crossings at
Dormer Green (161 m 23 ch), Noblethorpe
(161 m 35 ch), Barcroft (162 m 14 ch),
Heyworth (162 m 55 ch), Moss (163 m 2
ch), Fenwick (164 m 14 ch), Balne Lowgate
(165 m 22 ch) and Balne (165 m 70 ch).

The old link from the Great Central to
the Hull & Barnsley crossed the ECML
just before the Adwick-Stainforth line over-

bridge, Shaftholme and Joan Croft junctions then preceding the long, straight
stretch to Temple Hirst. On the latter, some
early crossing houses remain and the yard,
signal box and station house at Moss are
still apparent. Soon after, the River Went is
crossed and then the Aire & Calder
Navigation.

S.14   Shaftholme   Junction-
Knottingley Line
*East Coast Main Line, branch from
Shaftholme Junction. 10 m 55 ch*

Now a freight route, this line was one of the
original segments in what is now the East
Coast Main Line and carried its passenger
expresses between London and York for 21
years. Although the Great Northern Railway
succeeded in securing powers for its main
line to Doncaster in the 1846 session of
Parliament, it faired badly with a supplementary approach for branches to Sheffield and to the West Riding. Fortunately,
help was at hand in the form of the
Wakefield, Pontefract & Goole concern
which had obtained powers for a branch
from its line at Knottingley to join the GN
at Askern Junction, north of Doncaster.
The WP&G was absorbed by the Manchester & Leeds which was as keen to get to
Doncaster as the GN was to reach Leeds,
making an agreement between the two a
simple matter.

The Askern Junction-Knottingley line
was opened on 6 June 1848 and helped to
bring a change of heart in the conflict over
Great Northern access to York. The upshot
was a link from Knottingley to the York &
North Midland Railway at Burton Salmon
and GN trains running from London to
York from 8 August 1850. This arrange-
ment continued when the Manchester &
Leeds became part of the Lancashire &
Yorkshire Railway, but ended when the
North Eastern opened the more direct route
from Chaloners Whin, York to Shaftholme
Junction on 2 January 1871.

The 'Askern Branch', as the line was
sometimes known, declined in importance
after it lost its trunk route status but continued to carry a Doncaster-Wakefield
passenger service until 27 September
1948. It had stations at Askern (6¾ m from
Doncaster), Norton (8 m) and Womersley
(10½ m).

From Shaftholme Junction the double
line follows a straight and level course for
the section to Stubbs Walden which is all
on the Doncaster panel. On the way it has
level crossings at Thorpe (68 m 43 ch),

Haywood (67 m 57 ch), Askern (66 m 26 ch), Selby Road (65 m 73 ch) and Norton (65 m 12 ch). From between the last two a 32 chain connection to Askern Colliery trails off on the Down side. The two CCTV crossings at Stubbs Walden—South (64 m 28 ch) and North (64 m 11 ch)—lie on either side of the River Went and are followed by traces of the trackbed of the Hull & Barnsley line which formerly passed overhead.

From Womersley AHB LC (62 m 49 ch), through three more AHB crossings at Post Office Lane (62 m 14 ch), Spring Lodge (61 m 21 ch) and Cridling Stubbs (60 m 45 ch), and on to Knottingley South (58 m 66 ch) and West (58 m 20 ch) junctions, the route is controlled from the Knottingley end.

S.15 Sheffield-Barnsley Line

Section of Wincobank Junction-Horbury Junction (for Leeds) and Wincobank Junction-Huddersfield routes. 12 m 72 ch

The Blackburn Valley is one of the natural approach routes to Sheffield and today it is used by the M1 motorway as well as by the much older railway route, which carries a service to Leeds and to Huddersfield. The latter only dates from 1983 when the Barnsley-Penistone line was reopened and the route through the Don Valley closed as part of a restructured package between BR and the South and West Yorkshire PTEs. From 16 May 1983 this ended the passenger-carrying life of the former GC route between Penistone and Sheffield which had been opened on 14 July 1845 and had served Wortley (32½ miles from Manchester), Deepcar (33¼ m), Oughty Bridge (36½ m), Wadsley Bridge (38½ m), Neepsend (40 m) and then Sheffield Victoria (41¼ m).

The Don Valley is paralleled five miles to the north east by the Blackburn Valley and this formerly carried two railways northbound, the Great Central line which took an elevated course and the surviving ex-Midland Railway route which had to tunnel to get out of the valley. The GC inherited its interest from the South Yorkshire Railway which, in turn, had acquired the project from the Sheffield, Rotherham, Barnsley, Wakefield, Huddersfield & Goole concern. The latter began the original construction in 1847, but then had to choose a new route when it encountered tunnelling problems, hence the more elevated course. A passenger service, originally involving a reversal at Aldam Junction, began on 4 September

1854 and ended on 7 December 1953.

The GC route passenger service called at Broughton Lane (2¼ m from Sheffield Victoria), Tinsley (3¼ m), Meadow Hall & Wincobank (4¼ m), Grange Lane (5½ m), Ecclesfield (6¼ m), Chapeltown & Thorncliffe (8 m), Westwood (9½ m), Birdwell & Hoyland Common (10¾ m), Dovecliffe (13½ m), Stairfoot (15¾ m) and then Barnsley Court House (17¾ m). The five trains a day took 55 minutes for the journey compared with 46 on the Midland route, which also had twice as many trains to choose from.

Today's line started in a humble way as a Midland Railway mineral branch, serving the iron works at Thorncliffe for which it started supplying coal and removing the finished products from 30 August 1893. The route was linked from Chapeltown through Tankersley Tunnel to the Midland's line into Barnsley from 12 April 1897 and began to carry a through passenger service from 1 July of that year. It had a goods and coal branch west to Birdwell & Pilley and subsequently acquired an alternative link to the Barnsley-Cudworth line.

At Wincobank Junction, 161 m 52 ch from St Pancras, the local Leeds and Huddersfield trains transfer to the Slow line and then turn sharply into a cutting which marks the beginning of a curving rise up the Blackburn Valley. The ex-Great Central line is visible on the right as the rise continues, but straighter now, past Ecclesfield West signal box (164 m 24 ch) and high over the B6086 to the platforms and shelters of the simplified Chapeltown station (165 m 58 ch). Former platforms and station buildings just beyond mark the point at which the original route ran on to Thorncliffe, but today's services curve round into the 1,498 yd of Tankersley Tunnel (166 m 29 ch to 167 m 17 ch) which actually passes beneath the ex-GC route.

Tankersley Tunnel, which contains a summit, and a bend at the northern end, leads the route to an area of rolling wooded countryside and a section on which the site of the former Wentworth & Hoyland Common is followed by the crossover at Skiers Spring signal box (167 m 66 ch). There was a coal mine siding here and a mineral line connection beyond Elsecar (169 m), which comprises platforms and traditional Up side buildings and is approached by an embankment and cutting combination.

In railway circles a few names conjure up the whole coal-carrying activity, partly because they seemed to appear on so many private owners' wagons and wagon labels.

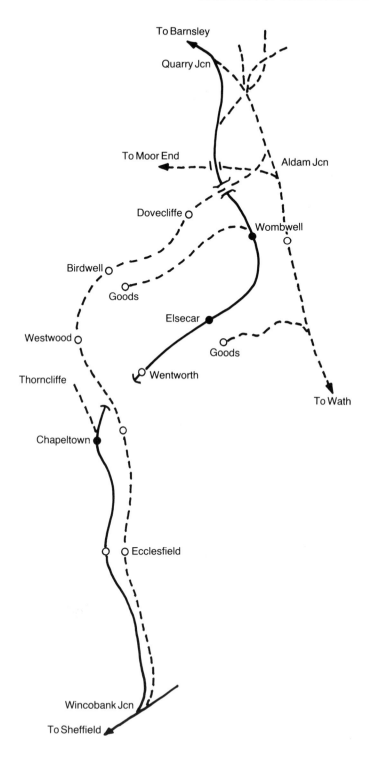

One of these was Wombwell, now just a modest station (170 m 45 ch) with platforms and shelters reached from the B6096 overbridge at the Sheffield end. The Midland had five colliery connections under the control of Wombwell and the Great Central three, and there was pottery and other traffic as well, all needing to be supplied with empties, labelled outwards, waybilled, entered in the wagon books and listed for invoicing and the eventual division of receipts between the companies hauling the traffic to its final destination.

Nowadays little evidence of all this remains, although the GC route's link to Worsbrough and Birdwell is marked by an overbridge just after the surviving line has reached the bottom of its descent from Elsecar. The following viaduct over the Dove also reveals the course of the other goods line from Aldam Junction out to Moor End and Penistone. Just beyond the viaduct was the route from Monkspring Junction over the River Dearne to Cudworth, but now our route continues forward to the remodelled Quarry Junction (173 m 48 ch/7 m 50 ch) near Barnsley Hospital and on past Jumble Lane barrier crossing (6 m 59 ch) which precedes Barnsley station (6 m 54 ch) (see separate entry).

The service on this line is mainly provided by the Sheffield-Leeds and Sheffield-Huddersfield through trains, but there are some services which work only as far as Barnsley.

S.16 Shell Junction—see Middlesbrough-Saltburn Line

S.17 Shepley—see Barnsley-Huddersfield Line.

S.18 Sherburn-in-Elmet
Normanton, Altofts Junction to Colton North Junction line, between Milford Junction and Church Fenton. 12 m 69 ch from York

Closed to passengers on 22 September 1930, this station has now come back into use and is served by the Sheffield-York local trains. The station site follows the connection from the Hull line at Sherburn Junction (13 m 21 ch) and has a CCTV level crossing in addition to its platforms and shelters. A portion of the older, low platform can still be seen, as can the old Up side dock and the base of the goods yard hand crane.

S.19 Shildon—see Bishop Auckland Branch

S.20 Shipley
Leeds-Skipton line, junction with branch to Bradford Forster Square. 205 m 71 ch from St Pancras

This interesting triangular junction owes its inclusion in the early railway network to the fact that the only reasonably level access to Bradford is from the north. This fact influenced the promoters of the Leeds & Bradford Railway who obtained their enabling Act on 4 July 1844 for a route which followed the River Aire into Leeds after this northern exit from Bradford, the change in direction from north to east occurring at the old market town of Shipley.

Construction of the Leeds & Bradford commenced in 1845 and public passenger services began on 1 July 1846 after formal opening ceremonies on the previous day. At this stage many of the works along the line were incomplete, but new railways desperately needed receipts at the earliest possible moment. Thus it was that Shipley did not get a station until 16 July, when a wooden island platform was provided.

The L&B was committed by its original legislation to building a line west from Shipley and this was ratified by the Leeds & Bradford (Shipley-Colne Extension) Act of 30 June 1845. Services commenced to Keighley on 16 March 1847 and on to Skipton on 28 August of that year. By 1849 a link with Colne and the East Lancashire Railway had been established, the new cross-country route bringing Shipley an improved station. It got a new one altogether in 1875, located slightly nearer Bradford and soon to see Settle & Carlisle route trains and locals on the Guiseley branch (from 4 December 1876) added to the St Pancras, east-west and original Leeds-Bradford services.

Just before the Midland Railway had opened its cut-off route from Shipley to Otley via Guiseley, the Great Northern Railway had reached Shipley by taking over two 1860s concerns, the Bradford, Eccleshill & Idle Railway and the Idle & Shipley Railway. Their steeply-graded route carried some 10 trains each way daily over the 8¼ miles from Shipley (Bridge Street) to Bradford Exchange and lasted until 1968, although latterly only for through and local freight, the passenger service having ended on 2 February 1931. The Great Northern terminus at Shipley was a separate station, although a connection between the two systems existed on the approaches from Thackley.

The peak rail development period at Shipley was around the turn of the century when the Leeds and Bradford lines were quadrupled, but the latest change is as recent as 1979 when a phase of general BR/PTE improvements added a single line platform on the Leeds-Skipton leg of the station triangle. This enabled through services to call at Shipley without reversing, a facility now used by the Carlisle, Morecambe and Keighley/Skipton trains.

The approach to Shipley along the Aire Valley still reveals evidence of its former four-track status. The Guiseley line junction follows Thackley Tunnel and then comes Leeds Junction (205 m 58 ch) at the east end of the station where the twin tracks of the Skipton and Bradford routes separate. Up trains on the former use Shipley's single Down platform, leaving the curving L&B route platforms to be used by the Ilkley trains which run hourly with extras in the peak. These arrive and depart via Shipley Bradford Junction (206 m 1 ch), at the south-west corner of the triangle and where a wooden signal box controls the remaining 2 m 54 ch to Forster Square.

The traditional stone buildings of Shipley station lie in the angle between the Bradford-Leeds/Ilkley and Bradford-Skipton platforms, the latter route having a 17 ch curve from Bradford Junction signal box to Shipley's second frame at Shipley, Bingley Junction (205 m 76 ch). On the Skipton route this is followed by the 55 yd Shipley Tunnel (206 m 6 ch to 206 m 9 ch).

From 3 October 1988, Shipley has been served by the 'Bradford Executive', rerouted to use Forster Square from that date.

S.21   Silkstone Common—see Barnsley-Huddersfield Line

S.22   Simonside—see Pelaw

S.23   Skellow Junction—see Stainforth-Adwick Line

S.24   Skelton—see York

S.25   Slaithwaite—see Manchester-Leeds Line

S.26   Sleights—see Middlesbrough-Whitby Line

S.27   South Bank—see Middlesbrough-Saltburn Line

S.28   South Elmsall—see Doncaster-Wakefield Line

S.29   South   Kirby   Junction—see Doncaster-Wakefield Line

S.30   South Shields—see Boldon

The original builders of the Leeds & Bradford Railway extension followed quite closely the course of the Leeds & Liverpool Canal, seen in the background here.

S.31 Sowerby Bridge
Manchester-Normanton/Bradford line, between Hebden Bridge and Milner Royd Junction. 28 m 51 ch from Manchester Victoria

There was a station at Sowerby Bridge on the original 1840 line of the Manchester & Leeds Railway, but this was located just west of Sowerby Bridge Tunnel and the present location dates from 1876. The new site east of the earlier station was chosen to fit in with a planned cut-off route up the Ryburn valley and across to the Manchester-Huddersfield-Leeds line, but in the end this got no further than Rishworth and served out its life as a modest branch line.

After a very difficult time with the construction of Ripponden Tunnel, the branch opened to Ripponden for goods on 15 July 1878 and then on to Rishworth for passengers and goods on 1 March 1881. The L&Y 'Motor Cars—One Class Only' which were used on the branch called at Triangle (1½ m), Ripponden & Barkisland (3¼ m) and Rishworth (3¾ m) and took 13 minutes for the outward journey and 11 for the downhill return. At one period the service stood at 18 trains each way daily and the branch also gained a halt at Watson's Crossing, but all this came to an end when the service ceased on 8 July 1929. Freight then continued until the branch was cut back to Ripponden in 1953 and closed completely on 1 September 1958.

Returning to the L&Y main line, there was a station at Luddenen Foot at one time, but railway, river and canal now make their uninterrupted way down the green Calder valley. The 657 yd Sowerby Bridge Tunnel (27 m 60 ch to 28 m 10 ch) precedes the station, which is something of a gloomy place with the main stone buildings on the Down side and a concrete canopy on the Up island. Prior to the advent of rail motors, trains for Rishworth left an *east* end bay and reversed on to the branch, but the rail motors used a separate wooden platform with a walkway out to it. The Down side bay used by the Halifax trains is still apparent and there are signs of the former coal drops.

There is much of industrial archaeological interest at Sowerby Bridge, including the former meeting point of the Rochdale Canal and the Calder & Hebble Navigation. The station also featured in Branwell Brontë's less-than-distinguished railway career, but is now more important for its regular service of Manchester-Leeds/York/Scarborough trains. Some of the Preston-Leeds trains call, as do the Hebden Bridge locals.

S.32 Springbank Junction—see Hull

S.33 Springwood Junction—see Barnsley-Huddersfield Line

S.34 Stainforth Junction-Adwick Junction Line
Links the Doncaster-Hull and Doncaster-Wakefield lines. 7 m

This double line freight route was originated by the South Yorkshire Railway to link with the West Riding, Hull & Grimsby company's line from Wakefield to Doncaster. It was opened on 1 November 1866 and closed to passengers on 14 May 1979. Local goods traffic ceased on 15 September 1980 but the route has remained open for the coal traffic from Hatfield Main Colliery and as an avoiding line which diverts traffic from the busy Doncaster area.

From Stainforth Junction (166 m 70 ch) the route runs west via Stainforth Road AHB level crossing (165 m 42 ch), Bramwith AHB LC (164 m 72 ch) near the site of a former goods depot, and Thorpe Road AHB LC (164 m 48 ch) to Thorpe Marsh Power Station (163 m 46 ch). At Applehurst Junction (163 m 27 ch) there is a double line connection for northbound movements to the East Coast Main Line, and then at Skellow Junction (160 m 59 ch) the original line turns northwards to connect with its companion route at Adwick Junction. The southbound curve from Skellow Junction to Carcroft Junction (160 m 9 ch) dates from 1969 and has the greater curvature of the two.

Controlled from Doncaster panel, the route has a line speed of 50 mph.

S.35 Standedge Tunnel
Manchester-Huddersfield-Leeds line, between Regional Boundary and Huddersfield. 15 m 11 ch from Manchester Victoria

The Huddersfield & Manchester Railway used the Tame Valley to approach the Pennine ridge from the Manchester direction and the Colne Valley on the Huddersfield side, but needed the 3 m 66 yd Standedge Tunnel to link the two. Like all the Pennine tunnels it was not easy to build, and although the route had reached Huddersfield from Heaton Lodge in 1847, it was another two years before the section

Relaying work taking place in Standedge Tunnel.

through the tunnel to Stalybridge was ready for opening on 1 August 1849.

Today the tunnel carries services from North Wales and Liverpool via Manchester, to Leeds and beyond. High above, where the air shafts emerge on Pule Hill, walkers on the Pennine Way are making another sort of dramatic journey as they cross from Close Moss to the reservoirs at Black Moss. Below them the railway is level between the two portals of the tunnel, but rises at 1 in 125 on the approach from Manchester and drops at 1 in 105 towards Huddersfield.

S.36   Starbeck
Leeds-York line, between Harrogate and Knaresborough. 18 m 27 ch from York

Today it is not too easy to visualize Starbeck as a major railway crossroads. It is now just a simple station on the route of the Leeds-York trains and consists of platforms, waiting shelters, a barrier crossing and a traditional signal box. Yet Starbeck was the first railhead for Harrogate and once lay on a main trunk route from the West Riding to the Tees.

The trunk route scheme was that of the Leeds & Thirsk Railway which obtained its Act on 21 July 1845, the same day that the York & North Midland company was authorized its line from Church Fenton to Harrogate. At the northern end of its route

the L&T planned an extension to the Tees, and eventually achieved this in 1852. Meanwhile the section through Starbeck came into use on 1 September 1848, with through services between Leeds and Thirsk from 10 July of the following year. Although the Leeds & Thirsk, which took the name Leeds Northern to match its heightened ambitions, was authorized to build branches to Harrogate and to Knaresborough, the former had to wait until the North Eastern Railway opened the Harrogate loop on 1 August 1862. The link to Knaresborough dates from 1 October 1851.

Starbeck declined in importance as more trains came to use the Harrogate loop, although freight and specials continued to use the Crimple Viaduct-Starbeck original route, including trains from 'foreign' railways which might otherwise have to pay charges for the use of the NER turntable at Harrogate. Starbeck had its own water supply reservoir located between the western approach routes, and the station itself had a substantial goods activity with full load yard, sundries shed and cattle dock. The loco shed and transfer yard was at the York end where the L&T line departed southwards, and the site is now marked by restoration work on some of the former shed features by the Great Yorkshire Railway Preservation Society.

The Starbeck-Crimple Viaduct section of the L&T route closed in 1951 and that north through Ripon in 1967.

S.37 Stocksfield—see Newcastle-Carlisle Line

S.38 Stocksmoor—see Barnsley-Huddersfield Line

S.39 Stockton

Northallerton-Newcastle line, between Eaglescliffe and Hartlepool. 60 m 4 ch from Leeds

The Stockton & Darlington Railway claimed its prime place in railway history with the opening of its line to carry coal to the Tees at Stockton on 28 September 1825. The unloading wharf lay on a bend in the river now claimed by the A1305 road, but the S&D museum at 48 Bridge Road still re-creates some of the atmosphere of those early days of rail transport. The passenger service on the section of the original line from Bowesfield Junction was cut back to a station south of the coal wharf when steam took over from horse traction and then ended altogether on 1 July 1848 with the opening of South Stockton (now Thornaby) on the Middlesbrough line. Goods traffic continued, though.

Another pioneer railway opened to Stockton in mid-1833. This was the Clarence Railway, built to provide a shorter coal route than that of the S&D and running via what are now Norton and North Shore junctions to a wharf just downstream from its rival. A passenger service was introduced on 11 July 1835, by which time the coal traffic was passing along the 29 October 1833 extension to Haverton Hill and Port Clarence.

Today's passenger line through Stockton dates from the opening of the Leeds Northern Railway's trunk route on 2 June 1852, the station being shared with the West Hartlepool Harbour & Railway. It lay just west of the present station which dates from 1893 and was originally provided with an overall roof. The retaining wall for this is still standing, with the main block, in red brick, on the Up side.

The NER's architect, William Bell, designed the 1893 Stockton station, which must have been an impressive affair in its

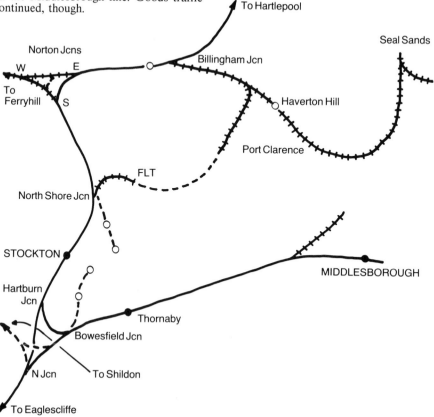

Above *Exterior view of Stockton station.*

Below *Two further views of the huge station at Stockton built in 1893, when it was provided with a double-span train shed.*

heyday. Nowadays it is somewhat care-worn and considerably over-large for the two-coach units which provide the bulk of the Middlesbrough-Newcastle and Darlington-Hartlepool services. The wide approach road leads to a sizeable portico, now spoilt by the bricking-up of the clock aperture, and then to the huge main block and the long platforms. Part of the Up platform is out of use and the country end bays are things of the past; even the avoiding lines around the Down side have now been cut to match traffic levels.

The approach to Stockton station passes the connection to the Thomson scrap yard and siding area. Through the station itself Permissive working is authorized on the Up and Down main lines which subsequently pass beneath a long footbridge which also spans the former yard area. North Shore signal box (61 m 71 ch) controls the One Train single line to the access ground frame (61 m 45 ch) of the Freightliner terminal which lies on the now-truncated riverside route to Haverton Hill but is being transferred to a new Cleveland depot at Wilton. The former 1833 Clarence Railway line also headed for the river from here, with the former Stockton & Hartlepool Railway's station located a little way along its course.

S.40   Stourton Junction—see Leeds

S.41   Sunderland

Northallerton-Newcastle line. 89 m 60 ch from Leeds

Saxon settlements at the mouth of the Wear were subsequently to grow into the town and port of Sunderland. With extensive coal deposits not far inland, early railways were constructed to link the mines with staiths on the river, and Sunderland quickly became a major port with substantial allied activities, notably shipbuilding.

The first line of the post-wagonway era was that opened by the Durham & Sunderland company in 1836. From 5 July of that year mineral traffic began to pass over the inclines of this undulating route, which included a branch to Haswell. The latter subsequently became part of the route to Hartlepool and carried a passenger service until 9 June 1952. On the original line the passenger service to Durham (Elvet) was cut back to Pittington from 1 January 1931, but the trains continued to serve Ryhope (3 m), Seaton (5 m), Murton (6¾ m), Hetton (8½ m) and Pittington (10¾ m) until 5 January 1953.

The Sunderland terminus of the Durham & Sunderland was near the South Dock, while that of the area's next railway, the Brandling Junction, was on the north side of the Wear. The BJR opened its line from the Tyne for goods traffic on 19 June 1839, using a site at Monkwearmouth for its terminal and adding, over the next three months, both passenger traffic and an extension to North Dock. The present Monkwearmouth site took over in 1848.

Another round of railway development took place at Sunderland in the 1850s and

The entrance to Sunderland station at street level.

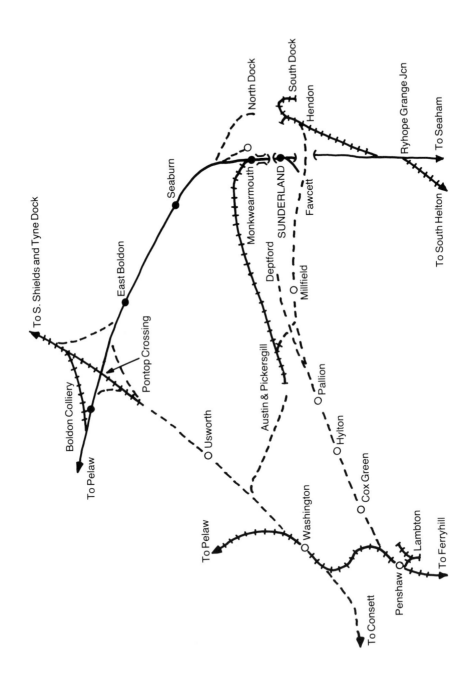

The arriving dmu at Sunderland station's island platform will shortly depart again for Hexham.

produced the Newcastle & Darlington Junction line west to Penshaw in 1852-3 (1 June 1853 for passengers), and the Marquis of Londonderry's railway up from Seaham which opened for goods on 3 August 1854 and for passengers on 2 July 1855. These various enterprises eventually passed, via the York & Newcastle grouping, to the North Eastern Railway which introduced its own round of changes which shaped the eventual railway network at Sunderland. After opening the goods route inland along the north bank of the river on 1 July 1876, the lines north and south of the Wear were connected from 4 August 1879 and the previous Hendon and Fawcett stations at Sunderland closed in favour of the present site. Another cross-river link was opened at Pallions in 1909.

On the N&DJ route in the 1930s 25-30 trains left Sunderland daily for Durham/Bishop Auckland, calling at Millfield (1 m), Pallion (1¾ m), Hylton (3¼ m), Cox Green (5¼ m), Penshaw (6¼ m), Fencehouses (8¼ m), Leamside (10¾ m) and then Durham (15 m). There was an intensive local service to Newcastle, another on the main line which included the Newcastle-Seaham Harbour trains, and a significant number of through services to Leeds, Liverpool and King's Cross. Sunderland at this period also had a half-hourly service over the 7¾ miles to South Shields, with calls at Monkwearmouth, Seaburn, East Boldon

and then Tyne Dock (5¾ m) and High Shields (7 m).

Today's line through Sunderland did not take up its present form until the coastal link from Hart was brought into use on 1 April 1905. It has steadily grown in stature ever since and continues to carry an excellent local service to Middlesbrough and Newcastle, giving a basic service of one train every 15 minutes to the latter point. Some services are extended west to Hexham and there is a daily through service to and from King's Cross.

On the Down direction approach to Sunderland the D&S and Londonderry routes survive in the form of a freight line from Ryhope Grange (87 m 63 ch) to Hendon and the South Dock area. The main line continues on through the 127 and 711 yd South Tunnels (89 m 6 ch to 89 m 45 ch) to some little-used Down side sidings just in advance of the station and where the connection from the N&DJ route is still in use for local purposes. Sunderland signal box (89 m 46 ch) is located here.

Sunderland station itself is a 1965 successor to one destroyed by wartime bombing. It now uses the two faces of one island platform just below street level and reached from a modern ticket concourse in a good central position. Leaving the station northbound trains pass through the 256 yd Sunderland North Tunnel (89 m 64 ch to 89 m 76 ch) and cross over the River Wear bridge which provides a view of the remains of the N&DJ route out to Pallion.

S.42   Swalwell Junction

Newcastle-Carlisle line, between Gateshead and Hexham. 3 m 78 ch from Gateshead, High Level Bridge Junction

Two One Train freight branches leave the Newcastle-Carlisle line at Swalwell Junction. Eastbound the main line forsakes the 1837 course here, leaving the little-used single line to the premises of T.J. Thomson to continue the 1837 direction nearer the south bank of the River Tyne. This it does from 3 m 78 ch to 3 m 15 ch, then continuing for another 55 ch to the Dunston loop and former staiths.

South of the main line, the 44 ch connection to Swalwell Opencast sidings is the modern successor to an 1847 line from Derwenthaugh Junction to the coal mines of the area.

S.43   Swinton Junction-Milford Line

Part of the Sheffield-York route. 22 m 40 ch

This south-north line carries substantial coal traffic, including despatches from collieries along the route. It is also used by other through freight services, eg, oil and stone trains, and by the Sheffield-York local passenger service. The section south of Moorthorpe, where the Wakefield line diverges, handles Leeds-Nottingham trains, plus those to and from Birmingham, South Wales and the South West.

The route was originally a joint Midland and North Eastern project designed to give an improved connection between the former at Swinton and the latter's line from Burton Salmon to Knottingley. The development was connected with the traffic easement on the latter as a result of the rerouting of ECML trains via Selby, and it received its enabling Act on 16 July 1874 as the Swinton & Knottingley Railway. The new line was then ready for goods traffic by 19 May 1879, with passenger services commencing on 1 July of that year. It quickly became busy not only as a through route, but also because of its links with other lines and for the collieries it came to service. In a sense the latter contributed to the recent decline in status, because the subsidence problem was one factor in the diversion of NE/SW services via Doncaster.

The local trains using the line start their journey at Sheffield and, after calling at Rotherham, pass via Aldwarke North Junction (164 m 48 ch), Swinton Junction (166 m 59 ch) and Dearne Junction (168 m 64 ch) into the ER Northern Operating Area, where the distances change to the 17 m 15 ch from the original S&K junction with the NER at Milford. The connection with Manvers Colliery on the Down side is followed further north by the platforms, shelters and overbridge of Bolton-on-Dearne station (16 m 56 ch) and its adjacent R/G crossing.

On the longer stretch north to Moorthorpe the S&K serves two active colliery groups. The first is Goldthorpe Colliery where a 1 m 62 ch One Train single line leaves the Up side and turns east around the perimeter of the colliery. This line is controlled by a small wooden signal box at Hickleton (15 m 5 ch) where the Hickleton Colliery Empty Wagon Sidings are now semi-derelict. After an elongated switchback section the main line collects the connection from Frickley Colliery which is also on

New sidings being installed near Milford Junction for use by merry-go-round trains and part of the works associated with the Selby coalfield diversion.

the Up side, although this time controlled by Moorthorpe box (11 m 63 ch). Up and Down Goods Loops then precede Moorthorpe station (11 m 29 ch), which still has its period station buildings, albeit now accommodating the Mallard pub.

At Moorthorpe Junction (11 m 24 ch) the twin track connection with the Doncaster-Wakefield line descends 52 ch to South Kirkby Junction, leaving the S&K to pass over the other route and continue north via the site of the now closed east-north spur between the two. Ahead lies a long section to Pontefract which twice has to cut deep through east-west ridges and then cross the ensuing plain with long, high embankments.

Just beyond Moorthorpe Junction traces of embankment earthworks are all that remain of the Hull & Barnsley's Stairfoot line which crossed the S&K here. The keen eye can also spot another embankment further north and on the opposite Down side. This marks the course of the Brackenhill Light Railway which served Hemsworth Colliery, some 2½ miles to the west and also had a goods depot branch part way along the line at Ackworth Moor Top. Although the Light Railway Order was obtained on 19 March 1901, extension of time orders were needed in 1904 and 1907, and the line was not finally opened until 1 July 1914, then lasting only until 1 January 1962. On the S&K north of Brackenhill Junction lay Ackworth station, whose brick goods shed still stands on the Down side of the line.

The remainder of the S&K route has just one station, at Pontefract Baghill (4 m 31 ch). This has a separate entry, as does Ferrybridge where the west and east spurs from the Goole line join at Ferrybridge South (2 m 38 ch) and North (2 m 27 ch) junctions respectively. The old buildings of Ferrybridge station are still visible on the Down side and are followed by Ferrybridge box (2 m 10 ch) and the merry-go-round lines into the power station. The S&K route then crosses the River Aire, still busy with commercial traffic, and plunges into the stone-lined 104 yd Brotherton Tunnel (1 m 24 ch to 1 m 19 ch) on the final approach to Milford.

At the zero distance point, the 16 m 69 ch distance of the original York & North Midland York-Normanton line takes over for the section through Hillam Gates CCTV LC (15 m 67 ch) to Milford Junction (15 m 7 ch). The two pairs of tracks from Normanton and from Pontefract run in parallel over this section, starting where Burton

Salmon Junction was formerly located. They separate at Milford signal box to run either to Sherburn and on to Church Fenton or to pass around the coal holding sidings to the Leeds-Selby line at Gascoigne Wood.

T.1   Tankersley Tunnel—see Sheffield-Barnsley Line

T.2   Tees
Darlington-Saltburn   line,   between Eaglescliffe and Middlesbrough. 13 m 59 ch from Darlington

Tees signal box controls not only the local passenger train movements on the Saltburn line but also freight traffic on the four additional goods lines between Thornaby East Junction (11 m 69 ch) and Newport East Junction (14 m 3 ch). North of these lies the sizeable complex of the Tees/Newport freight yard and traction depot.

The location, appropriate to the considerable industrial activity of the south bank of the Tees, increased in importance from 1915 with the introduction of the North Eastern Railway's experimental scheme of electrification for coal traffic from Shildon. Although electric traction was not perpetuated after 1935, Newport Yard continued to be busy and still has an important freight and traction role. The diesel maintenance depot is located at the west end of the complex, with the former steam roundhouse visible by the lineside. The marshalling yard beyond is laid out in the traditional form of reception, sorting and departure sidings although nowadays the main activities are the supply of empty tank, hopper and coal wagons and the provision of power for trainload movements. Railfreight activity has now been concentrated on the Up yard and most of the Down has been lifted.

Dating from 1958, the steam roundhouse was probably the last of its kind to be built in Europe.

T.3   Tees-side Airport
Darlington-Saltburn   line,   between Darlington and Middlesbrough. 5 m 43 ch from Darlington

The station is a simple affair of platforms and shelters significant only for its proximity to the airport which lies immediately south of the railway. The service derives from the Darlington-Hartlepool and Saltburn line trains. Originally Middleton St George and serving an RAF airfield, the present station dates from 3 October 1971.

Above *Newport Yard, Middlesbrough. Note the overhead electrification equipment for the pre-1935 coal trains from Shildon.*

Below *Interior of the engine sheds at Newport in 1942.*

T.4 Temple Hirst Junction

East Coast Main Line, junction with Selby line. 169 m 16 ch from King's Cross

Just before Temple Hirst Junction the East Coast Main Line passes over the Knottingley-Goole route, near the point where the Hull & Barnsley Railway used to connect with it. On this section the ECML also crosses the Aire and Ouse rivers and there are views of Eggborough power station to the west and of Drax to the east.

After 1964, when Temple Hirst station finally closed even for goods traffic, the name meant nothing in railway terms, until the opening of a new section of main line in 1983. The old route was truncated at Selby and a new stretch of line built around the western edge of the vast Selby coalfield. Temple Hirst now marks the divergence of the surviving double track to Selby from the point at which the new main line commences.

The story of the Selby diversion dates back to the mid-1970s when the Selby Coalfield Public Inquiry was held into the consequences of the then National Coal Board's decision to mine the vast coal deposits discovered north of Selby. To avoid either sterilizing 40 m tonnes of coal or risking subsidence along the course of the ECML between Selby and York, a decision was taken to build 14 miles of diversionary route capable of handling 125 mph services. The British Railways (Selby) Act was secured in 1978, followed by the purchase of the land required and the letting of contracts.

By 1982 the northern section between Colton Junction and Hambleton was ready for use, the through route being completed in time for a special ceremony on 29 September 1983 prior to public running from 3 October. As part of the opening ceremonials, the Eastern Region General Manager's saloon met the Chief Civil Engineer's tamping machine at Bridge No 1 which carries the main line over the River Aire. A plaque was affixed to this bridge and a special 'Completion of Line' certificate handed over.

T.5 Temple Hirst Junction-Selby Line

Branch from East Coast Main Line. 4 m 75 ch

This is the surviving portion of the cut-off route opened on 2 January 1871 between Shaftholme Junction north of Doncaster

and Chaloners Whin Junction south of York. East Coast Main Line trains were then to use the new line for 112 years, until the section north of Temple Hirst was rerouted to allow the unhindered development of the Selby coalfield. The old main line north of Selby was then closed completely—and much of its former course has now vanished under a new bypass road—but the portion covered by this entry was retained to permit the provision of a local passenger service between Selby and Doncaster.

Old and new main lines part company at Temple Hirst Junction (169 m 16 ch) with the former then heading direct for Selby via level crossings at Burn Lane (170 m 70 ch), Henwick Hall (172 m 20 ch) and Brayton (173 m 2 ch). Between the last two the line passes beneath the route of the former connection between the Leeds-Selby and Selby-Goole lines, the spur between the latter and that from Doncaster surviving for CCE purposes. The approach to Selby is via an embankment over the canal to Canal Junction (173 m 59 ch) and the single line spur round to West Junction on the Leeds line, and then on to join the latter at Selby South Junction (174 m 11 ch).

T.6 Thackley Tunnel—see Shipley

T.7 Thirsk

East Coast Main Line. 22 m 16 ch from York

Thirsk, a Norman town in the Vale of Mowbray, changed its stage-coach activities for railway ones when the Great North of England Railway began running passenger trains between York and Darlington on 30 March 1841. The rout of the stage-coaches was then completed a few years later when a second railway arrived at Thirsk, that of the Leeds & Thirsk company, which opened to a separate station east of the main line on 1 June 1848. Like the GNE line, the L&T had opened earlier for goods, and its Thirsk Town station was to continue handling goods after all passenger services had been transferred to the main line station in 1855. This transfer utilized an 1848 connection between the two routes and ended the previous practice of L&T line trains reversing there.

From 1856 to 1901 the main Leeds & Thirsk/Leeds Northern through services were routed via Melmerby, Thirsk and Northallerton. Subsequently an increasing number passed direct from Melmerby to Northallerton, although Thirsk continued

to enjoy some through services, including a Bradford-Berwick link, as well as the local ones. These eventually came to an end when the Melmerby-Thirsk line was closed on 14 September 1959.

Although Thirsk may now have lost its local services on the main line, as well as those to Malton and on the Leeds Northern route, it does still have good links with the InterCity network by courtesy of the Leeds-Newcastle trains, now running via York. These use the outer face of the island platforms which Thirsk received under a wartime route widening scheme.

On the approach to Thirsk from Tollerton, the ex-Leeds Northern trackbed can be seen to the west as the main line comes to the Slow to Fast and Fast to Slow connections at Green Lane Junction (21 m 45 ch). The footbridge-linked island platforms of the station are then followed by the Down side signal box (22 m 34 ch), with the main line then continuing north via four R/G level crossings—Nos 81 (22 m 73 ch), 82 (23 m 33 ch), 88 (27 m 16 ch) and 89 (27 m 58 ch)—and with more Fast-Slow links at Avenue Junction (23 m 60 ch) in between.

T.8   Thornaby
Darlington-Saltburn line, between Eaglescliffe and Middlesbrough. 11 m 63 ch from Darlington

Thornaby lies on the 1830 extension of the original Stockton & Darlington line, and the modern bridge over the Tees which precedes Thornaby station is on the same foundations as the original, and not entirely successful, suspension bridge provided by the S&D. The station itself, an island platform reached from a substantial footbridge, is served by the Newcastle-Middlesbrough and Bishop Auckland/Darlington-Saltburn trains.

The two goods lines which commence at Bowesfield pass round Thornaby station and are joined at Thornaby East Junction (11 m 69 ch) by additional lines serving Tees Yard.

Thornaby traction depot is part of the nearby Tees Yard complex. It is a 19-line 'Level 4' depot with 240 staff and handling Class 20, 37 and 47 locomotives plus multiple units and freight rolling stock.

On this section of the main line south of Thirsk, the NER installed automatic semaphore signals operated by high pressure gas. On the track nearby are the contacts of Raven's mechanical fog signalling apparatus.

T.9   Thorne
Doncaster-Hull line, junction with the Cleethorpes line. Junction 7 m 69 ch from Doncaster, Thorne North station 14 m 2 ch from Gilberdyke Junction

The line from Thorne Junction as far as 9 m 27 ch was owned by the Great Central, and that from 14 m 6 ch eastwards through Thorne North station to Gilberdyke Junction was opened by the North Eastern Railway on 1 October 1869.

From the ER Southern operating area the approach to Thorne Junction passes the junction with the Adwick-Stainforth freight line and then the loading sidings of Hatfield Main Colliery. Then after Thorne Junction the Doncaster-Hull line crosses the Stainforth & Keadby Canal and enters Thorne North station, which still has substantial Down side buildings. To the east, on the flat, open, drained marshland section to Goole the only railway features of note are the AHB level crossing at Thorne Moor (12 m 32 ch) and the R/G crossing at Creykes (10 m).

The 1869 Thorne-Staddlethorpe (now Gilberdyke) line was an interesting example of inter-railway co-operation which gave the NER running powers into Doncaster, the GCR access to Hull and the L&Y Goole-Hull running powers. The modern Sprinters on the Sheffield/Doncaster-Hull services have now inherited the benefits.

T.10   Thornhill   Junction—see Manchester-Leeds Line

T.11   Thurstonland Tunnel—see Barnsley-Huddersfield Line

T.12   Tollerton—see Pilmoor

T.13   Tursdale Junction—see Ferryhill

T.14   Tweedmouth
East Coast Main Line, between Alnmouth and Berwick. 65 m 78 ch from Newcastle

The long, gentle descent of the East Coast Main Line, followed by a rise at 1 in 230/190 to Tweedmouth, was brought into service by the Newcastle & Berwick Railway on 29 March 1847, with a temporary viaduct over the River Tweed opening in the following year. This section, covered by the 'control tower'-style signal box on the Down side, passes through Beal CCTV LC (58 m 52 ch), Beal Crossovers (59 m 32 ch), No 193 R/G LC (60 m 67 ch), Scremerston CCTV LC (63 m 46 ch) and Spittal LC (65 m 1 ch), and then continues through Berwick to the Regional Boundary. Beal, Goswick and Scremerston all used to have stations, Beal serving the Holy Island of Lindisfarne which is visible from the main line trains.

This border sign on the Kelso branch was devised with the axe double-headed in order to avoid controversy in an area where border skirmishing was once commonplace.

Tweedmouth's own passenger station closed on 15 June 1964 but the station buildings remain, together with coal and engineers' sidings. Behind the Up side goods and grain terminal lay the old 1878 dock line, but less trace remains of this than of the line west to Kelso which was opened on 27 July 1849. The trackbed of the latter is visible heading from the old Down side loco depot area to the south bank of the Tweed below.

The Berwick-Kelso trains used to reverse at Tweedmouth and had a timing allowance of five-seven minutes for doing so. After Tweedmouth they called at Velvet Hall (5¼ m from Berwick), Norham (7¾ m), Twizell (10¾ m), Coldstream (13½ m), Sunilaws (16¾ m), Carham (19 m), Sprouston (21¼ m) and then Kelso (23½ m), one train each way daily also covering the 11½ miles from Kelso to St Boswells. Passenger services ceased on 15 June 1964.

There was a bad accident on the ECML near Goswick crossing on 27 October 1947, 27 people being killed and 59 injured when the 11.15 am Edinburgh to King's Cross train was derailed during engineering work, due to taking the Main to Slow turnout too fast.

T.15　Tyne Coal Terminal—see Boldon

T.16　Tyne Yard
East Coast Main Line, between Durham and Newcastle. 75 m 62 ch from York

A four-track section of the main line commences at Ouston Junction (73 m 32 ch) and continues to Low Fell Junction (77 m 37 ch) where the connection to the Carlisle route departs. West of it lie the reception, sorting and departure sidings of Tyne Yard, built where the old Lamesley station used to be and designed to handle the freight traffic to and from the industries of the Tyne. Although not as big or as busy as it used to be, the yard still handles a significant volume of coal, oil, cement, sand and other traffics.

The modern Tyne signal box (75 m 62 ch) takes over from Ferryhill and controls the ECML as far as the King Edward Bridge Junctions where the Gateshead panel takes over.

U.1　Ulleskelf
Normanton-Colton North Junction line, between Church Fenton and Colton Junction. 8 m 70 ch from York

The island platforms at Ulleskelf are served by the Sheffield-York local trains and by some services on the Leeds-York route. The old brick goods shed still stands on the Up side.

W.1　Wakefield
Wakefield Westgate is on the Doncaster-Leeds line, 175 m 65 ch from King's Cross; Wakefield Kirkgate is on the Eastwood-Normanton line, 47 m 62 ch from Manchester

Wakefield lies on two main railway routes, the west-east route which originated with the Manchester & Leeds and later became L&Y and then LMS, and the former Great Northern line from Doncaster to Leeds which carries the London service.

Wakefield can trace its history back to Edward the Confessor. In later years it became an important centre for woven cloth with a great deal of agricultural activity in the surrounding area. Like neighbouring West Riding towns it attracted the attention of railway promotors quite early in the railway age, although initially the citizens of Wakefield used coach services into Leeds or the North Midland station at Oakenshaw to make their early train journeys. However, Wakefield soon got its own station at Kirkgate when the Manchester & Leeds Railway opened the Hebden Bridge-Goose Hill portion of its line on 8 October 1840.

By the time Wakefield got its next railway line, that of the Wakefield, Pontefract & Goole enterprise, the Lancashire & Yorkshire had taken over the M&L and acquired the near-finished route to Goole. When the latter opened on 1 April 1848 it gave the growing L&Y a route from west to east which came to carry a great deal of traffic.

The next round of railway development at Wakefield then waited until the 1850s when the Great Northern reached the town from Leeds. Through the medium of the Bradford, Wakefield & Leeds Railway its trains ran into a makeshift station at Westgate from 5 October 1857, with a line extended round to the joint L&Y and GN station at Kirkgate.

The next decade brought further change. The West Riding & Grimsby Railway's line was opened between Westgate South Junction and Doncaster North Junction on 1 February 1866, bringing into being the long viaduct section south of Westgate station. By this time the GN had acquired the BW&L (now the West Yorkshire) and, with the Manchester, Sheffield & Lincolnshire Railway, had also swallowed up the West Riding & Grimsby concern, putting a decidedly 'Great Northern' stamp on Wakefield. Despite a fair amount of squabbling, especially with the Midland, the town got a new station at Westgate, complete with a high clock tower.

While Wakefield has lost such services as the Leeds 'circular' and that to Bradford via Batley, it nevertheless does fairly well in terms of modern railway services. Stops by the Leeds-King's Cross trains put London almost within two hours' journey time, and the town has links to the North East and South West, as well as local Doncaster, Sheffield and Huddersfield services.

Westgate station on the west side of the town is approached in the Down direction by the long section on arches which crosses over the former L&Y line and is joined by the 26 ch, single line connection therefrom at Wakefield Westgate South Junction (175 m 38 ch), with Up and Down passenger loops then supplementing the main lines through the station (175 m 65 ch). In its reconstructed form this has a modernized entrance on the Up side, concrete framed canopies and a novel sculpture on the site of the former Down bays. Entitled *A Light Wave*, it consists of seven wooden 'spray' sculptures in blue placed at intervals along the bay area. At night they are lit from beneath in sequence to create an unusual spectacle of light and shadow.

On the Up side north of Westgate station are the lines serving Toleman's car terminal, while on the Down side, at Balne Lane (176 m 12 ch), Wrenthorpe Down Sidings marks the site of Wrenthorpe Junction where the GN line to Dewsbury formerly headed off via Alverthorpe, Flushdyke, Ossett and Earlsheaton. The route then continues, at high level, towards Leeds.

Kirkgate, to the south of Wakefield, now occupies a secondary role and presents a more traditional image dominated by the long block of buildings in red brick on the Down side. It has Up and Down L&Y lines to serve the platforms, plus two central Through lines, all running from Wakefield Kirkgate West Junction (47 m 43 ch)—where the Goole and Normanton lines separate—through the station (47 m 62 ch) to Kirkgate East (47 m 68 ch) and Kirkgate box (47 m 76 ch).

The Kirkgate end of the 26 ch bi-directional line between the two Wakefield stations is controlled by Kirkgate signal box and the other end by the Leeds panel (which also controls the whole Westgate layout). This line carries an hourly Huddersfield-Wakefield service which reverses at Kirkgate and connects at Westgate with the London and Leeds-Doncaster/Scunthorpe trains. Kirkgate also has an hourly Leeds-Sheffield stopping service, but no longer a service from Kirkgate through Westgate (1 m), Lofthouse & Outwood (3½ m), Stanley (5¾ m) and Methley (8½ m) to Castleford (10 m).

A new station at Outwood, 2½ miles north of Westgate, is served by Leeds-Wakefield locals and Leeds-Sheffield trains.

W.2   Wakefield-Goole Line

From Wakefield Kirkgate West Junction to Potters Grange Junction, Goole. 26 m 71 ch

This route was authorized to the Wakefield, Pontefract & Goole Railway on 31 July 1845 and became part of the Manchester & Leeds concern before opening on 1 April 1848. It thus became part of the Lancashire & Yorkshire Railway system and later of the London, Midland & Scottish Railway. The section west of Pontefract lost its passenger services on 2 January 1967, but the rest of the line carries a through Leeds-Goole service with extra workings between Leeds and Knottingley.

The route between Wakefield and Knottingley is described in various separate entries, the double line continuing from the latter point to Drax where it becomes single for the remaining eight miles to Goole. This route used to carry Liverpool/Manchester-Hull expresses in addition to its local services and the shipment coal to Goole, but now the main non-passenger activity is the movement of coal to the huge power stations along its course. All movements are under the control of signal boxes at Knottingley, Sudforth Lane and Hensall, the latter controlling entry to the single line with the Goole box then taking over from Engine Shed Junction.

A substantial quantity of the coal used at the local power stations comes from Kellingley Colliery, a modern pit just east of Knottingley and rail-connected at the Goole end. There are Up and Down Refuge Sidings, and the line crosses the Knottingley & Goole Canal which will be its companion for the rest of the journey. Then the signal box at Sudforth Lane LC (61 m 8 ch) is followed by Whitley Bridge station (62 m 55 ch) which has short platforms with shelters and a barrier crossing at the Goole end. The ex-L&Y signal box is followed by Whitley Bridge Junction (63 m 2 ch) and the connection used by coal and oil supplies to Eggborough power station.

Three more level crossings precede the next station: High Eggborough (63 m 33 ch), Eggborough Ings (64 m 5 ch) and Snaith and Pontefract Highway (64 m 14 ch). Then comes Hensall station (64 m 39 ch) itself, with another L&Y box, a level crossing and a fine station house complete with railway clock and enamel signs. Heck Lane (64 m 74 ch) and Heck Ings (65 m 40 ch) crossings follow on the next section which passes beneath the East Coast Main Line and has traces of the east-north spur that once linked the two.

At Drax Branch Junction (65 m 66 ch) the double line becomes single and the connection to the power station veers off north, using a portion of the old Hull & Barnsley

route, the abandoned course of which is also apparent south of the WP&G route. The latter continues its level easterly course over waterways and through pleasant villages with further level crossings at Gowdall Lane (66 m 51 ch) and Field Lane (66 m 66 ch).

Snaith station (68 m 13 ch) is a modern affair with short platforms and waiting shelters. It has an open crossing at one end and the remains of earlier platforms and a dock at the other. More level crossings follow at West Cowick (68 m 61 ch), East Cowick (69 m 48 ch) and Snaith Road (70 m 17 ch) before the route reaches Rawcliffe (70 m 75 ch) where it is crossed by the M62. The station uses the Down side platform, the other standing out of use opposite. The former has a waiting shelter and the old station house, built in brick with stone facings, stands nearby. There is an open crossing at the Goole end.

Past a former private siding connection the route now enters its final phase, still flat and now with its canal rival close by. At Engine Shed Junction (73 m 52 ch/64 ch) the single line turns to climb up to its connection with the Doncaster-Hull line at Potters Grange Junction (0 ch), leaving the original L&Y route to continue ahead to the docks and the former L&Y terminus there.

W.3   Wakefield-Pontefract Line

Links Wakefield with Leeds-Goole line.
9 m 5 ch

The Lancashire & Yorkshire Railway completed its west-east expansion by absorbing the Wakefield, Pontefract & Goole Railway which opened between the points named in its title on 1 April 1848. The section east from Pontefract still carries a (Leeds-Goole) passenger service while the western portion is a double line, 50 mph freight route serving several intermediate collieries.

The line commences south west of Wakefield, at Kirkgate West Junction (47 m 43 ch) where the Horbury and Westgate routes join. It then heads east through Kirkgate station (47 m 62 ch), past Kirkgate box (47 m 76 ch) and on to Calder Bridge Junction (48 m 28 ch) and its Turners Lane Curve connection with the Normanton line. At Oakenshaw Junction (48 m 67 ch), the link towards the ex-MR Cudworth route departs and our line passes on to Crofton West (49 m 40 ch) and East (50 m 23 ch) junctions, the former giving access to Sheffield and Doncaster and the latter picking up the Down link from the Cudworth direction. Now clear of the Wakefield area junctions, our ex-WP&G railway passes through level crossings at Crofton Old Station (50 m 25 ch), Streethouse (52 m 11 ch), Red Lane (52 m 27 ch) and Featherstone (53 m 71 ch) to join the passenger line from Castleford at Pontefract West Junction (56 m 36 ch), before continuing into Pontefract Monkhill station (56 m 48 ch).

In LMS days the passenger trains on this line called at Sharlston (4 m), Featherstone (6 m) and Pontefract Tanshelf (8 m), but the route lost its passenger services on 2 January 1967.

W.4   Walton Street—see Hull

W.5   Weeton—see Leeds-York Line

W.6   West Parade Junction—see Hull

W.7   West Sleekburn Junction—see North Blyth Branch

W.8   Wetherall—see Newcastle-Carlisle Line

W.9   Whitby
Terminus of branch from Middlesbrough.
30 m 62 ch from Pickering

Local interest in the Stockton & Darlington Railway went on to prompt ideas for a railway line for Whitby and resulted in an Act of 6 May 1833 for a line to Pickering, where it was planned to make connection with the York & North Midland Railway. The line was opened with horse traction on 26 May 1836, although the easy bit inland

from Whitby to Grosmont had been brought into use 11 months earlier.

The original line from Whitby to Pickering was to become the main outlet for rail travel to the Midlands and South until its closure on 8 March 1965. Indeed, it was 30 years before the historic port got its second rail connection, when the Castleton to Grosmont gap in the Esk Valley line was bridged from 2 October 1865. By this time Whitby's third railway had been authorized in the form of the Whitby, Redcar & Middlesbrough Union Railway.

The WR&MU had taken on a daunting task, because the cliff-top route involved many earthworks, tunnels and viaducts. Following the enabling Act of 16 July 1866 a start was made on the construction work, but the company got into such hopeless physical and financial difficulties that it was glad to sell out to the North Eastern Railway in 1875. Even that concern needed eight years to complete the work, and the line was not finally opened until 3 December 1883.

The final railway to reach Whitby was the Scarborough & Whitby's coastal route from the south. This, too, gave its engineers and backers a few headaches, with the work started in great expectation in 1872 soon grinding to a halt for lack of funds. Completion was eventually achieved to permit opening from 16 July 1885, the route being worked by the NER from the beginning and taken over fully from 1898.

In the settled LNER days, Whitby had five or six trains each way daily on each of its routes, supplemented by the through services from the York direction and by substantial additions on summer Saturdays,

The gloomy interior of Whitby station photographed in 1952 before the removal of the roof.

LNER Sentinel railcars Hope *and* Courier *fill the air with smoke as they connect Whitby's two stations.*

particularly on the Scarborough-Whitby-Middlesbrough line. Whereas trains from the Grosmont direction approach at town level along the course of the Esk, the coastal line crossed the valley by a high viaduct to West Cliff station, whence a shuttle worked down to the main station below.

Local services north from Whitby used the main river route inland for the first half mile or so and then ran parallel with it to a point beneath the high level viaduct where the rising curve to West Cliff (21½ miles from Scarborough) began. Heavier trains needed banking on this section, but a long cutting then eased the gradient at the beginning of the cliff top route and through Sandsend (24 m) to Kettleness (26½ m). A sharply curving loop took the line behind the heights and clefts of Hob Holes before it continued on through Hinderwell (30 m) and back to the coast at Staithes (31¾ m). The section on from Grinkle (35¼ m), through Loftus (36½ m) and Skinningrove (37½ m) to Brotton and thence to Saltburn or Middlesbrough was reopened in 1973 to serve Boulby Mine, after the route had lost its passenger services south of Loftus on 5 May 1958 and altogether from 2 May 1960.

The high-level station at West Cliff sur-

vived until 12 June 1961, after which the Scarborough trains reversed at Prospect Hill Junction for their descent to town level. In less than four years, on 8 March 1965, both that service and the main route out via Pickering were also to go.

The original Whitby & Pickering line was taken over by the York & North Midland from 30 June 1845 and converted from horse to locomotive working. The town also got a new station building two years later and this still survives, although only one operational track remains of the once-busy complex of platforms, bays, stabling, locomotive and goods lines. With a five-arched *porte-cochère* entrance and Georgian-style windows, the station building is an attractive example of the work of G.T. Andrews surviving amid changes, the latest of which involve a supermarket development and possible access to Whitby for North Yorkshire Moors Railway trains.

W.10   Whitehall Junction—see Leeds

W.11   Whitley Bridge—see Wakefield-Goole Line

W.12   Whitwood—see Normanton

W.13   Widdrington

East Coast Main Line, between Morpeth and Alnmouth. 23 m 20 ch from Newcastle

Lying on the 1 July 1847 stretch of the Newcastle & Berwick Railway, Widdrington station has been simplified in recent years, although the former station house, one of the series designed for the line by Benjamin Green, survives in private hands. Calls by some of the Newcastle-Alnmouth/Berwick trains provide the service.

From the south, the approach to Widdrington is via the barrier crossing (and house) at Ulgham Lane (20 m 52 ch), with the station and CCTV crossing and then Widdrington Crossover (24 m 64 ch) following. A little further to the north lie Felton Lane LC (25 m 16 ch) and the barrier crossing and signal box at Chevington (25 m 49 ch). The latter controls the Up and Down Passenger Loops and the Up side coal sidings and connection to Widdrington Colliery.

W.14   Wombwell—see Sheffield-Barnsley Line

W.15   Woodlesford

Sheffield-Wakefield-Leeds line, between Normanton and Leeds. 190 m 2 ch from St Pancras

Woodlesford is now just a simplified station with platforms and waiting shelters, but there are signs of a more elaborate past, particularly on the Down side where the plinth and core spindle of a former hand crane can still be seen in the stone cobbled dock area. The platform which follows has an earlier, low-height section, a reminder that early trains were generally lower and narrower than those of today. The 190 milepost stands on the Up platform.

The Sheffield-Wakefield-Leeds trains serve Woodlesford which is on the 1840 North Midland Railway route and stands amid an industrial landscape of mining spoil, opencast quarrying, a canal and a tank farm.

W.16   Woolley Tunnels

Wincobank Junction, Sheffield to Horbury Junction line, between Barnsley and Horbury Junction. 49 m 29 ch from Manchester Victoria

Periods of financial stringency are not the sole prerogative of the twentieth century. The general shortage of investment capital which followed the railway mania spending spree meant that the Sheffield, Rotherham, Barnsley, Wakefield, Huddersfield & Goole Railway promoters of the line from Horbury Junction to Barnsley could only afford to lay a single track, which they opened on 1 January 1850. Five years later increasing traffic necessitated doubling, but the second tunnel was not added until 1902.

The route itself, having descended to the floor of the Dearne Valley after leaving Barnsley, has to cross the Woolley Edge escarpment to get into the valley of the Calder. It uses the two 1,745 yd Woolley North and South Tunnels (47 m 33 ch to 46 m 34 ch) to achieve this. The approach to the tunnels has Bretton Country Park on the west side of the line and the massive Woolley Colliery complex to the east. The rail connection with the latter is controlled by Woolley Coal Siding signal box (48 m 55 ch) which is followed by a crossover at the Up side loading point and its twin stabling lines. The latter are also connected to the main line at the north end, before the physical separation of the two tracks to pass through either the tall, narrow bore of the original Down tunnel or the simpler alignment and profile of the Up one.

There were stations at Haigh to the south of the tunnels and Crigglestone to the north, but these closed on 13 September 1965. The route now just continues to Crigglestone Junction (45 m 56 ch), where the single line 1902 freight spur taking traffic for the west round to Horbury Station Junction (44 m 13 ch) maintains the Manchester-based distances. On the remaining 1 m 53 ch of the original route east to Horbury Junction, Royal Oak coal sidings connect on the Down side and there is a view of a viaduct of the former MR route to Dewsbury. The connection from the Procor wagon works is made in the vee of the junction.

W.17   Wortley Junction—see Leeds

W.18   Wressle—see Leeds-Hull Line

W.19   Wyke Tunnel—see Halifax

W.20   Wylam—see Newcastle-Carlisle Line

Y.1   Yarm

Northallerton-Newcastle line, between Northallerton and Eaglescliffe. 55 m 76 ch from Leeds

The original Stockton & Darlington project included a modest branch from its main line to the north side of the River Tees at Yarm and there was later a Yarm station on the

1852 Leeds Northern line, the former closing in 1862 and the latter in 1960 (goods
1964). The Leeds Northern line, still open
as a double track freight route, bisects a
loop of the Tees and rises to cross it by
means of Yarm Viaduct. The two spans
over the river are of stone and there are 41
others in brick. There is also a small, 75 yd
Yarm Tunnel (55 m 76 ch to 55 m 79
ch).

Y.2   York
*East Coast Main Line, junction with
Harrogate and Scarborough lines. 188 m
40 ch from King's Cross*

The Romans made York their military
centre, to the Saxons it was the capital of
the kingdom of Northumbria, the Vikings
conducted their commerce there, and
Norman William was building a castle at
York within three years of his landing at
Pevensey Bay. The early railways continued the emphasis that previous ages had
put upon York and the eastern routes
planned between London and Scotland all
headed for the elegant and important
city.

The discussions of prospective railway
promoters in York began to crystallize as
first the Leeds & Selby Railway became a
reality and then the North Midland's
Derby-Leeds scheme emerged to offer a
link to London via Birmingham. In 1835 a
meeting in York's Guildhall led to the formation of the York & North Midland
Railway enterprise, and on 21 June 1836 to
the passing of its Act for a line from York to
Altofts (Normanton) and connections to
Leeds and the route of the Leeds & Selby.
The company's chairman was York draper
George Hudson, soon to be labelled the
'Railway King', and George Stephenson
was the engineer.

Northwards from York the Great North
of England Railway secured authorizations
in 1836 and 1837 for a route via Croft to
Gateshead. The two companies agreed to
share a station just inside the walls of York,
but the city's first trains, which ran to and
from the Leeds & Selby Railway at
Milford, used a temporary wooden station
from 29 May 1839 until 4 January 1841
when the new station designed by G.T.
Andrews was brought into use. By this time
Y&NM trains were running to Altofts, and

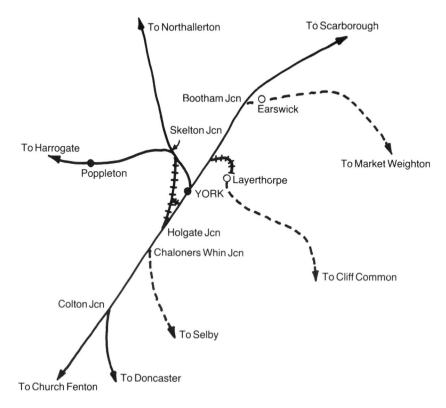

Above *NER 25 ton departmental bogie van based on York North Junction Shed.*

Below *The interior of Locomotive Yard signal box at York. A moment of quiet when even the train register boy has nothing to do.*

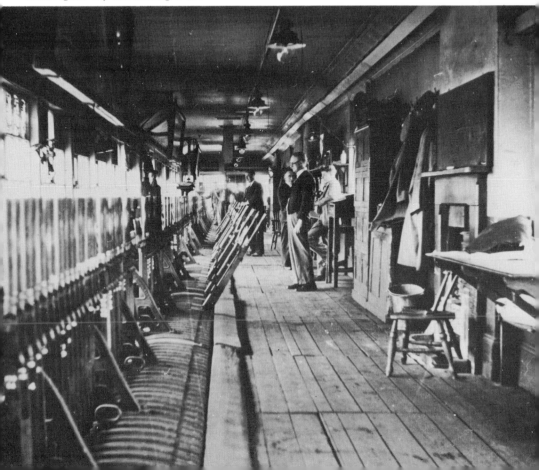

The porte-cochère *frontage of York station with the hotel just beyond.*

from 30 March 1841 the link to London was extended north as far as Darlington, fitting reasons for a festive official opening of the joint station.

The 1840s also gave York three more railway lines, the Y&NM's York-Scarborough route opening on 7 July 1845, that from York to Market Weighton on 4 October 1847 (with a link on to Beverley and Hull from 1865), and the East & West Yorkshire Junction's York-Knaresborough line on 30 October 1848. Later dates of note include the routing of East Coast Main Line trains via Selby from 1871, the 1880 branch to Foss Islands goods depot, and the opening of the Derwent Valley Railway connecting with it in 1913.

Inevitably growing traffic levels and the awkward traffic movements always associated with a terminal led to the need for a better station at York; and the present station was built between 1874 and 1877. As opened it consisted of 11 bays and two through platforms, including No 8 which was used for the refreshment stops of the developing Anglo-Scottish traffic. The new station was provided with an 800 ft overall glazed roof divided into spans of 43 ft, 55 ft and 81 ft, and 48 ft high at the highest point.

York's new station enjoyed a best timing of around four hours to London. A hundred years later, HSTs took over the honourable traction mantle of the LNER 'Pacifics' and

their 'Deltic' successors, and by 1982 had cut the four hours to two. In addition to the glamorous express services on the East Coast Main Line, a variety of running powers into York and of working arrangements between the NER/LNER and their neighbours gave the city a great variety of long distance, through and excursion services. From the Leeds, Sheffield and Liverpool directions dozens of trains arrived and departed again for Scarborough or the North, there were links to the Great Eastern system to serve Harwich and Liverpool Street, and many strange 'through carriages' like the link from Barry Island to Newcastle.

The passenger services on York's local branches were augmented by the additional summer workings to the Yorkshire resorts, York having a substantial level of day and evening excursion business along the Scarborough line. Local services out to Strensall, Earswick and Copmanthorpe were worked by push-pull sets and various types of railcar appeared on such workings as the circular route to Leeds.

Apart from the Rowntree confectionery business and sugar-beet from BSC Poppleton, York's domestic freight traffic involved the usual mixture associated with a large city. It was dealt with mainly at Leeman Road depot until 1972 when the surviving business was added to the bulk traffic activity at Foss Islands. In the early part of the century freight wagons to and from the local sidings and conveyed on the branch pick-up services were dealt with at several small York yards, but this work, including the attaching to and detaching from main line services, was increasingly concentrated on the Dringhouses Yard built to the south of the station during the First World War and provided with a hump in 1961.

The Foss Islands branch was opened on 1 January 1880, partly to serve the cattle market, but it came to be important for its sidings, the connections to Rowntree's Works, and the link with the Derwent Valley Light Railway. The sidings included those of York Corporation, York Gas Company, Anglo-American Oil and the Station Hotel Laundry, and the branch gained a halt in 1927 to cater for the Rowntree's work people. Originally called Rowntree's Cocoa Works, this lay on the initial 15 ch double track section of the branch and was followed by the ground frame controlling the siding access. From 38 ch to the buffer stops at 1 m 29 ch, the branch was single track and worked on the One Train basis. It had a line speed maximum of 20 mph and was controlled by the Burton Lane signal box. Closure followed a 'last train' on 8 July 1988.

At one period York had no less than six engine sheds, but the emphasis changed to the north end with the building of a new shed there under an authorization of March 1878. The situation was to change many times subsequently and in pre-grouping days as many as six railways had some sort of locomotive facilities at York. The York railway complex also included carriage and wagon works to the west of the main line and, to the east, what was originally the Y&NM locomotive works eventually became the Queen Street Museum, established by the enterprise and public spiritedness of the old North Eastern Railway. The National Railway Museum is its modern successor.

The approach to York is via Dringhouses Junction (186 m 67 ch) where crossovers link the Main and Leeds lines, and where the former Down yard is now marked only by its lighting towers. Over the years York local and transfer traffic was concentrated on the Up side Dringhouses Yard where the raised 'knuckle' helped to increase wagon separation during the shunting process without creating the sort of braking requirements needed in full hump yards. There is now little activity here and the York approaches will be further simplified in the forthcoming remodelling scheme.

Near Holgate Junction (188 m 8 ch) an Up side flower bed with 'York' lettered in stone is a reminder of the LNER efforts to landscape the lineside. There are Up and Down Goods Loops here, as well as the 1 m 46 ch loop west to rejoin the main line beyond the station at Skelton. The latter accommodates the sidings of the various engineering functions and runs via York Yard South (25 ch) and York Yard North (79 ch) boxes. Track Circuit Block applies over most of the avoiding line and on the 41 ch second access to Clifton Carriage sidings (now closed).

Prior to remodelling, York station consisted of the main Up side administrative area, where the important services used the long, through No 8 platform line, and two Down side islands, the main one offering

The remains of the old station at York, seen through the arch in the city walls.

Ornamentation at York, with the former tea bar on the left, the span over the north end bays in the centre, and the hotel to the right.

through lines to platforms 9 and 14 and the outer island accommodating further through lines at platforms 15 and 16. All the through lines were bi-directional and Permissive, ie able to take more than one train in the section, including the Up and Down Main lines which lay beneath the station's main span and between platforms 8 and 9. Subsidiary spans and canopies covered the bays, three at each end on the Up side and two at each end of the inner Down side island.

From the city of York the approach to the station tends to involve passing the headquarters offices which were built in 1906 for the North Eastern Railway to the designs of Horace Field and William Bell, and now house its Eastern Region successor. It is an imposing building with considerable but tasteful decoration, and makes the former offices nearby seem drab by comparison. The station itself is then preceded by what used to be the railway hotel, a handsome four-storey building with some excellent interior features.

Thomas Prosser originated the design of the main station and William Peachey completed the 1877 construction. The subdued *porte-cochère* frontage leads to a circulating area and then to the station proper where the great roof spans are raised on massive Corinthian columns and provided with end screens which skilfully enhance their stature. On the wide footbridge and in the support spandrels appear monograms and coats of arms, and the 1906 tea room building is very evocative of past catering of the best kind—including the availability of a luncheon hamper, with wine, for only 2/6d (12½p)!

Among the many interesting features of York station are a NER tiled map and a hundred-year-old semaphore signal brought from Haxby and erected in the concourse. There is also a plaque in the wall of a new waiting building which acts as a reminder of the bombing of the station in the small hours of 29 April 1942, and of Station Foreman William Milner, a member of the LNER Ambulance Movement who gave his life in an effort to help others. Other buildings and places of railway interest in York include the National Railway Museum, the old Station Hotel, the access arch in the city wall leading to the old station, and the 1924 NER War Memorial by Sir Edwin Lutyens.

North from York the Scarborough line turns sharply east and the ECML mileage of 188 m 40 ch from King's Cross starts again at zero where lines X/Y provided the second access route to Clifton sidings. The National Railway Museum premises on the Down side are followed by the loco fuelling sidings, those of the civil engineer, coal sidings, and the BSC access, with the Harrogate line departing west at Skelton (1 m 51 ch).

The whole York area is affected by a remodelling scheme which started in 1988.

To go with electrification the area will benefit from an £18 million resignalling and track simplification programme which will help to improve train approach speeds and operational flexibility and to reduce track maintenance costs. A new signalling centre will control 42 route miles of railway and also supply comprehensive train information to the station, which has already benefited from a £950,000 scheme of improvements to the travel centre, waiting room and left luggage office. The scheme will remove surplus running lines and sidings and reduce the station lines to five through and five bay lines.

As befits such an important geographical and railway centre, York enjoys a very good train service both on the East Coast route between London and Scotland and across country, to Liverpool/Manchester and via the NE/SW route to Derby, Birmingham and beyond. It has some very useful local services to Hull, Sheffield, Leeds, etc. The modern *Flying Scotsman* covers the 188½ miles to King's Cross in 2 hours and 1 minute, and even better things are due under electrification. By comparison, the loss of the ticket revenue from the daily train to the Rowntree halt seems of importance only to its three regular users.

Y.3   York-Scarborough Line
East Coast Main Line, branch from York.
42 m 6 ch

Scarborough, a settlement since very early times, was quick to convert its spa tradition into one of catering for the visitors brought by the railway age. There had been railway talk in the town early in the 1830s and by the end of the decade George Hudson and his York & North Midland Railway were committed to building a line from York. The enabling Act was obtained on 4 July 1844 and only one year and three days later the opening was being celebrated.

The 42-mile line has no gradients of significance, but achieves this only by following a section of the winding course of the River Derwent. The original plan had been to tunnel through the high ground near Kirkham Abbey, but this cost was avoided at the expense to future generations of a drop from the 60-70 mph line speeds applying elsewhere along the route to 40-45 mph between the 13¾ and 18¾ mileposts.

By the last quarter of the nineteenth century and on into this one, holiday and excursion traffic to Scarborough had reached very high levels, completely swamping the modest local traffic on the route. Thus, in

A1 'Pacific' 60126, appropriately named Sir Vincent Raven, *pulls out of York station with the Up* Northumbrian *in 1951.*

an early piece of railway rationalization, the wayside stations along the Scarborough line lost their passenger service as early as 22 September 1930, although an alternative station-to-station bus service was provided and the goods facilities were maintained until 1964.

The route leaves the East Coast Main Line at the north end of York station, immediately crosses the River Ouse, and then passes the now-closed Burton Lane signal box where the Foss Islands branch used to connect. Bootham Lane level crossing with its traditional gates and signal box (1 m 51 ch) marks the departure point for the trackbed of the former line to Market Weighton (22¼ m) via Earswick (2½ m), Warthill (6 m), Holtby (8 m), Stamford Bridge (9¼ m), Fangfoss (11¾ m), Pocklington (16 m), Nunburnholme (18½ m) and Londesborough (20½ m). This opened on 4 October 1847, with the Market Weighton-Beverley extension then waiting until 1890. The route lost its York-Hull service with the closure on 29 November 1965.

Heading almost due north, the York-Scarborough line passes Haxby Road (3 m 27 ch) and Haxby (4 m 18 ch) crossings and station remains, and then curves north east to Strensall's three crossings, No 1 (6 m), No 2 (6 m 11 ch) and Strensall proper (6 m 48 ch). The latter, with its signal box, lies east of the station site where the station house survives in a red brick form typical of the line. More station buildings and crossings appear on the section ahead to Malton, some retaining the 'viewing' bays which

probably owed something to earlier toll house designs.

After Common Road LC (7 m 52 ch) comes Flaxton (9 m 21 ch), where the crossing gates follow the old station platforms, and then Barton Hill (11 m 48 ch) where the Up side station house survives and the small, square signal box controls the barrier crossing, as well as the Absolute Block section from Strensall and on to Kirkham Abbey. A short distance to the south of Barton Hill, along the course of the River Derwent, lies the Scrayingham burial place of George Hudson, the 'Railway King' who helped to create the original line.

Near Howsham Hall and Howsham LC (13 m 28 ch) the Scarborough route begins a long S bend with the Derwent on its right. Before Kirkham Abbey LC and signal box (15 m 1 ch), where the former station buildings still display their clock, there is an excellent view of the ruins of the twelfth century priory and of a weir on the river. The route is now wooded and an elaborate stone lodge acts as a reminder that Castle Howard lies just a short distance north of the railway. Another stone building marks the site of Castle Howard station and the line then continues its riverside course, past a small suspension footbridge and on to the former Huttons Ambo station where the double curve gives way to a final straight approach to Malton (21 m 12ch). Castle Howard station had been designed by G.T. Andrews in an elaborate style to match its role of serving a great country house.

Malton, former junction for Driffield and

Built at York two years after the formation of the NER, this York & North Midland Class '254' locomotive would have worked on almost any of the NER Yorkshire lines up to 1890.

Scarborough forms the eastern starting point for some cross-Pennine services. Here, a Sprinter set for Manchester waits to depart from Platform 3 at the end of 1987.

Pilmoor, has a separate entry. Its Up side signal box (21 m 32 ch) is followed by traces of the former connecting routes before the Scarborough line sets off via the ex-railway cottage at West Moor to Rillington (25 m 42 ch). Here the station house still stands on the Up side, in addition to the level crossing and signal box. Beyond the station is the site of the junction for the old branch to Pickering.

The Rillington-Pickering line was opened at the same time as the Scarborough line and was part of the package that had persuaded the railway promoters of Whitby to build their rail outlet southwards to Pickering. It became part of an important rail route, carrying the through service from London and the West Riding to Whitby as well as a York/Malton-Whitby local service. The latter called at Marishes Road, 7½ miles from Malton and the only stop on the Rillington-Pickering portion. The route closed on 8 March 1965.

Between Rillington and Seamer there were formerly stations at Knapton, Heslerton, Weaverthorpe and Ganton, all with goods facilities. They remain marked by the section's intermediate crossings which are located at High Scampston (26 m 19 ch), Knapton (27 m 41 ch), Heslerton Station (29 m 32 ch), West Heslerton (30 m 52 ch), East Heslerton (31 m), Weaverthorpe (32 m 68 ch) and Ganton (34 m 34 ch). Weaverthorpe signal box is still operational.

Seamer West signal box (38 m 63 ch) marks the junction between the Scarborough line and the one from Hull via Bridlington. The location, which has its own entry, was also linked with Pickering by a single line which had opened on 1 May 1882 and which lost its passenger services on 5 June 1950. The final stretch from Seamer to Scarborough (42 m 6 ch) runs between the Mere Lake and 500 ft high Oliver's Mount on the seaward side and tumuli-ridden high ground inland.

The Scarborough line has been used for some years for steam-hauled weekend excursion services, maintaining its past traditions as a leisure route. But more important are the Sprinter trains which run to Liverpool via Huddersfield and Manchester via Halifax and which give Scarborough excellent national connections along the way. There are also some additional York services and, of course, those to and from Hull via Seamer and Bridlington.

Tyne & Wear Metro

The Metro system of Tyneside consists of 55 km (34.18 miles) of modern, rapid transit electric railway which is broadly integrated with other train, bus and ferry transport in the area through special interchange centres, lesser interchange points, and common publicity. The system derives from a study of the transportation needs of Tyneside which resulted in strategic recommendations for implementation by the Passenger Transport Authority of the Tyne & Wear region. The enabling Act for the Metro scheme, the Tyneside Metropolitan Railway Act, was obtained in 1973 and by the following year the implementing Passenger Transport Executive had placed the first contract.

Although it used existing technology, the new system evolved its own special design standards aimed at reducing construction and operating costs. It had the immense advantage of being able to base 42 km (26 miles) of its route on existing BR lines, leaving only 13 km (8 miles) of new construction. Needless to say, however, the new construction was in the most difficult places, mainly Newcastle city centre where a new bridge over the Tyne and a new underground section were required. There were major and difficult works beneath Newcastle Central station, for example.

The former North Eastern Railway had electrified the suburban lines out to Tynemouth and the coast at the beginning of the century, and the LNER had added the line to South Shields in 1938. Diesel multiple units were more recently put to work on the local system, but it badly needed investment and revision if it was to compete effectively with road transport and properly meet the social and economic needs of the area. The inputs of finance and an overall view of transport requirements became available through the Metro scheme and, after detailed BR/PTE discussions, the suburban rail lines were transferred to new ownership.

After the years of construction and testing, the final section of the Metro system came into use in March 1984 and it now carries over 60 million passengers a year. It is the most intensively used local transport system in Britain and takes some £78 m annually towards its £109 m costs. Allowing for savings in other areas it is reckoned that the Metro earns a return of 8 per cent on capital.

The system uses an overhead electric power supply at 1,500 V dc, drawn through nine substations, to feed the paired, articulated lightweight passenger vehicles. Each double vehicle runs on three bogies, weighs 39 tonnes, and has a seating capacity of 84 with a crush load capacity of 200. There are 88 cars in the fleet, all fitted with pneumatic sliding doors. Sixty-eight cars are needed to make up the 34 trains of the normal Monday to Saturday service.

Above *The former NER station at Whitley Bay, now carrying the M logo of the Tyne & Wear Metro system.*

Below *Metro train arriving at South Shields station, located close to the town shopping centre.*

Metro trains are controlled by two and three-aspect colour light signalling, and operate within automatic speed limitation and emergency braking parameters. Regulation is from an illuminated panel in the Central Control Room, each train feeding its number and running data into control computers via trackside transponders. Signalling and route setting is then automatic unless a manual override is needed at the panel or to deal with local emergencies.

Many of the stations on the system are new and exploit modern materials to give them functional utility without sacrificing a pleasant appearance. The ex-BR stations have been sympathetically modernized. Ticketing is by zone with tickets obtained from change-giving machines and then used to secure access to the platform, where train information is displayed. There are frequent on-train ticket checks.

The Metro has one route south of the Tyne, that out to South Shields. This leaves the city centre and crosses the river via the new Queen Elizabeth Bridge and then passes through a short tunnel section in which Gateshead station is located. The course then runs parallel with the BR Sunderland line, taking the space occupied by two of the former four tracks, passing through Felling to the BR/Metro interchange point at Heworth where the stations of the two systems are side by side. Pelaw Metro station is next, with carriage sidings following and then a crossing of the BR Ferryhill and Sunderland lines in order to continue the course along the south bank of the river.

The BR freight line to Simonside runs along the north side of the Metro route beyond Pelaw, the latter being built single with long double-line station sections in order to accommodate both systems on the available trackbed. There are Metro stations at Hebburn and Jarrow, the latter incorporating a mural remembering the Jarrow March of the depression years. At Bede the Simonside BR line ends, but the Metro acquires a fresh companion in the coal route from Boldon which joins after the short Tyne Dock Tunnel. Dean Road ER/NC exchange sidings follow Tyne Dock station, dusty coal hopper wagons contrasting with the white and orange livery of the Metro trains. These provide another view of coal activity as they pass over the National Coal electrified link to Crossgate sorting sidings and the staiths beyond.

The eastern end of the South Shields route has forsaken the course of the former BR line through the declining riverside industrial area in favour of a new elevated approach to the town. This curves into a station above the main shopping area and comprises just a single platform with three carriage sidings beyond. There is a 10-minute interval service from South Shields station, and the ferry to North Shields is only five minutes walk away.

The other end of Metroline 1 will take the passenger back from South Shields to the busy Metro station below Newcastle Central and then on in the tunnel, first to the Monument interchange with Metroline 4 (St James-North Shields), and then to Haymarket. The route on to Bank Foot first follows the course of the old Blyth & Tyne and then turns west to pick up the Ponteland branch.

Between Jesmond and West Jesmond a single line over the course of the ex-BR connection to Manors is now used for empty stock movements. Beyond the latter the Metro route then passes through a new station at Ilford Road to South Gosforth, which the LNER made its main electric stock depot after a fire at Walkergate. Today the triangle between the Metro lines from the city, east to Whitley Bay and west to Bank Foot is the heart of the Metro system, housing its stock, engineering and control facilities. The depot sidings extend along Metroline 1 towards Regent Centre after the Bank Foot line has been joined by the BR freight line from Benton Junction, which has passed behind the main Gosforth depot building.

There are modern Metro stations at Wansbeck Road, Fawdon and Kingston Park after the interchange complex at Regents Centre. This was a single line BR freight route before doubling for Metro use and BR services to ICI at Callerton still use the line under Metro operating regulations. They continue beyond Bank Foot where the Metro services currently terminate at a single platform, although extension of the Metro to Newcastle Airport has now been approved.

The service on Metroline 2 runs between Pelaw and Benton, following the same route as Metroline 1 as far as South Gosforth where the trains turn east on to what was originally an 1864 B&T line to Monkseaton; the BR origins show in the stations at Longbenton and Benton. The latter has cranage and dock facilities and is followed by two spurs, a dead-end north to two carriage servicing platforms, and the connection south to the BR main line at Benton Quarry Junction.

The route east of Benton is part of Metroline 3, the trains from Pelaw leaving Benton, passing over the East Coast Main Line, and continuing through Palmersville to Shiremoor. Along here a new line was laid to carry the BR freight connection to the B&T lines, running on the north side of the former trackbed which was taken over by the Metro. The two systems part company at Shiremoor with the Metro trains then continuing to West Monkseaton, where the trackbed of the old line from Hartley can still be seen.

The original 1860/1 route to Tynemouth was altered in 1882 to create a loop which would link up with the North Shields line. Along this section of the Metro system the NER origins are more apparent than anywhere else. Rebuilt in 1915, Monkseaton has long brick buildings with a traditional booking hall and a pre-

The Metro station at Bank Foot with a South Shields train at the single platform. The BR single freight line to Callerton is on the left.

platform arcade. Whitley Bay, modified in 1910, has a tall, decorated clock tower as well, while the 1882 Tynemouth is a riot of under-utilized accommodation, including former bays, vast canopies and highly elaborate ironwork. The 1882 rerouting overlaid an 1865 extension of the Blyth & Tyne to North Shields and displaced three B&T locations plus that of the Newcastle & North Shields Railway's 1847 terminus.

Beyond Tynemouth the Metro route passes beneath the main Tynemouth Road to pick up the course of the N&NS and reach the present North Shields station. Before the tunnel section here there are traces of the ex-B&T junctions where freight used to reverse to get to the goods depot. The Metro has an engineers' depot between North Shields and Smith's Park and then, near the elevated platforms of Percy Main, there are traces of the mineral line network that originated as the Seghill Railway portion of the Blyth & Tyne and reached inland to bring coal from as far away as Seaton and Cramlington for shipment at Northumberland Dock.

The course of the old Riverside Branch can be seen after Percy Main, the Metro then continuing through modern stations at Howdon, Hadrian Road, Wallsend and Walkergate and its elevated course providing an interesting view of the industrialized north bank of the Tyne. A rusting British Steel siding heralds the meeting of Metro and ECML, where Chillingham station serves the transport needs of the nearby Heaton depot. Through Byker and Manors the Metro exchanges the vantage point of the stylish, slimline Ouseburn Viaduct for a descent underground which finally leads to Monument and then the streamlined terminus at St James.

To the north of the Metro route on this section the heyday of coal movement to Percy Main is recalled at Middle Engine Lane where the George Stephenson Railway Museum project contains vintage locomotives and rolling stock, including *Killingworth Billy*. Middle Engine Lane was also the site of the Metro system's test track in 1975.

The routes

The geography of the Northern Operating Area of the Eastern Region is such that it is dominated by the East Coast Main Line and by the cross-Pennine routes on which the network of West Riding railways is centred. Indeed, so far as north-south routes are concerned, virtually all the others have gone, the Leeds Northern cut between Harrogate and Northallerton, the coastal link from Hull to Middlesbrough deprived of the portion north of Scarborough, and lesser routes, like the ones via Wetherby, Market Weighton, Gilling and Pickering, now little more than a memory. However, the Northallerton-Eaglescliffe (N.11), Ferryhill-Pelaw (F.6) and Blyth & Tyne (B.16) lines do still survive as freight routes, and there are excellent services along the Yorkshire coast between Hull and Scarborough (H.35).

The east-west route picture has also changed dramatically over the years. Of the five routes across the country between Wensleydale and the Tweed only the earliest, that between Newcastle and Carlisle (N.5), has survived. Further south, rationalization victims have included the Hull & Barnsley system and the eastern end of the pioneer Manchester & Leeds line, now handling a few freight trains instead of the 200 passenger trains a day that once used it. On the credit side are the useful Bishop Auckland-Saltburn route described below, the delightful Esk Valley line to Whitby (M.15), the ex-L&Y line to Goole (W.2) and, of course, the busy and thriving Liverpool/Manchester-Leeds-Scarborough/Hull complex, also covered below.

East Coast Main Line

North of Doncaster and the lines off to Hull and Wakefield, the East Coast Main Line passes beneath the West Riding & Grimsby line and comes to Shaftholme Junction. Here the former course over the L&Y line to Knottingley is still in use for freight, but present ECML services take the 1871 route towards Selby, through a flat landscape of west-east waterways and huge power stations. After crossing over the Knottingley-Goole line, trains pick up the 1983 Selby Diversion at Temple Hirst Junction, and then the course of the 1839 York & North Midland Railway at Colton Junction. Via the site of the former Chaloners Whin Junction they then complete the section into York, historic cathedral city, railway headquarters, home of the National Railway Museum and currently having its layout remodelled.

At the north end of York's imposing station the main line swings away from the Scarborough line and then sheds the route to Harrogate and Leeds at Skelton Junction. The ensuing section over the Plain of York was built by the Great North of

A view of the High Level Bridge at Newcastle with the castle keep in the background.

England Railway and opened in 1841. It passes through Alne, where the modest Easingwold Railway branched off, and Pilmoor which was once a junction with lines east via Gilling to Malton and Pickering and west to Boroughbridge and Knaresborough. One of the two routes of the Leeds Northern trunk route from Leeds and Harrogate used to join the ECML at Thirsk, with the other joining at Northallerton, the courses of both still being visible. The onward route of the Leeds Northern survives as a freight-only line to Eaglescliffe, leaving the ECML just before the surviving single freight line into Wensleydale.

The former Richmond branch used to leave the main line at Eryholme, but now its course continues untrammelled to a bridge over the Tees at Croft and then joins the Saltburn line for the entry into Darlington, where avoiding lines pass east of the station. Here there are several reminders of the place of Darlington in railway history, including a sign marking the point where the Stockton & Darlington Railway crossed the main line in one of the most famous of railway right angle crossings. The S&D enterprise is perpetuated by the course of the branch to Bishop Auckland, in part of the route east to Middlesbrough, and in a museum project housed in the former S&D station at North Road, Darlington.

On the main line north of Darlington, the original GNofE enterprise was handed over to the Newcastle & Darlington Junction company which opened a line via Ferryhill to Rainton Crossing in 1844. The onward course to Gateshead was via Brockley Whins (Boldon) until 1849, and then via Pelaw. On the first part of this Darlington-Newcastle section today's trains pass beneath the route of the old Clarence Railway just north of Aycliffe and then meet that company again at Ferryhill, in the form of the freight line from Stockton. Another east-west route at

Ferryhill is still marked by the Kelloe Bank Foot Branch, which once continued east to Hartlepool and west to the Wear Valley and the West Durham coalfields.

The Old Main Line leaves the 1871/2 new one at Tursdale Junction north of Ferryhill, the latter descending and rising again to the former Relly Mill Junction at Durham. Here the Bishop Auckland, Crook and Newcastle via Blackhill routes used to join, the 1856/7 course of the former being used over Durham's high viaduct and through the station as far as Newton Hall Junction. It then continues to Leamside, leaving the present 1868 route to drop at 1 in 150 to Chester-le-Street.

The ECML, having crossed the Tees at Darlington and the Wear at Durham, now heads past Tyne Yard and the junctions with the Carlisle line for the dramatic bridges across the Tyne and the equally dramatic station which follows them. The earlier, High Level bridge and the link between Newcastle Central and Manors date from 1848, and the King Edward Bridge upstream from 1906. East of Manors, where the Blyth & Tyne network used to connect and the Quayside and Riverside lines depart, the ECML uses the 1839 route to North Shields as far as Heaton Junction, site of Newcastle's main carriage depot.

From Heaton to Berwick the original line was built by the Newcastle & Berwick Railway and was opened in 1847. At Benton Junction the present link with the surviving B&T lines heads off east and that via the Metro system to ICI Callerton turns west, leaving the main line to head for Morpeth where the B&T system

A Deltic speeds south along the East Coast Main Line south of Darlington in 1975.

rejoins and the North British line from Scotsgap used to make its junction. A second B&T connection follows at Butterwell.

North of Morpeth the ECML runs close to the Northumberland shore line using viaducts to cross rivers like the Wansbeck, Coquet and Aln. After former branches to Amble and Newton-on-the-Moor, the Aln commands a dip down to the picturesque site of Alnmouth station, once the junction for Alnwick and the scenic route to Coldstream. Alnmouth has a new, modern and quite attractive station, but other N&B stations provide a considerable contrast, their elaborate period architecture representing some of the best examples of railway buildings in the country.

On the final English portion of the East Coast Main Line, the former North Sunderland Railway left for Seahouses at Chathill and there is a view of Holy Island soon afterwards. Then comes Tweedmouth where the trains along the Tweed from Coldstream used to reverse before completing their journey to Berwick over the Royal Border Bridge. Following the excellent view that this affords comes Berwick station, historically situated on a castle site which saw its share of the border strife between England and Scotland. The border and the Regional Boundary follow.

S.13	Shaftholme Junction (160 m 16 ch)	F.6	Ferryhill-Pelaw Line
S.14	Shaftholme Junction-Knottingley Line	D.14	Durham (66 m 13 ch)
		C.10	Chester-le-Street (71 m 72 ch)
T.4	Temple Hirst Junction (169 m 16 ch)	T.16	Tyne Yard (75 m 62 ch)
		L.8	Low Fell Junction (77 m 37 ch)
T.5	Temple Hirst Junction-Selby Line	N.4	King Edward Bridge South Junction
H.3	Hambleton South Junction (174 m 10 ch)		(79 m 42 ch)
		N.5	Newcastle-Carlisle Line
L.3	Leeds-Hull Line	N.4	King Edward Bridge North Junction
H.3	Hambleton North Junction (174 m 75 ch)		(79 m 57 ch)
		N.4	Newcastle West Junction (80 m 5 ch)
C.14	Colton Junction (182 m 79 ch) Leeds and Sheffield Lines	N.3	Newburn Branch
Y.2	Holgate Junction (188 m 8 ch)	N.4	Newcastle (80 m 16 ch/0 ch)
Y.2	York (188 m 40 ch/O ch)	N.4	Newcastle East Junction
Y.3	York-Scarborough Line		Newcastle-Middlesbrough/North-
Y.2	Skelton (1 m 51 ch)		allerton Line
L.4	Leeds-York Line	N.4	Manors (46 ch)
T.12	Tollerton (9 m 40 ch)	N.4	Riverside Junction (1 m 25 ch)
T.7	Thirsk (22 m 16 ch)	R.5	Riverside Branch
N.10	Longlands Junction (28 m 71 ch)	N.4	Heaton (2 m 16 ch)
N.10	Northallerton (29 m 76 ch)	B.15	Benton South Junction (4 m 20 ch)
N.10	High Junction (30 m 9 ch)	C.1	Callerton Branch
N.11	Northallerton-Eaglescliffe Line	B.15	Benton North Junction (4 m 24 ch)
N.10	Castle Hills Junction (30 m 63 ch)	B.16	Benton-Morpeth Line
R.3	Redmire Branch	C.18	Cramlington (9 m 74 ch)
E.10	Eryholme (38 m 72 ch)	M.23	Morpeth (16 m 50 ch)
D.2	Darlington South Junction (43 m 61 ch)	B.16	Benton-Morpeth Line
		P.3	Pegswood (18 m 44 ch)
M.14	Saltburn Line	B.41	Butterwell Junction (20 m 63 ch)
D.2	Darlington (44 m 10 ch)	A.12	Ashington Branch
D.2	Parkgate Junction (44 m 58 ch)	W.13	Widdrington (23 m 20 ch)
B.22	Bishop Auckland Branch	A.2	Acklington (28 m 43 ch)
F.4	Ferryhill South Junction (56 m 17 ch)	A.5	Alnmouth (34 m 69 ch)
		C.9	Chathill (45 m 78 ch)
F.5	Ferryhill-Norton-on-Tees Line	B.11	Belford (51 m 45 ch)
F.4	Ferryhill (56 m 70 ch)	T.14	Tweedmouth (65 m 78 ch)
K.2	Kelloe Bank Foot Junction (57 m 50 ch)	B.17	Berwick (67 m)
		B.17	Regional Boundary (69 m 67 ch)
K.2	Kelloe Bank Foot Branch		

Above *An Up HST speeds past the sign marking the halfway point between London and Edinburgh on the East Coast Main Line.*

Below *Ancient and modern architectural styles on the concourse of Newcastle station.*

A tubular pile being lifted from the Self Contained Piling Vehicle as part of the preparatory work for electrification.

Middlesbrough-Newcastle

Soon after leaving Middlesbrough, the Middlesbrough-Newcastle local trains pick up the course of the 1830 Stockton & Darlington extension, and follow this past Tees Yard to the junction with the original S&D line at Bowesfield. From there the Hartburn Curve carries the trains round to meet the Leeds Northern line and into the massive, under-utilized station at Stockton. The section on to Hartlepool is also served by the Darlington-Hartlepool trains. It uses part of the 1833 Clarence Railway to get to Norton, where the freight line for Ferryhill departs, and then continues on to Billingham.

Beyond Billingham the course of the 1840/1 Stockton & Hartlepool Railway, rid of the Clarence Railway route which now serves the freight needs of Haverton Hill and Seals Sands, turns north east for the Hartlepool conurbation via the connections for the British Steel works and the Hartlepool nuclear power station. There has been much rationalization in the area and this is very apparent either side of Hartlepool, where the Newburn Yard area now lies desolate and the route of the docks lines is bare of activity. Beyond Hartlepool station the important surviving line takes an elevated course around the docks area to get to Cemetery North, where the siding connection to the Steetley works marks the course of the 1835 coal route from Haswell pits into Hartlepool proper. Present day trains use this as far as the former junction at Hart.

The line from Hart, on the Hartlepool-Ferryhill/Sunderland route, to Seaham was opened by the North Eastern Railway in 1905 and passes several collieries on its coastal journey. The port at Seaham has handled coal since wagonway days and there is still a considerable volume of coal movement by rail in this area. Between Seaham and Sunderland the rail route is that opened in 1854/5 by the Marquis of Londonderry—again for coal movement—and one of his stations still exists as the accommodation at Hall Dene level crossing. Then comes Ryhope Grange, where the present rail connection from National Coal's Hawthorn plant was once part of the Durham & Sunderland Railway's 1836 line to the South Dock area of Wearside.

Sunderland's present sub-surface city centre station is on a site brought into use when the lines north and south of the Wear were linked in 1879. The two routes inland along the Wear are closed (apart from a short shipyard branch), as is the Brandling Junction Railway's route to North Dock, Wearmouth, but rail freight traffic is still handled in the South Dock area and Sunderland has an excellent passenger service to Newcastle and Hexham, as well as to Middlesbrough.

The classical station at Monkwearmouth is now used for museum purposes and the next stops on the original 1839 line are Seaburn and East Boldon. The latter heralds a highly interesting railway area where the right angle Pontop Crossing marks the point at which the Stanhope & Tyne and Brandling Junction lines crossed. To the south west lies the former ore route to Consett and Stanhope, while the surviving line towards the Tyne connects with Tyne Dock and National Coal's lines around South Shields. Boldon Colliery station, as Brockley Whins, was on the first railway route from London to the Tyne.

At Pelaw Junction our route is joined by the freight line from Ferryhill which was used by main line trains until the route via Durham was created. The Metro system crosses the two BR lines east of Pelaw, now sharing the course of the South Shields route which the LNER electrified in 1938 with the surviving single freight line to Jarrow, Hebburn and Simonside.

Above *A two-car Class '143' Pacer set pauses at Stockton on its way from Middlesbrough to Newcastle.*

Below *Elegant ironwork and a sturdy Potts clock at Hartlepool.*

West along the Tyne from Pelaw there is an interchange station with the Metro at Heworth before the ex-BJR route passes Tyneside Central Freight Depot, crosses the river by means of the High Level Bridge, and completes its course at Newcastle's imposing and complex station.

M.13	Middlesbrough (15 m from Darlington)	R.8	Ryhope Grange (87 m 63 ch)
		S.5	Seabanks Branch
T.2	Tees (13 m 59 ch)	R.8	Hawthorn Branch
T.8	Thornaby (11 m 63 ch)	S.41	Sunderland South Tunnels (89 m 6 ch to 89 m 45 ch)
B.27	Bowesfield (10 m 76 ch/44 ch)		
H.7	Hartburn Junction (0 ch/59 m 14 ch from Leeds)	S.41	Sunderland (89 m 60 ch)
		S.41	Sunderland North Tunnel (89 m 64 ch to 89 m 76 ch)
S.39	Stockton (60 m 4 ch)		
S.39	North Shore (60 m 47 ch)	M.20	Monkwearmouth (90 m 26 ch)
S.39	Freightliner Terminal Branch	A.14	Austin & Pickersgill Shipyard Branch
N.15	Norton-on-Tees South (61 m 71 ch)		
		S.6	Seaburn (91 m 33 ch)
N.15	Norton-on-Tees East (62 m 19 ch)	E.3	East Boldon (93 m 17 ch)
F.5	Ferryhill-Norton Line	B.24	Boldon Colliery (95 m 12 ch)
B.19	Billingham (63 m 60 ch)	B.24	Boldon West Junction (95 m 16 ch)
B.19	Billingham Junction (63 m 69 ch)		
B.20	Billingham-Seal Sands Storage Line	B.24	Tyne Coal Terminal Branch
G.12	Greatham (67 m 28 ch)	P.4	Pelaw Junction (98 m 7 ch)
S.11	Seaton Snook Junction (68 m 60 ch)	S.22	Simonside Branch
		P.4	Pelaw Junction (98 m 16 ch)
S.10	Seaton-on-Tees Branch	F.6	Ferryhill-Pelaw Line
S.9	Seaton Carew (69 m 36 ch)	H.21	Heworth (99 m)
C.13	Cliff House (68 m 60 ch)	N.4	St James Bridge Junction (100 m 23 ch)
H.8	Hartlepool (71 m 55 ch)		
H.8	Cemetery North (73 m 49 ch)	N.4	Park Lane Junction (100 m 68 ch)
H.30	Horden (78 m 58 ch)	N.4	High Level Bridge Junction (101 m 33 ch)
E.2	Easington (80 m 35 ch)		
D.4	Dawdon (84 m 22 ch)	N.4	Newcastle East Junction (101 m 59 ch)
S.7	Seaham (84 m 44 ch)		

Bishop Auckland-Saltburn

Sections of this route east and west from Darlington perpetuate the original course of the Stockton & Darlington Railway which subsequently extended its main line to Middlesbrough, and then through associated schemes to the coast at Redcar and west into Weardale and through Barnard Castle to the West Coast Main Line. Today the route carries Bishop Auckland and Darlington to Saltburn services, plus Darlington-Hartlepool trains over its centre section.

At the simple, modern station at Bishop Auckland the single line freight route from the Wear Valley joins the passenger line to Darlington. Opened in 1842/3, this passes through Shildon Tunnel to join the original S&D route from West Auckland just beyond Shildon station. The services via Barnard Castle used to join here and then, like today's services, turn south via the site of Simpasture Junction, start of the 1833 Clarence Railway route to Port Clarence and the line used by the Shildon-Newport electrically-hauled coal trains of the NER/LNER era. Beyond Simpasture Junction lie Newton Aycliffe and Heighington stations, with the other former route from Barnard Castle joining just before the veteran North Road station.

After shedding the Darlington 'depots' branch, the 1825 S&D line left North Road station and headed east to Albert Hill Junction. There the main line continued its course and crossed the ECML on the level, whereas present services take the route of the S&D's Croft branch to join the ECML at Parkgate Junction and the following island platform of Darlington Bank Top. South of this is the Saltburn line trains use an 1887 line to rejoin the original S&D course at Oak Tree Junction.

The half-hourly Saltburn trains pass Tees-side Airport which has a simple station nearby and then continue through the MoD station at Allen's West. At Eaglescliffe the Leeds Northern route from Northallerton joins briefly, departing again for Stockton beyond the island platform of Eaglescliffe station. A spur from the Stockton direction joins at Bowesfield Junction, which is where the Saltburn trains abandon the original S&D route to the Tees staiths in favour of an 1830 extension through Thornaby and past the marshalling yard and traction depot at Tees. As Newport Yard this was the eastern end of the electrified coal route from Shildon until 1935, and it still handles substantial volumes of freight to and from the extensive industrial sites dominating the section along the south bank of the Tees.

Although badly bombed in the war, Middlesbrough is still an impressive station. It is the starting point for the service through Hartlepool and Sunderland to Newcastle and for the trains along the beautiful Esk Valley to Whitby. These turn away south at Guisborough Junction opposite Middlesbrough Dock, leaving the Saltburn services to continue east through Cargo Fleet, past the erstwhile Cleveland Railway junction and on through the new station at South Bank to the junctions with the freight lines to the British Steel, ICI and Shell complexes around Grangetown and its station.

After the British Steel station at Redcar the route heads for the gentler coastal area and the period station at Redcar Central. The sea becomes visible from the line at Redcar East, with the line then continuing through Longbeck and Marske to Saltburn West Junction. There the former coastal route to Whitby survives in part as a freight line serving Boulby Potash Mine, leaving a short, separate single line to continue to the pleasant resort of Saltburn, another S&D enterprise prudently 'fronted' by an associated company.

B.22	Bishop Auckland (11 m 23 ch)		Hartlepool Line
E.4	Eastgate Branch	B.27	Bowesfield (10 m 76 ch)
B.22	Shildon Tunnel (8 m 66 ch to 9 m 42 ch)	B.27	Hartburn Curve
		T.8	Thornaby (11 m 63 ch)
B.22	Shildon (8 m 28 ch)	T.2	Tees (13 m 59 ch)
B.22	Newton Aycliffe (6 m 30 ch)	M.13	Middlesbrough (15 m)
B.22	Heighington (5 m 8 ch)	M.13	Guisborough Junction (15 m 23 ch)
B.22	Hopetown Junction (75 ch)		
B.22	North Road Station (49 ch)	M.15	Middlesbrough-Whitby Line
B.22	Albert Hill (32 ch)	M.14	Cargo Fleet (16 m 6 ch)
B.22	Parkgate Junction (O ch/44 m 64 ch/44 m 58 ch)	M.14	South Bank Junction (17 m 31 ch)
		M.14	South Bank (17 m 40 ch)
D.2	Darlington North Junction (44 m 36 ch)	M.14	Beam Mill Junction (18 m 3 ch)
		M.14	Grangetown (18 m 41 ch)
D.2	Darlington (44 m 10 ch)	M.14	Grangetown Junction (18 m 76 ch)
D.2	Darlington South Junction (43 m 61 ch/29 ch)	M.14	Shell Junction (19 m 29 ch)
		M.14	British Steel Redcar (20 m 56 ch)
D.8	Dinsdale (3 m 65 ch)	R.2	Redcar Central (22 m 64 ch)
D.8	Oak Tree Junction (4 m 28 ch)	R.2	Redcar East (23 m 60 ch)
T.3	Tees-side Airport (5 m 43 ch)	M.14	Longbeck (25 m 29 ch)
A.3	Allen's West (8 m 9 ch)	M.14	Marske (25 m 65 ch)
E.1	Eaglescliffe South Junction (8 m 58 ch)	S.2	Saltburn West Junction (27 m 5 ch)
N.11	Northallerton-Eaglescliffe Line	B.26	Boulby Potash Mine Branch
E.1	Eaglescliffe North Junction (9 m 2 ch)	S.2	Saltburn (27 m 57 ch)

Manchester-Leeds-Scarborough/Hull

The original route from Manchester to Leeds was brought into full use on 1 March 1841 when Summit Tunnel was finally completed and trains could make the throughout journey via Milner Royd Junction, Normanton and the North Midland route thence to Leeds Hunslet. Today, the section between Milner Royd and Heaton Lodge Junction is only used for freight, and the cross-Pennine passenger trains travel instead through Halifax and its following tunnels to Bradford, and then over the local route via New Pudsey to Leeds. Like its canal predecessors, this Summit route uses the valley of the River Calder and it offers some spectacular views, as well as a variety of stations as extreme as the contrasting L&Y features of Hebden Bridge and the modernity of Bradford Interchange.

The 1847/9 Colne Valley route from Manchester is equally dramatic with its summit following the climb to Standedge Tunnel and then a narrow valley course through Marsden and Slaithwaite to the tunnel and viaduct approach to Huddersfield, in which it is joined by the route from Sheffield and Barnsley. The platforms at Huddersfield stand between the majestic station buildings on the Up side and a great goods warehouse on the Down.

The exit from Huddersfield is over a long viaduct with this ex-London & North Western line then passing through Deighton to make use of the former Manchester & Leeds route through Mirfield as far as Ravensthorpe, where the direction changes from east to north. The route is now that of the Leeds, Dewsbury & Manchester concern, opened in 1848 and carrying the railway through the heart of the Dewsbury and Batley wool areas to a summit in Morley Tunnel and then down into Leeds.

Today's single central station at Leeds is the culmination of a long period of change and evolution, but it now offers easy interchange between a dozen major

A Leeds-Morecambe train in 1987.

Journey's end for one cross-Pennine route, Scarborough, where the station buildings are dominated by the great clock tower added to the original Andrews block in 1884.

routes and bustles with HSTs, Sprinters, Pacers and dmus. The Liverpool/ Manchester-York/Scarborough Sprinters and the companion Chester-Hull services interconnect with Manchester-Rochdale-York trains and the through Liverpool-Newcastle ones, as well as with the King's Cross services and the local workings to Bradford and on via Skipton, to Barnsley and Sheffield, to Doncaster, to Harrogate, to Ilkley and to Goole.

Leaving Leeds, the Scarborough and Hull trains use the route of the 1834 Leeds & Selby Railway, first passing its original Marsh Lane terminus on the Down side, and then Neville Hill locomotive and carriage depot with its adjoining goods branch to Hunslet East. Former branches departed at Cross Gates for Wetherby and Garforth for Castleford, with the York and Hull routes then separating at Micklefield where the original L&S buildings still survive.

The line to Hull crosses the York-Sheffield line at Milford where the two routes made early connection. Immediately afterwards comes the Gascoigne Wood loading point for the huge Selby coalfield for which the East Coast Main Line was diverted in 1983. Junction is made with the latter's new course at Hambleton, the Hull route then continuing its easterly course to Selby. There, the 1871-1983 course of the ECML from Doncaster remains in use, but the section beyond the station and its swing-bridge over the River Ouse has been abandoned. The same applies to the old Market Weighton line, leaving just the Hull line to follow a course through Wressle, Howden and Eastrington and below the ill-fated Hull & Barnsley Railway to meet the 1869 NER route from Doncaster at Gilberdyke Junction. The final course along the north bank of the Humber estuary shows evidence of the days when docks traffic was heavy, but now even the great Paragon station has been reduced in size.

The section of the York route between Micklefield Junction and Church Fenton dates from 1869, but at the latter point it joins the 1839 York & North Midland Railway line which gave York its first railway link with London. Beyond Church Fenton the trackbed of the 1847 line to Wetherby and Harrogate is visible, the Scarborough trains then continuing through Ulleskelf to meet the East Coast Main Line at Colton Junction. Ahead lies York, where the grand station is matched by the adjoining hotel and the nearby Eastern Region headquarters, and where the National Railway Museum is located.

The present station at York dates from 1877. The Scarborough line and the ECML part company immediately beyond it with the former crossing the River Ouse and heading north west to Burton Lane Junction where the Foss Islands Branch departed (and formerly gave access to the Derwent Valley Light Railway), and then through Bootham Junction where the 1847 line to Market Weighton began. The intermediate stations on the Scarborough line were closed in favour of a bus alternative back in 1930, leaving today's trains to speed on to the curving section along the River Derwent near Kirkham Abbey.

Malton retains its G.T. Andrews station, and bridge abutments mark the course of its former branches to Gilling and Driffield. Through Saturday holiday trains from the north to Scarborough used to travel via the former. On the surviving Scarborough line, Rillington used to mark the divergence of the line to Pickering and Whitby, but the next stop is now at Seamer, where the Hull line joins. Along the final stretch to Scarborough there is more evidence of the volume of the former rail activity, including extensive sidings and the Londesborough Road excursion station, with its adjoining Whitby line tunnel. A locomotive turntable is still used by steam specials and the interesting Scarborough station is still popular and busy.

H.16 Eastwood (22 m 3 ch from Manchester Victoria)
H.16 Weasel Hall Tunnel (23 m 12 ch to 23 m 17 ch)
H.16 Hebden Bridge (23 m 50 ch)
M.22 Mytholmroyd (24 m 68 ch)
S.31 Sowerby Bridge Tunnel (27 m 60 ch to 28 m 10 ch)
S.31 Sowerby Bridge (28 m 51 ch)
M.18 Milner Royd Junction (29 m 21 ch)
M.18 Milner Royd Junction-Mirfield Line
H.1 Bank House Tunnel (30 m 57 ch to 30 m 67 ch)
H.1 Dryclough Junction (31 m 63 ch)
H.1 Halifax (32 m 28 ch)
H.1 Beacon Hill Tunnel (32 m 40 ch to 33 m 10 ch)
H.1 Hipperholme Tunnel (34 m 5 ch to 34 m 22 ch)
H.1 Lightcliffe Tunnel (34 m 67 ch to 34 m 70 ch)
H.1 Wyke Tunnel (36 m 12 ch to 36 m 74 ch)
L.9 Low Moor (37 m 37 ch)
B.29 Bowling Tunnel (38 m 18 ch to 39 m 13 ch)
B.29 Bowling Junction (39 m 20 ch)
B.29 Mill Lane Junction (39 m 79 ch/40 m 3 ch)
B.29 Bradford Interchange (40 m 27 ch)
L.2 Mill Lane Junction (40 m 3 ch/191 m 78 ch)
L.2 Wakefield Road Tunnel (191 m 36 ch to 191 m 42 ch)
Change of mileage 190 m 24 ch to 6 m 49 ch
L.2 Stanningley Tunnel (5 m 22 ch to 5 m 43 ch)
L.2 New Pudsey (4 m 77 ch)
L.2 Bramley (3 m 15 ch)
L.1 Holbeck West Junction (2 ch/185 m 1 ch)
L.1 Holbeck East Junction (185 m 4 ch/42 m 5 ch)
L.1 Whitehall Junction (42 m 23 ch/25 ch)
L.1 Leeds North Junction (5 ch)
L.1 Leeds West Junction (0 ch/20 m 70 ch)
L.1 Leeds (20 m 47 ch)

M.2 Diggle Junction (14 m 59 ch)
S.35 Standedge Tunnel (15 m 11 ch to 18 m 14 ch)
M.2 Marsden (18 m 54 ch)
M.2 Slaithwaite (21 m 19 ch)
H.33 Gledholt North and South Tunnels (25 m 4 ch to 25 m 15 ch)
H.33 Springwood Junction (25 m 20 ch)
B.4 Barnsley-Huddersfield Line

H.33 Huddersfield North and South Tunnels (25 m 20 ch to 25 m 15 ch)
H.33 Huddersfield (25 m 60 ch)
H.33 Hillhouse Junction (26 m 26 ch)
M.2 Deighton (27 m 60 ch)
B.30 Bradley Junction (28 m 39 ch)
H.15 Heaton Lodge South Junction (28 m 78 ch)
H.15 Heaton Lodge Junction (29 m 54 ch)
M.18 Milner Royd Junction-Mirfield Line
M.19 Mirfield East Junction (39 m 26 ch)
Mirfield-Normanton Line
M.2 Thornhill LNW Junction (39 m 72 ch/32 m 16 ch)
M.2 Ravensthorpe (32 m 28 ch)
D.7 Dewsbury (33 m 62 ch)
B.5 Batley (35 m 9 ch)
M.22 Morley Tunnel (36 m 25 ch to 38 m 19 ch)
M.22 Morley (38 m 24 ch)
L.1 Farnley Branch Junction (40 m 65 ch)
L.1 Farnley Branch
L.1 Holbeck East Junction

L.1 Leeds (20 m 47 ch)
L.1 Leeds East Junction (20 m 26 ch)
L.3 Marsh Lane Junction (19 m 48 ch)
L.3 Richmond Hill Tunnel (19 m 44 ch to 19 m 39 ch)
L.3 Neville Hill West Junction (18 m 74 ch)
L.3 Hunslet East Branch
C.23 Cross Gates (16 m 11 ch)
G.1 Garforth (13 m 23 ch)
M.12 Micklefield (10 m 69 ch)
M.12 Micklefield Junction (10 m 63 ch)
L.3 South Milford (7 m 57 ch)
G.2 Gascoigne Wood (6 m 27 ch)
H.3 Hambleton West Junction (4 m 43 ch)
H.3 Hambleton East Junction (3 m 34 ch)
East Coast Main Line
S.12 Selby West Junction (36 ch)
S.12 Selby South Junction (0 ch/31 m 12 ch)
S.5 Temple Hirst Junction-Selby Line
S.12 Selby (30 m 79 ch)
S.12 Selby Swing Bridge (30 m 70 ch)
L.3 Wressle (25 m 3 ch)
L.3 Howden (22 m 27 ch)
L.3 Eastrington (19 m 23 ch)
G.4 Gilberdyke Junction (17 m 7 ch)
Doncaster Line
G.4 Gilberdyke (16 m 76 ch)
B.38 Broomfleet (14 m 33 ch)
B.39 Brough (10 m 38 ch)
M.9 Melton Halt (8 m 46 ch)

F.2 Ferriby (7 m 42 ch)
H.20 Hessle (4 m 64 ch)
H.34 Hessle Road (1 m 74 ch)
H.34 King George Dock Branch
H.34 Anlaby Road Junction (73 ch)
H.34 Hull (0 ch)

M.12 Micklefield Junction (15 m 62 ch)
C.11 Church Fenton (10 m 58 ch)
C.11 Church Fenton North Junction (10
       m 31 ch)
       Sheffield Line
U.1 Ulleskelf (8 m 70 ch)

C.14 Colton Junction (5 m 41 ch/182 m
       79 ch)
       East Coast Main Line
Y.2 York (188 m 40 ch/0 ch)
Y.2 Burton Lane (1 m 9 ch)
Y.2 Foss Islands Branch
M.1 Malton (21 m 12 ch)
Y.3 Rillington (25 m 42 ch)
S.8 Seamer West (38 m 63 ch)
H.35 Hull-Scarborough Line
S.8 Seamer (39 m 17 ch)
S.4 Scarborough (42 m 6 ch)

ER traffic, operation and engineering

Prior to the separation of the new Anglia Region, the Eastern Region 'territory' totalled over 20,000 square miles. The 5,386 single track miles of railway in that area represented 26 per cent of the British Rail total and carried over 150 million passenger journeys a year. The Eastern Region's annual 140,000 freight trains accounted for 43 per cent of the BR total.

The Northern Area of the revised ER is responsible for much of that freight train business which is made up of merry-go-round trains, company trains, Speedlink and Freightliner services. Coal traffic predominates, with iron and steel next in order of volume, followed by petroleum products and then a mix of other bulk commodities like aggregates, chemicals, cement, cars, grain and so on. The coal business is especially important in South Yorkshire.

Passenger business within the ER Northern Area has a number of important elements, chief among them the long distance movements over the East Coast Main Line. But the volume of cross-Pennine traffic is also very significant with Hull, Scarborough/York, Manchester/Liverpool and Chester line flows boosted at places like Halifax, Huddersfield and Bradford and interchanging at Leeds. The North East/South West services plus those on the Summit and Skipton routes add to the importance of Leeds which also has a very large amount of local travel on its Metrotrain services. Darlington is fed similarly by the Bishop Auckland-Saltburn, Whitby and Hartlepool routes, and Newcastle by the Carlisle and Sunderland lines and by the Tyne & Wear Metro trains.

Local traffic is of considerable importance to the ER Northern Area, particularly in the West Riding and on Tyneside. Many such flows now lie within the spheres of the Passenger Transport Authorities established by the 1968 Act, and the Passenger Transport Executives through which they operate. BR deals with three such bodies in the area under notice, South and West Yorkshire and Tyne & Wear, acting as operating agents for routes on which the PTEs provide financial underwriting which may include the purchase of stock, eg, the West Yorkshire Metrotrains, and the provision of stations, eg, Frizinghall. The BR/Local Authority relationship extends beyond the PTE areas, of course, but those areas have seen some dramatic increases in the level of local travel and have produced some major interchange benefits such as those at Bradford Interchange (B.29) and Newcastle (N.4) stations.

After the years of rationalization and contraction, the rail network is expanding again with a significant number of new stations opening. An example is the pleasant, modern station serving the new Gateshead Metro Centre (N.5)—light, airy,

Routine HST inspection, part of a precise, planned and carefully carried out traction maintenance activity.

colourful, and linked by dedicated walkway to the vast, imaginative shopping and leisure centre nearby. On stations generally, passenger information and ticketing facilities have been brought up to high standards with new travel centres at major locations, up-to-date visual display panels and manned platform information booths to add personalized advice to that of the technological systems.

Of all the rail changes, the most important and dramatic is, of course, the electrification of the East Coast Main Line, the physical evidence of which became increasingly apparent as this book was being written. In overall terms, the £300 million scheme will replace already excellent HST services with electric trains hauled by Class 91 Electra locomotives between King's Cross and Leeds and north through York and Newcastle to Edinburgh. Improvements in the original timescale have given Leeds the new services early, and completion of the rest of the scheme is scheduled for 1991. Accompanied by an increasing range of fares and facilities, the new electric trains should help to maintain the significant growth experienced in ER passenger traffic levels.

Electrification means a vast preparatory task involving the installation of 29,500 masts for the overhead current supply, 1,400 miles of overhead wiring, and 400 miles of fibre optic cable for communication. In addition to the raising, lowering or rebuilding of 157 bridges, a great deal of track renewal and realignment is involved, including major track remodelling at York and Newcastle. In addition, new main-

Above *HST prototype at York on 11 June 1973.*

Below *The Self Contained Piling Vehicle has produced dramatic savings in the time taken to erect the steel masts for the East Coast electrification.*

tenance and control centres are needed at Doncaster, Newcastle and Edinburgh, together with four new telephone exchanges for the signalling and communications activity of what is almost a new railway.

The electrified routes will eventually need 31 new passenger sets and their locomotives and 21 freight locomotives. The Class 91 Electras, after initially running with existing Mark 3 coaching stock, will subsequently haul Mark 4 sets capable of running at 140 mph. By use of a remote control 'time division multiplex' (TDM) link between a driving van trailer and the electric locomotives, the new sets can be driven from either end, thereby maintaining the turnround time advantages of the HST sets and saving some £3 million in locomotive capital.

The East Coast Main Line is not the only part of the Eastern Region to experience dramatic change. The cross-Pennine routes and other local and cross-country services have been revolutionized by the advent of Sprinters and Pacers, new types of multiple unit replacing the life-expired dmu fleet. Based on bus construction principles, the new units incorporate the latest in design and engineering technology to produce fast, modern services over medium distance routes, eg, Hull-Scarborough, Leeds-Morecambe etc.

Like the electrification programme, the replacement of the old dmu fleet and some cross-country coach sets involves an investment of £300 million to re-equip BR's Provincial sector passenger services. The first generation of Pacers and the larger Sprinters is being followed by more advanced designs; eg, the Leyland Class 155 Sprinters have been followed by the longer Class 156 Metro Cammell Super Sprinters and the higher classification 158 Express units are due in May 1989. These will be air-conditioned and capable of running at 90 mph, and will take over former locomotive and coaches routes like that from Newcastle to Liverpool. Major features of the new units include air suspension, three-step brakes,

The modernization of level crossings has been an important part of the changes in railway practice. This is a typical open crossing.

Pacer unit interior – clean, bright and spacious.

automatic couplers, power-operated doors, and a light, colourful interior design.

Although traditional signal boxes and semaphore signals are still commonplace on the secondary routes, changes in the spheres of operational control and signalling have matched those of traffic and traction. At one end of the scale there has been great simplification; at the other immense sophistication. Most single freight lines, for example, are now worked on a One Train basis with the train crew normally operating the crossings. On the Redmire Branch (R.3), for example, a Travelling Chargeman draws keys for himself and the guard for unlocking and relocking the crossings on the route into Wensleydale. On other local lines, special instructions, appliances and speeds match the operation to the traffic in the simplest and safest way.

On the main routes, entrance-exit, push-button, route-setting panels—frequently able to set 1,000 routes or more—have been with us for some time. Now, the next generation of signalling control is arriving, exemplified by the scheme due for introduction as part of the changes at York in 1989. York signalling involved the

Above *Preview* Tees-Tyne Pullman *entering York on 27 September 1985 as part of a run which took the world start-to-stop speed record for long-distance diesel trains.*

Below *A new Pacer unit on the Whitby line on 5 April 1986 just after their introduction.*

The Newcastle signalling panel pictured at the beginning of the mas era.

biggest route relay interlocking system in the world when it was introduced in 1951, and the solid state interlocking system now due to replace it will be equally in the van of signalling technology.

York's new integrated signalling control centre will cover over 100 route miles, linking up with Doncaster to the south and with another new ISCC to be built at Newcastle. It will be based on interlocking systems for each sub-area covered plus four special interface processors to forward 'instructions' to the signalling hardware via fibre optic cables. Telephone links to signals and stations will also employ the latest equipment and there will be a new, electronic passenger information system. When completed the installation will control some 230 miles of track.

The resignalling at York is linked to remodelling of the whole layout there in a scheme costing £18 million. With the ER's main lines all laid with continuous welded rail, civil engineering attention has been increasingly concentrated on layout simplification and more efficient and economical maintenance. These two elements are closely linked in so far as simpler layouts frequently reduce track wear as well as raising speeds over curves and through points and crossovers. At York the running lines through the station are being reduced from nine to five, with fewer bay platform lines, only one diamond crossing (for the Down Scarborough line) and the running lines reduced to two over most of the two routes between Holgate Bridge and Skelton.

The civil engineer is making other major contributions to traffic movement. A notable example is in the sphere of track renewal which is now being completed much faster and the track being returned to traffic without imposing speed restrictions while the ballast settles. This is being achieved by a concentration of resources to speed up the cleaning-renewal-relaying cycle, and by the use of a Dynamic Track Stabilizer Machine which is able to achieve mechanically the ballast compaction that would previously have been done by the passage of trains during a period of imposed slower running.

The evidence of the Eastern Region's progress in traffic and technology is not hard to find. Remodelling and electrification works are very apparent at York (Y.2) and Newcastle (N.4), while for sheer passenger traffic variety Leeds (L.1) takes some beating. Passenger station architecture is a delight at period locations like Huddersfield (H.33) and Scarborough (S.4), while Alnmouth (A.5), Gateshead Metro Centre (N.5) and some of the new, simple and clean PTE stations, reveal the best of unions between good architectural practice, modern materials and competent construction. Those who delight in classical architecture should savour Benjamin Green's work for the Newcastle & Berwick Railway (C.9, M.23, W.13), G.T. Andrews's stations on the York & North Midland lines (B.18, F.7, H.34, H.35, M.1, R.2, S.4, W.9), and the stations on the Newcastle-Carlisle route (N.5).

The Region has a full share of notable tunnels, viaducts, bridges and other track

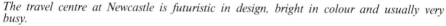

The travel centre at Newcastle is futuristic in design, bright in colour and usually very busy.

Above *Class 141 Metrotrain unit of the West Yorkshire PTE.*

Below *A commonplace Eastern Region freight scene – merry-go-round coal train and power station.*

features. The spectacular include structures like the Royal Border Bridge (B.17), Standedge (S.35) and Bramhope (B.31) tunnels, the swing-bridges at Goole (G.8) and Selby (S.12), and locations like Pontop Crossing (B.24). Other lines and locations of higher-than-average interest include the delightful Ilkley Branch (I.2), the real beauty of the Esk Valley route to Whitby (M.15), the pleasant simplicity of Saltburn station (S.2) and town, and the earthy activity of the Tees-bank section which precedes it (M.14).

The importance of coal to the ER is nowhere more apparent than at the Gascoigne Wood (G.2) loading point for the Selby coalfield output. In contrast, the former Blyth & Tyne system produces movements as varied as the shipment flows to Blyth staiths (N.13) and the flow via Butterwell (B.41) to ICI Wilton. ICI traffic supports the Callerton Branch (C.1), as APCM does that beyond Bishop Auckland to Eastgate (E.4) where two daily cement trains are loaded. The Boulby Branch (B.26) produces up to seven trains a day for Tees Dock, Tees Yard and Middlesbrough, and the Wensleydale line (R.3) carries regular 33-wagon trains of limestone hauled by pairs of Class 20 locomotives and destined for Lackenby steelworks, which then produces large quantities of outward bloom, coil and slab steel movements (M.14). Other important freight flows include oil and petrochemicals from the Seal Sands Storage line (B.20), Speedlink and petroleum trains from ICI Haverton Hill (B.20), cars from Goole (G.8) and Freightliner movements from Leeds and Tees-side (L.1, S.39).

In contrast the past is still interestingly evident in examples as diverse as the huge Huddersfield warehouse (H.33), the water crane at Battersby (M.15), vintage water reservoirs at several locations (N.4, N.5, S.36), and the remains of coal drops at others (H.1, M.14). The contrast between the latter and the modern movements to the large power stations (D.10, E.6, F.3) is one of the fascinations of the ER railway system.

Early and closed lines

The whole development of the North East owes much to its early wagonways, the first of which dates back to around 1605—some 200 years before any thought of railways as we know them! The lines were built to serve the modest collieries of the period and carry their output to the nearest waterway. They were generally short, of very basic wooden construction, and anything but a 'permanent way' as we know it today. The course of these early lines would be altered as old seams gave out and new ones were exploited, or sometimes just because a particular stretch of terrain proved unsuitable in practical use.

Then around the beginning of the nineteenth century, the picture began to change. A major growth in the demand for coal made it profitable to mine deeper or further from a waterway, and unprofitable to hold up larger ships while the flat-bottomed keels carried coal from the upstream wagonways to the downstream anchorages. The availability of iron rails improved the prospects for longer rail lines and the development of steam locomotives offered the prospect of longer trains. By mixing locomotive sections with powered or self-acting inclines, it was possible to work worthwhile 'trains' over quite difficult countryside. The railway age was about to dawn.

The Stockton & Darlington is, deservedly, the best known of the pioneer railways to emerge from the changes, but there were others. The Middleton Railway at Leeds referred to in the next section was one, and there were several more in the North-East. In the area south of the Tyne, for example, the valley of its Derwent tributary was used to feed Derwenthaugh staiths, and the Tanfield Wagonway linked collieries of the Pontop, Tanfield and Marley Hill areas to the Dunston staiths a little further down the river. The Tanfield line reached a throughput of a quarter of a million tons of coal annually at quite an early stage, and was to become part of the Brandling Junction Railway system. Dating from the 1730s, it had some claim to be the oldest line inherited by BR in 1948.

When the wagonways from the pits around Mount Moor and Washington, County Durham, to the Wear became inadequate, their output and that from the new pit opened at Springwell in 1821 was conveyed to Jarrow by the new Bowes Railway. George Stephenson was engineer for the Bowes project, as he was for the Hetton Colliery Railway which took coal to Seaham for shipment. These lines were followed by others, like the Stanhope & Tyne and the mineral route from Haswell to Hartlepool. Such lines were the embryo from which the North Eastern Railway was to emerge a quarter of a century later.

Above *A typical railway 'pick-up' goods train, in this case on the Pickering-Whitby line near Goathland.*

Below *The swing bridge over the River Ouse at Naburn just south of York, a thing of the past since the rerouting of the East Coast Main Line over the Selby diversion.*

Not only did railways begin much earlier than one is apt to think, but so did railway closures. The Leeds & Selby lost its passenger service west of Milford in 1840 in favour of routing via Methley, but admittedly this was only temporary, whereas quite a few early passenger services were abandoned in the North East, eg, over the Clarence Railway (1842), to Tanfield (1844), Waskerley Park-Crawley (1846), Washington-Brockley Whins (1853), and that into Durham Gilesgate (1857). However, the main pre-BR closure period resulted from the 'depression' years after the First World War and saw the end of passenger services on quite a few lightly used lines, most of which were still retained for freight. The principle pre-BR closures were:

Closed to passengers	Line or branch
1929	17 June	South Gosforth-Darras Hall
	8 July	Rishworth Branch
	23 September	Stainland Branch
1930	1 January	Selby-Cawood
		Pateley Bridge-Lofthouse
	7 July	Amble Branch
	28 July	Kirkburton Branch
	22 September	Allendale Branch
		Alnwick-Coldstream
	1 December	Dewsbury Market Place Branch
1931	1 January	Melmerby-Masham
		Pittington-Durham
	2 February	Bradford-Shipley (GN)
	2 November	Stockton-Wellfield
1932	1 January	South Howden-Cudworth
1939	1 May	Durham-Blackhill
	11 September	Haverton Hill-Port Clarence
	4 December	Ferryhill-Bishop Auckland
1941	28 July	Ferryhill-Leamside
1947	16 June	Hartlepool Branch

Those of the BR era were:

1948	27 September	Doncaster-Knottingley
	29 November	Alne-Easingwold
1949	23 May	Meltham Branch
1950	5 June	Malton-Driffield
		Seamer-Pickering
	25 September	Knaresborough-Pilmoor
1951	22 January	Garforth-Castleford
	2 April	Harrogate-Pateley Bridge
	10 September	Wakefield-Edlington
	29 October	Seahouses Branch
		Durham-Waterhouses
1952	31 March	Ferryhill-Stockton
	9 June	Ferryhill-Hartlepool

Maintenance men wave for the photographer as a train thunders over Deepdale Viaduct on the Darlington-Tebay line.

1956	15 October	Hexham-Reedsmouth
1957	25 February	Bradford-Otley-Harrogate
1958	5 May	Whitby-Loftus
1959	29 June	Doncaster-Penistone
	14 September	Melmerby-Thirsk
	2 November	Holmfirth Branch
1960	2 May	Loftus-Guisborough
	13 June	Halifax-Sheffield
1962	1 January	Thornhill-Heckmondwike
		Keighley-Oxenhope
1963	9 September	Durham/Ferryhill-Pelaw
1964	6 January	Cross Gates-Wetherby
		Church Fenton-Harrogate
	2 March	Nunthorpe-Guisborough
	5 May	Durham-Sunderland
	15 June	Leeds-Pudsey-Bradford
		Selby-Goole
		Berwick-Kelso
	7 September	Bradford-Dewsbury-Wakefield
	19 October	Hull-Hornsea
		Hull-Withernsea
	2 November	Newbiggin Branch
		Blyth & Tyne
	30 November	Middleton-in-Teesdale Branch
1965	8 March	Scarborough-Whitby
		Malton-Whitby
	22 March	Arthington-Burley-in-Wharfedale
	14 June	Bradford-Mirfield
		Selby-Driffield
	29 November	Beverley-York
1966	4 July	Bradford-Gildersome-Wakefield
1967	2 January	Wakefield-Pontefract
	6 March	Harrogate-Northallerton
1968	1 January	Sheffield-Cudworth-Leeds
	29 January	Alnwick-Alnmouth
	10 March	Scotswood-Wylam
1969	3 March	Richmond Branch
1970	5 January	Manchester-Sheffield (GC)
		Barnsley-Penistone
		Castleford-Burton Salmon
		Milner Royd Junction-Mirfield
1973	23 July	Newcastle Riverside Branch
1976	3 May	Alston Branch
1977	26 November	Filey Holiday Camp Branch
1979	14 May	Northallerton-Eaglescliffe
1983	24 January	Clayton West Branch
	16 May	Sheffield-Penistone (GC)

Preservation and non-BR lines

The old North Eastern Railway was a proud company which showed great respect for its heritage. It was involved in active preservation as early as 1901 when it retained the Stockton & Darlington Railway's iron bridge over the River Gaunless after it had been replaced by a more modern one. The LNER maintained this responsible interest in the past, staging an active celebration of the Stockton & Darlington's centenary in 1925 and running an excellent museum in the old station premises at York. York is today the home of the national railway collection, and there are many more preservation locations in the Humber-Tweed region:

National Railway Museum
Leeman Road, York YO2 4XJ. Opened in 1975, this major museum is the home of the national railway collection and is appropriately housed on a former locomotive and goods depot site. The collection embraces over 50 locomotives, 40 coaches and nearly 100 other items of rolling stock, with prime exhibits arranged round two original turntables in the main hall. A viewing gallery presents the social and economic story of railways, and there are many smaller displays to enhance the understanding of the working life of railways and railwaymen. Picture galleries, models, audio-visual presentations and many other facilities support the dramatic presence of exhibits like the early horse-drawn vehicles, the Royal Saloons and fine steam locomotives such as the world steam record holder *Mallard*. The museum is open daily except at Christmas and New Year.

North Yorkshire Moors Railway
Pickering Station, Pickering, North Yorks YO18 7AJ. The North York Moors Historical Railway Trust operates this 18 mile route from Pickering, through Newtondale to Goathland and Grosmont, on BR's Esk Valley line. The railway is home to some 20 preserved steam locomotives, plus diesels and around 40 coaches, and trains operate on most days from the end of March to October. The line dates right back to a horse-worked railway of 1836, and was reopened by the preservation body in 1973. One of its major attractions is the landscape it traverses, the pleasant dale and meadow scenery of the end sections becoming quite majestic where the route passes through the rolling wooded moors of the once-glacial Newtondale. Appropriate to its past, the railway has a strong North Eastern flavour.

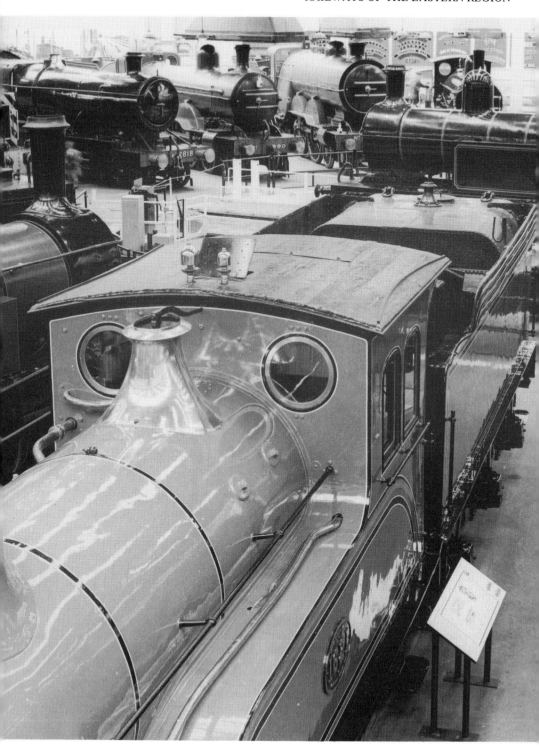

Keighley & Worth Valley Railway

Haworth Station, Keighley, West Yorks BD22 8NJ. This major preservation scheme rescued the former Midland branch line from Keighley to Oxenhope in 1968. The 5 mile single line route winds through an area of wooded meadows surrounded by towering moorlands and carries regular services at weekends from March to October and on weekdays, too, in July and August. The railway is home to some 40 locomotives and services operate with a considerable variety of traction, from express passenger engines to industrial types and railbuses.

North of England Open Air Museum

Beamish Hall, Stanley, Co Durham. The Beamish museum complex graphically portrays the past life and work of the North East, bringing together a host of influences including mining, agriculture and transport. The site includes a colliery line, a typical North Eastern station (Rowley) and an electric tramway. Steam services operate to and from the station, which includes a goods yard and all the paraphernalia of a working railway, and the tramway is also operational. The site has many other absorbing 're-creations' including a Co-operative store, period housing, farm stock and buildings, the colliery and its pit cottages, horse-drawn vehicles, and the elegant Beamish Hall.

Left *Interior of the National Railway Museum's Main Exhibition Hall* (National Railway Museum Photograph).

Below *Live steam operation on the Keighley & Worth Valley Railway* (K&WVR/John Sagar).

Middleton Railway Trust

Moor Road, Hunslet, Leeds LS10 2SQ. The first railway scheme to be presented to Parliament involved the construction of a wagonway from Middleton Colliery to Leeds and received the Royal Assent on 9 June 1758. This pioneering tradition was maintained when Matthew Murray introduced Blenkinsop steam locomotion on the line in 1812, and again when the Middleton Railway Preservation Society revived the line in 1960 and became the first preservation body to operate a freight activity. The Trust now has 1¾ miles of operational standard gauge line and some 15 steam and diesel locomotives. Public opening is at summer weekends from Easter to the end of September.

Monkwearmouth Station Museum

North Bridge Street, Sunderland, Tyne & Wear. Six years after its closure in 1967, Monkwearmouth station was reopened as a museum by Sunderland Corporation. Actually standing on the route of an early wagonway, it is an imposing classical building dating from 1848 and built for the York, Newcastle & Berwick Railway to the designs of local architect Thomas Moore. The museum displays include a ticket office of the 1865 period, a 1915 guard's van and a car van of 1939, and there are many smaller displays and exhibits.

South Tynedale Railway

The Railway Station, Alston, Cumbria CA9 3JB. The steep and winding branch line from Haltwhistle to Alston was closed in 1976, but a 1¾ mile line section at the Alston end has been reopened by the preservation society. A 2 ft gauge is now used and the line is operational most weekends in the summer, daily in July and August and on some weekdays in other peak months.

Darlington Railway Museum

North Road Station, Station Road, Darlington DL3 6ST. Lying on the course of the Stockton & Darlington Railway's original line of 1825, the very atmospheric station at North Road was revived by the Darlington Railway Museum Trust after becoming surplus to operational requirements on BR's simplified Bishop Auckland branch working. The location, which has many S&D connections, has now become the home of Stephenson's *Locomotion*, Hackworth's *Derwent*, and various other interesting displays and exhibits.

Tanfield Railway

Marley Hill Station, Sunniside, Gateshead, Tyne & Wear. The original Tanfield Wagonway dates back to 1725 and quickly became a major artery for moving coal from the area north of Stanley to the Tyne at Dunston. It was worked by a mixture of horse-power, stationary engines and self-acting inclines until locomotives appeared in 1881, and then continued as an ordinary BR coal line until the pit closures era. Following the closure of the NCB Marley Hill shed in 1970, locomotives and rolling stock were accumulated there for preservation and a section of Tanfield track to Bowes Bridge was reopened. The site is open on Sundays with operation in the peak summer months.

Bowes Railway

Bowes Railway Site, Springwell Village, Gateshead NE9 7QJ. From the original 1826 section from Mount Moor to Jarrow, the Bowes Railway system developed to serve 13 collieries, using seven rope-worked inclines and three locomotive sections. Pit closures from 1968 onwards brought about the end of the system which was then revived by courtesy of local councils and the Tyne & Wear Industrial Monuments Trust. Subsequent work on the project has given it a section of working line from Springwell to Blackham's Hill, operational inclines on either side of the Blackham Hill engine house, active workshops and a collection of locomotives and rolling stock, the latter including some unique freight wagons. Although restricted by funds, this is an important and developing site which is open throughout the year, with the railway operational on the first Sunday of the month and Bank Holidays from Easter to September.

In addition to these specific preservation centres there are quite a few other specialized and local collections. They include the Timothy Hackworth Museum at Shildon, which recognizes the contribution Hackworth's engines made to hauling the coal production of Durham, and a small museum devoted to the Stockton & Darlington Railway in an ex-S&D building at 48 Bridge Road, Stockton. George Stephenson's works are remembered in the railway museum at his native Wylam and in the Stephenson Railway Museum at Middle Engine Lane, Newcastle. Many of the conventional museums, at Hull and Newcastle for example, include railway items, while specialist preservation activity includes examples like the work of the Vintage Carriages Trust at Haworth and that of the Great Yorkshire Railway Preservation Society at the site of Starbeck loco depot.

New-BR railway systems are now few in number and modest in activity. The pits of National Coal might be excepted from this generalization since a number of mines, stockyards and coking plants have at least one diesel locomotive for internals movement. The nationalized coal concern also uses electric traction on its network at South Shields.

British Steel is another private railway operator, and has quite a sizeable railway network at its Hartlepool South Works. A less obvious operator is the Tyne & Wear Metro which has a fleet of five O-6-ODE locomotives for stock and engineering movements. Built by Brush Electrical Machines Ltd and based on a design for Nigerian Railways, these units have 427 hp Rolls-Royce engines and are geared to produce up to 30 mph. Examples of the smaller locations with their own power include the Procor wagons works at Horbury, and Melmerby Estates at Selby.

Addenda

Recent and forward developments

During this book's compilation period, work on the electrification of the East Coast Main Line has been in full swing. By the end of 1988, progress on the West Riding route was sufficiently advanced for the power to be switched on and for test running to then commence. Class 91 locomotives had started to arrive and were put to work with HST sets, first for driver training and then, from Spring 1989, on selected public services. There was a progressive introduction of more electric workings to Leeds from the May timetable, followed by the first deliveries of the new Mark 4 coaches during the summer. By the time this book is published, power will have been switched on to feed the overhead wiring as far as York, where the solid state interlocking signalling centre has already been commissioned, and about half the wiring to Edinburgh will have been installed.

Progress has also been notable in the works associated with electrification. By the middle of 1989, the main features of the new, simplified layout at York station had emerged, while changes further north included alterations on Durham Viaduct which had been closed for a week in March to permit track realignment for higher electrification speeds. In January 1989 work began at Newcastle on a scheme of alterations designed to improve the through lines and to provide an extra through island platform, primarily for services on the Sunderland-Newcastle-Carlisle route. The start of work on the SSI signalling centre here was slightly delayed by the need to remove rare orchids found growing on the site. A small modification of the original electrification plans was authorized to link Leeds station and Neville Hill depot.

The general trend towards station improvements has continued on the Eastern Region. At Thirsk the station buildings damaged by fire in 1987 were rebuilt in 1988. On the Scarborough line the remodelling of Scarborough itself, which included the provision of retail units on the station, was completed in the first half of 1989. At Malton a £250,000 refurbishing programme was begun, including modernization of the station entrance and the provision of a new canopy using materials redundant at Whitby. Further improvements were announced for Middlesbrough, Sunderland and Seaburn stations, but consent to demolish the listed G.T. Andrews roof at Filey station was refused.

In West Yorkshire, station improvements at the down-at-heel Bradford Forster Square have coincided with the provision of InterCity 125 services to Kings Cross and St Pancras. The picture at Interchange has been less rosy due to doubts raised about the financial viability of the whole complex. New life is returning to the station buildings at Halifax where work has started on a £175,000 scheme of improvements. The original station buildings and adjoining warehouse form part of the first stage of the Eureka project, designed to provide a pioneer early informal centre for children. The old station at Ilkley has been completely modernized and major improvements are planned for Dewsbury.

The western boundary of the Eastern Region has been extended by the transfer of Skipton from the LMR, and there is a general air of expansion in the sphere of the West Yorkshire PTE. New stations continue to be added to the network and there are forward plans for the restoration of passenger services to the Wakefield-Pontefract route. Looking further ahead, thought is now being given to the possibility of providing a new Leeds-Halifax service over the Dryclough-Heaton Lodge freight line. The PTE is also considering the feasibility of some local electrification, with Leeds-Bradford at the top of the list for investigation.

Further north the prospects for running North Yorkshire Moors Railway trains through from Grosmont to Whitby have receded as a result of the feasibility study showing no viable options. There have been operational changes on the Esk Valley line involving the closure of two signal boxes. Passing loops, operated by the train crews, have been retained. West of the ECML, the summer Sunday-only service beyond Bishop Auckland to Stanhope has produced encouraging results. In 1989 running commences in March, with an additional train each way and better main line connections at Darlington.

Other alterations in passenger services include major changes on the Newcastle-Carlisle line which now carries Sprinter workings through to Glasgow via Kilmarnock and the old G&SW route, and to Stranraer Harbour. The cross-Pennine service was revised with the May 1989 timetable, many trains running to and via Manchester Piccadilly over the new Windsor link line, instead of into Victoria as previously. The familiar 'Trans-Pennine' brand name, first used in connection with the pioneer dmu services nearly 30 years ago, is to be phased out as the service becomes integrated with the 'Express' network and locomotive-hauled trains are gradually replaced by Class 156 and 158 units.

On the black side, Goole Swing Bridge was in trouble again on 23 November 1988 when it was rammed by the 3,500 ton cargo vessel *Samo*. One of the fixed spans was knocked 30 feet out of alignment by the impact. Services were maintained by providing an alternative bus link and BR are to repair the damaged bridge under an agreement by which the premiums on future insurance will be found by the local authorities.

The first regular Down Yorkshire Pullman *electric service approaching Leeds on Monday 10 April 1989.*

Bibliography and sources

A book of this sort inevitably involves travelling over all the lines still open for passenger traffic, and the basic information on the current status of the system derives from this process. Further information on the current scene has been obtained from press releases and other BR sources, including *Rail News*. Other railway journals have also been consulted.

Location data is based on the *Sectional Appendix to the Working Timetables and Books of Rules and Regulations* which details lines, stations, junctions and other physical features, along with their distances, line speeds and other basic information. A total of 116 lines and branches appear in the ER Northern Area version.

Domestic railway material also provides a great deal of information on past railway activity. The various timetables give a very useful picture of past routes and train services, while publications like the Railway Clearing House *Handbook of Stations* provides data not only on stations and goods depots, but also on their facilities and private sidings. A large number of such sources have been consulted, including the handbooks issued annually under the title *Ports of the LNER*.

There are a great many sources of historical information on the area covered by this book. Reliable, factual and interesting coverage of *South and West Yorkshire* is given in Volume 8 of David & Charles's 'Regional History of Great Britain' series, and of *The North East* in Volume 4. The respective authors are David Joy and Ken Hoole, the latter also offering a deep insight into the North Eastern Railway territory through books such as *Railway Stations of the North East* (David & Charles, 1985) and 'Forgotten Railways' Volume 1, *North East England* (David & Charles, 1984).

The North Eastern Railway has been treated by quite a few writers, starting with W.W. Tomlinson's 1914 book of great stature, *The North Eastern Railway: Its Rise and Development* (now reprinted by David & Charles). The economic history of that company was dealt with by R.J. Irving in *The North Eastern Railway 1870–1914* (Leicester University Press, 1976), while Cecil J. Allen dealt with the North Eastern Railway and the LNER in volumes for Ian Allan in 1964 and 1966 respectively. Books on other individual lines in the area include the Turntable volumes on *The Hull & Barnsley Railway*, G. Whittle's *The Railways of Consett & North West Durham* (David & Charles, 1971), and the same author's *The Newcastle & Carlisle Railway* (David & Charles, 1979).

Major sources on specific aspects of railway activity must start with reference to *Clinker's Register of Closed Stations*, recently reprinted by Avon-Anglia in an edition covering the 150 years up to 1980. Other senior works on individual railway subjects include George Dow's *Railway Heraldry* and Gordon Biddle's *Victorian Stations* (both David & Charles), the former also contributing the substantive history of the Great Central Railway.

The smaller works which make some contribution to the understanding of the railways in the area covered are legion, with Oakwood Press, Wyvern Publications and Hendon Publishing offering a number of worthwhile books. Individual publications of stature include the *North Eastern Railway Historical Maps* of the Railway & Canal Historical Society, Colin Mountford's *The Bowes Railway* (Industrial Railway Society and Tyne & Wear Industrial Monuments Trust) and the 'by Rail' guides of the Railway Development Society.

Information on the preservation scene comes best from the material made available by the individual preservation bodies, most of whom publish booklets on their origins and activities.

Supplementary index

Modern arrivals at Newcastle.